WONDER WOMAN

A CELEBRATION OF 75 YEARS

WONDER WOMAN CREATED BY WILLIAM MOULTON MARSTON

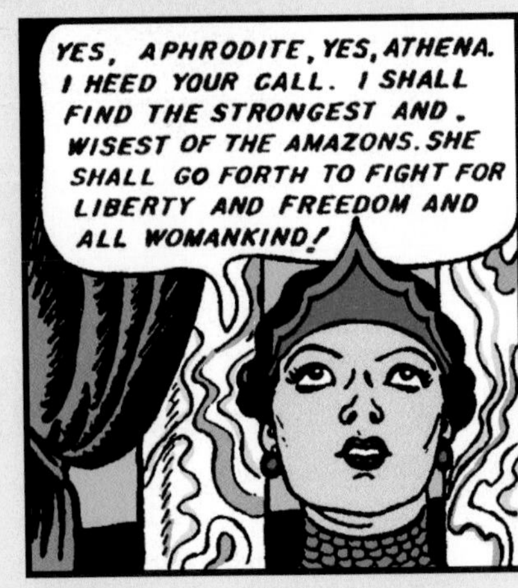

DC COMICS

SHELDON MAYER
ROBERT KANIGHER
JACK MILLER
LEN WEIN
KAREN BERGER
DAN THORSLAND
PAUL KUPPERBERG
JASON HERNANDEZ-ROSENBLATT
IVAN COHEN
EDDIE BERGANZA
MATT IDELSON
KRISTY QUINN
Editors – Original Series

MIKE W. BARR
ALICE MARBLE
Associate Editors – Original Series

DEBORAH ANDERSON
MAUREEN McTIGUE
TOM PALMER JR.
CHRIS CONROY
JESSICA CHEN
Assistant Editors – Original Series

JEB WOODARD
Group Editor – Collected Editions

ROBIN WILDMAN
Editor – Collected Edition

STEVE COOK
Design Director – Books

RANDALL DAHLK
Publication Design

BOB HARRAS
Senior VP – Editor-in-Chief, DC Comics

DIANE NELSON
President

DAN DiDIO and JIM LEE
Co-Publishers

GEOFF JOHNS
Chief Creative Officer

AMIT DESAI
Senior VP – Marketing & Global Franchise Management

NAIRI GARDINER
Senior VP – Finance

SAM ADES
VP – Digital Marketing

BOBBIE CHASE
VP – Talent Development

MARK CHIARELLO
Senior VP – Art, Design & Collected Editions

JOHN CUNNINGHAM
VP – Content Strategy

ANNE DePIES
VP – Strategy Planning & Reporting

DON FALLETTI
VP – Manufacturing Operations

LAWRENCE GANEM
VP – Editorial Administration & Talent Relations

ALISON GILL
Senior VP – Manufacturing & Operations

HANK KANALZ
Senior VP – Editorial Strategy & Administration

JAY KOGAN
VP – Legal Affairs

DEREK MADDALENA
Senior VP – Sales & Business Development

JACK MAHAN
VP – Business Affairs

DAN MIRON
VP – Sales Planning & Trade Development

NICK NAPOLITANO
VP – Manufacturing Administration

CAROL ROEDER
VP – Marketing

EDDIE SCANNELL
VP – Mass Account & Digital Sales

COURTNEY SIMMONS
Senior VP – Publicity & Communications

JIM (SKI) SOKOLOWSKI
VP – Comic Book Specialty & Newsstand Sales

SANDY YI
Senior VP – Global Franchise Management

WONDER WOMAN: A CELEBRATION OF 75 YEARS

PEFC Certified
Printed on paper from sustainably managed forests and controlled sources
PEFC
PEFC/29-31-75
www.pefc.org

DC Comics, 2900 West Alameda Ave., Burbank, CA 91505
Printed by RR Donnelley, Salem, VA, USA. 8/26/16. First Printing.
ISBN: 978-1-4012-6512-0

Library of Congress Cataloging-in-Publication Data is available.

TABLE OF CONTENTS

Collection cover art by Cliff Chiang
Case art by H.G. Peter

DC strives to be as thorough as possible in its effort to determine creators' identities from all available sources. This process is not perfect, and as a result, some attributions may be incomplete or wrongly assigned.

The comics reprinted in this volume were produced in a time when racism played a larger role in society and popular culture both consciously and unconsciously. They are reprinted without alteration for historical reference.

**Stories in parentheses were originally untitled.*

PART I: 1941-1957
THE AMAZON

In 1941, William Moulton Marston introduced the idea of a female super-powered crime-fighter to the world, one just as powerful as her male counterparts. A hero that would inspire a whole generation of readers, both male and female.

At this time, Marston was already a renowned psychologist, practicing since the end of World War I, and had famously been part of the team that invented the lie detector. He was also a supporter of the comic book cause at a time when comics were starting to be judged offensive for children. In a 1940 issue of *The Family Circle* magazine, Marston defended the popularity of the medium in an article called "Don't Laugh at the Comics."

He commended Superman as a bold new character and congratulated editor Max Gaines for having seen the great potential of this whole generation of heroes. After reading the article, Gaines contacted Marston and offered him a gig writing for his company, All-American Publications.

Gaines and editor Sheldon Mayer gave Marston the unique opportunity to create his own character, which he decided to make the embodiment of feminism and empathy. Adding a taste for mythology in the mix, Marston tied his creation to the ancient Greek gods, strengthening the links already in place between super-powered individuals of antiquity and modern comic book heroes. The first Flash wears a winged helmet resembling Mercury's, and the first Green Lantern got his powers from a magic lamp. Wonder Woman would gain her abilities from the Greek Olympians themselves.

At first, Marston toyed with the idea of calling his heroine "Suprema, the Wonder Woman," but after discussing it with his editors, settled on simply "Wonder Woman." The author also chose the artist himself, someone who could give life to his Amazon Princess: Harry G. Peter, an illustrator who mainly worked in newspapers. Just like Marston, Peter was a bit older than the rest of the comic book creators of these times. Even Mayer, who supervised the series, was only 24 years old.

Wonder Woman, a character who, mirroring her editorial team, combined tradition and modernity, debuted in ALL-STAR COMICS #8 alongside the Justice Society, All-American Publications and National Comics' premier superhero team. Her origin story was rather short and served as a backup adventure for the Justice Society. Nonetheless, a month later, Wonder Woman became the star of SENSATION COMICS, a new monthly book.

Wonder Woman was the star of that series until issue #106, published late 1951. Her success became so spectacular that, in addition to SENSATION, she also got her own title in Summer 1942. First published quarterly, it was upgraded to a bimonthly by the end of World War II. The Amazon Princess was also a recurring star in COMIC CAVALCADE, where she shared the spotlight with Flash and Green Lantern, from 1943 to 1948.

NEVER BEFORE HAVE I KILLED A HUMAN BEING--
--AND I DON'T INTEND TO NOW !

She also had a spot on the superhero team, the Justice Society, starting with ALL STAR COMICS #11 (June 1942). A sign of those times, her role was anything but major. Appearing in a few panels or pages, sometimes without a single line of dialogue, she was appointed as the team's secretary, writing and recording their adventures. But after the war Wonder Woman was brought back to the forefront, taking active duty in their last battles. At the peak of her popularity, like Batman and Superman before her, the Amazon Princess was given her own newspaper strip, created by Marston and Peter on top of everything else. Unfortunately, this strip only lasted for a year due to paper rationings experienced by publishers during the war.

Still, this incredible popularity, never seen before for a female character, carried on until the 1950s, when Wonder Woman's style and tone were tweaked for the first time.

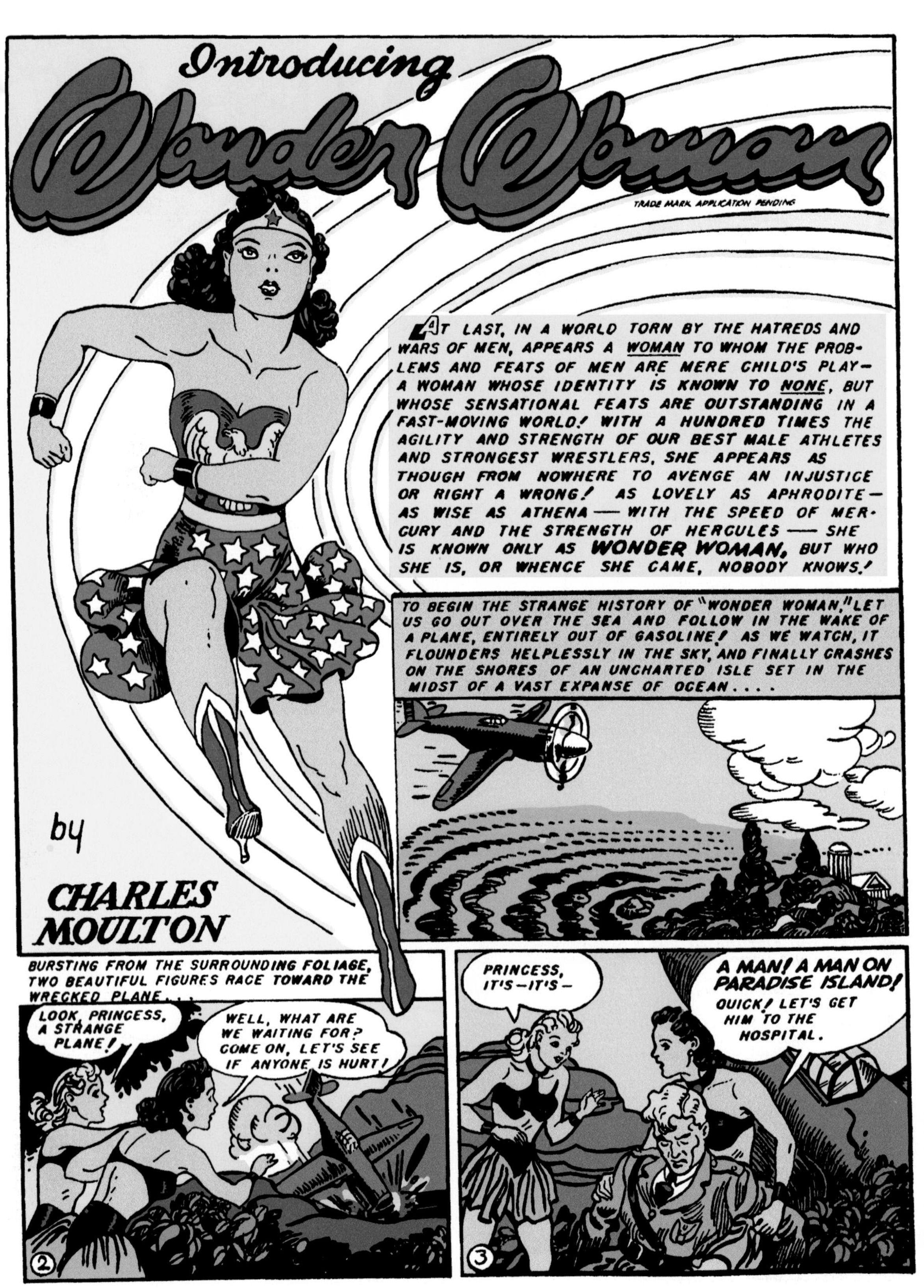
Introducing
Wonder Woman
TRADE MARK APPLICATION PENDING
At last, in a world torn by the hatreds and wars of men, appears a woman to whom the problems and feats of men are mere child's play—a woman whose identity is known to none, but whose sensational feats are outstanding in a fast-moving world! With a hundred times the agility and strength of our best male athletes and strongest wrestlers, she appears as though from nowhere to avenge an injustice or right a wrong! As lovely as Aphrodite—as wise as Athena—with the speed of Mercury and the strength of Hercules—she is known only as Wonder Woman, but who she is, or whence she came, nobody knows!
To begin the strange history of "Wonder Woman," let us go out over the sea and follow in the wake of a plane, entirely out of gasoline! As we watch, it flounders helplessly in the sky, and finally crashes on the shores of an uncharted isle set in the midst of a vast expanse of ocean . . .
by
CHARLES MOULTON
Bursting from the surrounding foliage, two beautiful figures race toward the wrecked plane . . .
Look, Princess, a strange plane!
Well, what are we waiting for? Come on, let's see if anyone is hurt!
2
Princess, it's—it's—
A man! A man on Paradise Island!
Quick! Let's get him to the hospital.
3

CARRYING THE FULL GROWN MAN AS IF HE WERE A CHILD, THE YOUNG WOMAN STEPS THROUGH THE FOLIAGE AND ENTERS THE STREETS OF A CITY THAT FOR ALL THE WORLD SEEMS TO BE BORN OF ANCIENT GREECE!
A MAN!
HOW DID HE GET HERE?
SOMEONE TELL THE QUEEN THERE'S A MAN ON PARADISE ISLAND!
AT THE HOSPITAL —
IS HE ALL RIGHT? WILL HE LIVE?
I DON'T KNOW. HE'S HAD A CONCUSSION. WE WON'T KNOW ANYTHING FOR DAYS. I WONDER WHAT THE QUEEN WILL DO WITH HIM. HE CAN'T BE MOVED.
SUDDENLY, HIPPOLYTE, THE QUEEN, ENTERS THE HOSPITAL ROOM...
MOTHER!
THE QUEEN!
I HEARD THAT THERE WAS A MAN HERE, BUT I COULDN'T BELIEVE IT. WHO IS HE?
HIS PLANE CRASHED ON THE BEACH OF THE ISLAND THIS MORNING. THE PRINCESS AND MALA BROUGHT HIM HERE. I FOUND THESE PAPERS IN HIS POCKET.
"CAPT. STEVEN TREVOR, U.S. ARMY INTELLIGENCE SERVICE." HMM. WE CAN'T LET HIM DIE. SEE THAT HE GETS THE BEST OF ATTENTION. KEEP HIS EYES COVERED SO THAT, IF HE SHOULD AWAKE, HE WILL SEE NOTHING! HAVE HIS PLANE REPAIRED, FOR HE MUST LEAVE AS SOON AS HE IS WELL! KEEP ME INFORMED OF HIS PROGRESS!
IN THE ENSUING DAYS, THE PRINCESS, THE QUEEN'S ONLY DAUGHTER, IS CONSTANTLY AT THE BEDSIDE OF THE UNCONSCIOUS MAN, HELPING — WATCHING —
YOU OUGHT TO GET SOME SLEEP, PRINCESS. YOU HAVE BEEN ON THE JOB NOW FOR FOURTEEN HOURS.
NEVER MIND ME. WE - WE MUST MAKE HIM WELL.
LEAVING THE PRINCESS TO WATCH OVER THE INJURED PILOT, THE DOCTOR SEEKS AUDIENCE WITH THE QUEEN....
WHAT HAS HAPPENED THAT YOU DISTURB ME AT THIS HOUR? IS THE MAN—
NO, HE IS ALIVE. IT IS THE PRINCESS I AM WORRIED ABOUT. I DON'T THINK SHE OUGHT TO BE ALLOWED IN THE HOSPITAL ANYMORE. SHE ACTS RATHER STRANGELY ABOUT THAT MAN.
2
SO SHE IS IN LOVE! I WAS AFRAID OF THAT! YOU ARE QUITE RIGHT, DOCTOR. I SHALL TAKE STEPS IMMEDIATELY.
THAT WOULD BE WISE. IT'S FOR THE CHILD'S OWN GOOD.

AND SO THE PRINCESS, FORBIDDEN THE PLEASURE OF NURSING THE ONLY MAN SHE CAN RECALL EVER HAVING SEEN IN HER LIFE, GOES TO HER MOTHER, HIPPOLYTE, THE QUEEN OF THE AMAZONS!
BUT MOTHER — I DON'T UNDERSTAND— I MUST SEE HIM! I MUST KNOW WHO HE IS, HOW HE GOT HERE! AND WHY HE MUST LEAVE? I-I LOVE HIM!
I WAS AFRAID, DAUGHTER, THAT THE TIME WOULD SOME DAY ARRIVE THAT I WOULD HAVE TO SATISFY YOUR CURIOSITY. COME— I WILL TELL YOU EVERYTHING!

AND THIS IS THE STARTLING STORY UNFOLDED BY HIPPOLYTE, QUEEN OF THE AMAZONS, TO THE PRINCESS, HER DAUGHTER !

In the days of Ancient Greece, many centuries ago, we Amazons were the foremost nation in the world. In Amazonia, women ruled and all was well. Then one day, Hercules, the strongest man in the world, stung by taunts that he couldn't conquer the Amazon women, selected his strongest and fiercest warriors and landed on our shores. I challenged him to personal combat—because I knew that with my MAGIC GIRDLE, given me by Aphrodite, Goddess of Love, I could not lose.

And win I did! But Hercules, by deceit and trickery, managed to secure my MAGIC GIRDLE—and soon we Amazons were taken into slavery. And Aphrodite, angry at me for having succumbed to the wiles of men, would do naught to help us!

Finally our submission to men became unbearable—we could stand it no longer—and I appealed to the Goddess Aphrodite again. This time not in vain, for she relented and with her help, I secured the MAGIC GIRDLE from Hercules.

With the MAGIC GIRDLE in my possession, it didn't take us long to overcome our masters, the MEN—and taking from them their entire fleet, we set sail for another shore, for it was Aphrodite's condition that we leave the man-made world and establish a new world of our own! Aphrodite also decreed that we must always wear these bracelets fashioned by our captors, as a reminder that we must always keep aloof from men.

And so, after sailing the seas many days and many nights, we found Paradise Island and settled here to build a new World! With its fertile soil, its marvelous vegetation—its varied natural resources—here is no want, no illness, no hatreds, no wars, and as long as we remain on Paradise Island and I retain the MAGIC GIRDLE, we have the power of Eternal Life—so long as we do not permit ourselves to be again beguiled by men! We are indeed a race of Wonder Women!

That was the promise of Aphrodite—and we must keep our promise to her if we are to remain here safe and in peace!

That is why this American must go and as soon as possible!

Come, let me show you the Magic Sphere you've heard me talk about. It was given to me by Athena, the Goddess of Wisdom, just after we conquered the Herculeans and set sail for Paradise Island! It is through this Magic Sphere that I have been able to know what has gone on and is going on in the other world, and even, at times, forecast the future!

That is why we Amazons have been able to far ,surpass the inventions of the so-called man-made civilization! We are not only stronger and wiser than men—but our weapons are better—our flying machines are further advanced! And it is through the knowledge that I have gained from this Magic Sphere that I have taught you, my daughter, all the arts and sciences and languages of modern as well as ancient times!

But let us see where your American captain came from and how he got here. Watch closely—

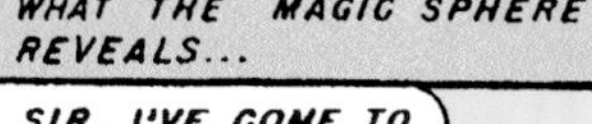

WHAT THE MAGIC SPHERE REVEALS...
SIR, I'VE COME TO REPORT THAT I HAVE AT LAST UNCOVERED INFORMATION AS TO WHO THE LEADERS OF THE SPY RING ARE. I'D LIKE PERMISSION TO CLOSE IN ON THEM PERSONALLY!
BUT THAT'S RIDICULOUS, CAPTAIN. YOU'RE THE MOST VALUABLE MAN IN THE ARMY INTELLIGENCE DEPARTMENT. WE CAN'T RISK LOSING YOU!

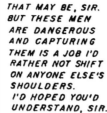

THAT MAY BE, SIR. BUT THESE MEN ARE DANGEROUS AND CAPTURING THEM IS A JOB I'D RATHER NOT SHIFT ON ANYONE ELSE'S SHOULDERS. I'D HOPED YOU'D UNDERSTAND, SIR.
HMM. I BELIEVE I DO, SON. . . I BELIEVE I DO.. GO TO IT, AND THE BEST OF LUCK TO YOU!

THAT NIGHT, STEVE TREVOR DRIVES TO A HIDDEN AIRFIELD NOT FAR FROM AN ARMY AIR BASE...
THOSE RATS HAVE THEIR PLANES HIDDEN HERE. VON STORM SHOULD DRIVE PAST HERE ANY MINUTE. IF I CAN CAPTURE HIM—THEIR LEADER—A CLEAN-UP JOB WILL BE SIMPLE.

MEANWHILE IN ANOTHER CAR, APPROACHING STEVE'S HIDING PLACE . . .
TONIGHT WE STRIKE. WE SEND OUR PLANES INTO THE STRATOSPHERE WHERE THEY CANNOT BE SEEN, AND BOMB AMERICAN AIR FIELDS AND TRAINING CAMPS. SINCE OUR PLANES WILL NOT BE IDENTIFIED, IT CANNOT BE CONSTRUED AS AN ACT OF WAR—

SUDDENLY, AS THE CAR PASSES STEVE'S HIDING PLACE . . . .
VAS IST?
JUST TAKE IT EASY, BOYS - YOU'VE GOT COMPANY!

IF YOU'LL BE GOOD ENOUGH TO STOP THE CAR AND STEP OUT QUIETLY, THERE WON'T BE ANY TROUBLE, GENTLEMEN—

THE DRIVER SWERVES THE CAR SUDDENLY AND CRASHES INTO A TREE . . . . .
GOOT WORK, FRITZ!

HA, GENTLEMEN! THE QUICK THINKING OF OUR DRIVER HAS NETTED FOR US AN AMERICAN OFFICER.
HE IS NOT HURT, JUST UNCONSCIOUS. HE WILL COME IN HANDY FOR OUR PLANS, NICHT WAR?

VON STORM AND HIS MEN ENTER THE SECRET AIRFIELD WITH THEIR CAPTURED PRIZE . . .
HE IS THAT CAPTAIN TREVOR WHO HAS BEEN GIVING US SO MUCH TROUBLE. IT IS A GOOD THING THAT WE HAVE ONE OF THE AMERICAN ROBOT PLANES THAT WE STOLE.
YOU, FRITZ, GET THE AMERICAN PLANE READY AND SET THE ROBOT CONTROLS. I WANT IT TO BE FLYING SO THAT IT CAN BE SEEN OVER THE AMERICAN AIRDROME WHILE YOU, IN THE STRATOPLANE, DROP BOMBS FROM WAY ABOVE!
AH! AND SO WE PUT OUR AMERI-CAN OFFICER IN THE ROBOT PLANE!
THE MALIGNANCE OF YOUR IDEAS IS REFRESH-ING, MEIN HERR.
A FEW MINUTES LATER AT THE AMERICAN AIRDROME—
HEY, LOOK! ISN'T THAT ONE OF OUR PLANES?
YEAH, BUT IT DOESN'T LOOK LIKE IT'S GOING TO LAND!
AND AT THAT MOMENT . . .
THE ROBOT PLANE IS DIRECTLY OVER THE AIRDROME, MEIN HERR.
GOOD! RELEASE YOUR BOMBS!
WHAT IN THE WORLD! ONE OF OUR OWN PLANES DROPPING BOMBS ON US!
THERE'S SOMETHING QUEER GOING ON HERE!
DUCK! RUN FOR COVER. THAT PILOT, WHOEVER HE IS, IS CIRCLING TO DROP ANOTHER LOAD—
AND IN THE ROBOT PLANE, STEVE TREVOR BEGINS TO REGAIN CONSCIOUSNESS—
WHERE AM I? I'M CIRCLING MY OWN FIELD! WHY, THIS IS A ROBOT-CONTROLLED PLANE! LET'S SEE IF I CAN MAKE THE THROTTLE WORK—
SUDDENLY, THE PILOT OF THE SPY PLANE BECOMES ALARMED . . .
VAS IST! THE PLANE IS NOT OBEYING THE ROBOT CONTROL! SOMETHING IS WRONG!
6
SOMETHING IS WRONG— RADICALLY WRONG— FOR STEVE TREVOR HAS SIZED UP THE SITUATION, AND IS AT ONCE ON THE TAIL OF THE SPY PLANE . . .

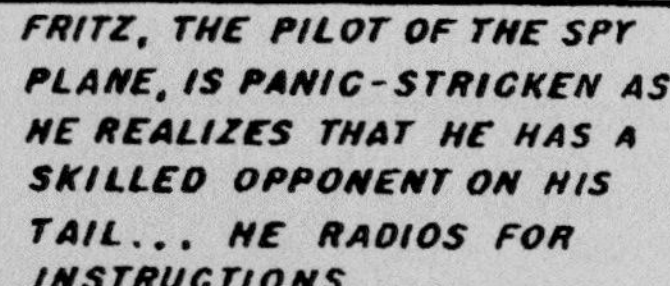
FRITZ, THE PILOT OF THE SPY PLANE, IS PANIC-STRICKEN AS HE REALIZES THAT HE HAS A SKILLED OPPONENT ON HIS TAIL... HE RADIOS FOR INSTRUCTIONS...

VON STORM! THE AMERICAN HAS RECOVERED CONSCIOUS-NESS. HE IS TURNING THE ROBOT PLANE AGAINST ME. I CAN'T SHOOT HIM DOWN! WHAT SHALL I DO? HELLO VON STORM, DO YOU HEAR ME?
VON STORM IS FURIOUS AT THE WAY HIS PLANS ARE GOING —
YOU FOOL! DON'T LET HIM SHOOT YOU DOWN! THEY MUST NOT FIND OUT THIS PLAN! THEY MUST NOT KNOW YOU DROPPED THOSE BOMBS! GET HIM AWAY FROM HIS FIELD—

THE STRATOPLANE TURNS TAIL AND RUNS — STEVE FOLLOWS...
HE'S TURNED TAIL, THE SKUNK! I'VE GOT TO SHOOT HIM DOWN, BUT HE KEEPS MOVING TOO HIGH FOR ME. I'LL CATCH HIM IF IT'S THE LAST THING I DO!

ALWAYS OUT OF SHOOTING RANGE, THE BLACK PLANE KEEPS STEVE FOLLOWING UNTIL THEY ARE FAR OUT AT SEA
I WONDER HOW LONG HE'S GOING TO KEEP THIS UP! WELL, AS LONG AS THERE IS GAS LEFT IN THIS CRATE, I'M GOING TO STAY WITH HIM—

HOURS PASS AND MANY MILES— HUNDREDS OF MILES — PASS WITH THEM, BUT STEVE KEEPS DOGGEDLY ON THE TRAIL OF THE ENEMY PLANE UNTIL FINALLY HIS GAS BEGINS TO RUN LOW ——
RUNNING SHORT OF GAS! LOOKS LIKE HE HAS ME LICKED! WAIT! WHAT'S THAT BELOW? CAN IT BE AN ISLAND? IT SEEMS SURROUNDED BY CLOUD FORMATIONS!

WELL, DAUGHTER, THERE'S THE HISTORY OF YOUR CAPTAIN UP TO THE VERY MOMENT HIS PLANE CRASHED ON PARADISE ISLAND!
BUT MOTHER, HE MUST BE TAKEN BACK TO AMERICA TO FINISH THE JOB HE STARTED!
7
GETTING HIM BACK WOULD BE A PROBLEM. LEAVE ME ALONE, MY DAUGHTER. I MUST CONSULT WITH APHRODITE AND ATHENA, OUR GOD-DESSES. I MUST SEEK THEIR ADVICE!
YES, MOTHER.
IT WOULDN'T BE ANY TRICK AT ALL FOR ME TO FLY HIM BACK MYSELF, BUT MOTHER WOULD NEVER HEAR OF IT.

IN THE QUEEN'S SOLITUDE, THE SPIRITS OF APHRODITE AND ATHENA, THE GUIDING GODDESSES OF THE AMAZONS, APPEAR AS THOUGH IN A MIST . . .

HIPPOLYTE, WE HAVE COME TO GIVE YOU WARNING. DANGER AGAIN THREATENS THE ENTIRE WORLD. THE GODS HAVE DECREED THAT THIS AMERICAN ARMY OFFICER CRASH ON PARADISE ISLAND. YOU MUST DELIVER HIM BACK TO AMERICA — TO HELP FIGHT THE FORCES OF HATE AND OPPRESSION.

YES, HIPPOLYTE, AMERICAN LIBERTY AND FREEDOM MUST BE PRESERVED! YOU MUST SEND WITH HIM YOUR STRONGEST AND WISEST AMAZON — THE FINEST OF YOUR WONDER WOMEN! — FOR AMERICA, THE LAST CITADEL OF DEMOCRACY, AND OF EQUAL RIGHTS FOR WOMEN, NEEDS YOUR HELP!

YES, APHRODITE, YES, ATHENA. I HEED YOUR CALL. I SHALL FIND THE STRONGEST AND WISEST OF THE AMAZONS. SHE SHALL GO FORTH TO FIGHT FOR LIBERTY AND FREEDOM AND ALL WOMANKIND!

AND SO THE AMAZON QUEEN PREPARES A TOURNAMENT TO DECIDE WHICH IS THE MOST CAPABLE OF HER SUBJECTS . . .

BUT MOTHER, WHY CAN'T I ENTER INTO THIS TOURNAMENT? SURELY, I HAVE AS MUCH RIGHT —

NO, DAUGHTER, NO! I FORBID YOU TO ENTER THE CONTEST! THE WINNER MUST TAKE THIS MAN BACK TO AMERICA AND NEVER RETURN, AND I COULDN'T BEAR TO HAVE YOU LEAVE ME FOREVER!

THE GREAT DAY ARRIVES! FROM ALL PARTS OF PARADISE ISLAND COME THE AMAZON CONTESTANTS! BUT ONE YOUNG CONTESTANT INSISTS ON WEARING A MASK . . .
IF YOU ARE ALL READY, LET THE TOURNAMENT BEGIN — AND MAY THE BEST MAIDEN WIN!

THE TESTS BEGIN! FIRST...THE FOOT RACE! A TRAINED DEER SETS THE PACE! AS THE DEER EASILY OUTRUNS THE PACK, SUDDENLY THE SLIM MASKED FIGURE DARTS FORWARD, HER LEGS CHURNING MADLY . . .

AND NOT ONLY CATCHES UP WITH THE DEER — BUT PASSES IT!

AS THE TESTS OF STRENGTH AND AGILITY GO ON THROUGHOUT THE DAY, MORE AND MORE CONTESTANTS DROP OUT WEARILY, UNTIL NUMBER 7, THE MASKED MAIDEN, AND MALA — NUMBER 12 — KEEP WINNING EVENT AFTER EVENT . . . UNTIL EACH HAS WON TEN OF THE GRUELLING CONTESTS!

AND NOW A DEADLY HUSH BLANKETS THE AUDIENCE. THE QUEEN HAS RISEN . . .

8

BULLETS AND BRACELETS!
BULLETS AND BRACELETS!
CONTESTANTS 7 AND 12. YOU ARE THE ONLY SURVIVORS OF THE TOURNAMENT! NOW YOU MUST GET READY FOR THE 21ST, THE FINAL AND GREATEST TEST OF ALL — BULLETS AND BRACELETS!
BULLETS AND BRACELETS!
BULLETS AND BRACELETS

EACH OF YOU WILL SHOOT FIVE TIMES. YOUR OPPONENT MUST CATCH THE BULLETS ON HER BRACELET - OR ELSE EXPECT TO BE WOUNDED! NOW TAKE YOUR PLACES NUMBER 12 WILL SHOOT FIRST.
THE COMMAND...AND THE GIRL FIRES POINT-BLANK AT NUMBER 7, THE MASKED MAIDEN!
THE ULTIMATE TEST OF SPEED OF BOTH EYE AND MOVEMENT! NO.7'S BRACELETS BECOME SILVER FLASHES OF STREAKING LIGHT AS THEY PARRY THE DEATH-THRUSTS OF THE HURTLING BULLETS!
NOT PASSES THE TEST UNSCATHED! NOW IT IS HER TURN TO FIRE. HER OPPONENT'S FAST— BUT NOT FAST ENOUGH!
NUMBER TWINS
NUMBER 7
UGH! MY SHOULDER!
THE WINNER... CONTESTANT NO.7 — THE MASKED MAIDEN!
YOU MAY REMOVE YOUR MASK, NUMBER 7! I WANT TO SEE THE FACE OF THE STRONGEST AND MOST AGILE OF ALL THE AMAZONS.
DAUGHTER! YOU!
I KNEW IT— I FELT IT! I THOUGHT PERHAPS - WELL, IT'S TOO LATE NOW! YOU'VE WON AND I'M PROUD OF YOU! IN AMERICA YOU'LL INDEED BE A "WONDER WOMAN", FOR I HAVE TAUGHT YOU WELL! AND LET YOURSELF BE KNOWN AS DIANA, AFTER YOUR GODMOTHER, THE GODDESS OF THE MOON! AND HERE IS A COSTUME I HAVE DESIGNED TO BE USED BY THE WINNER, TO WEAR IN AMERICA.
WHY MOTHER, IT'S LOVELY!
AND SO DIANA, THE WONDER WOMAN, GIVING UP HER HERITAGE, AND HER RIGHT TO ETERNAL LIFE, LEAVES PARADISE ISLAND TO TAKE THE MAN SHE LOVES BACK TO AMERICA—THE LAND SHE LEARNS TO LOVE AND PROTECT, AND ADOPTS AS HER OWN!
9

NO.1 JANUARY
The newest of the DC magazines
SENSATION COMICS
A SUPERMAN DC PUBLICATION
10¢
Featuring
THE SENSATIONAL
NEW ADVENTURE
STRIP CHARACTER-
Wonder Woman!

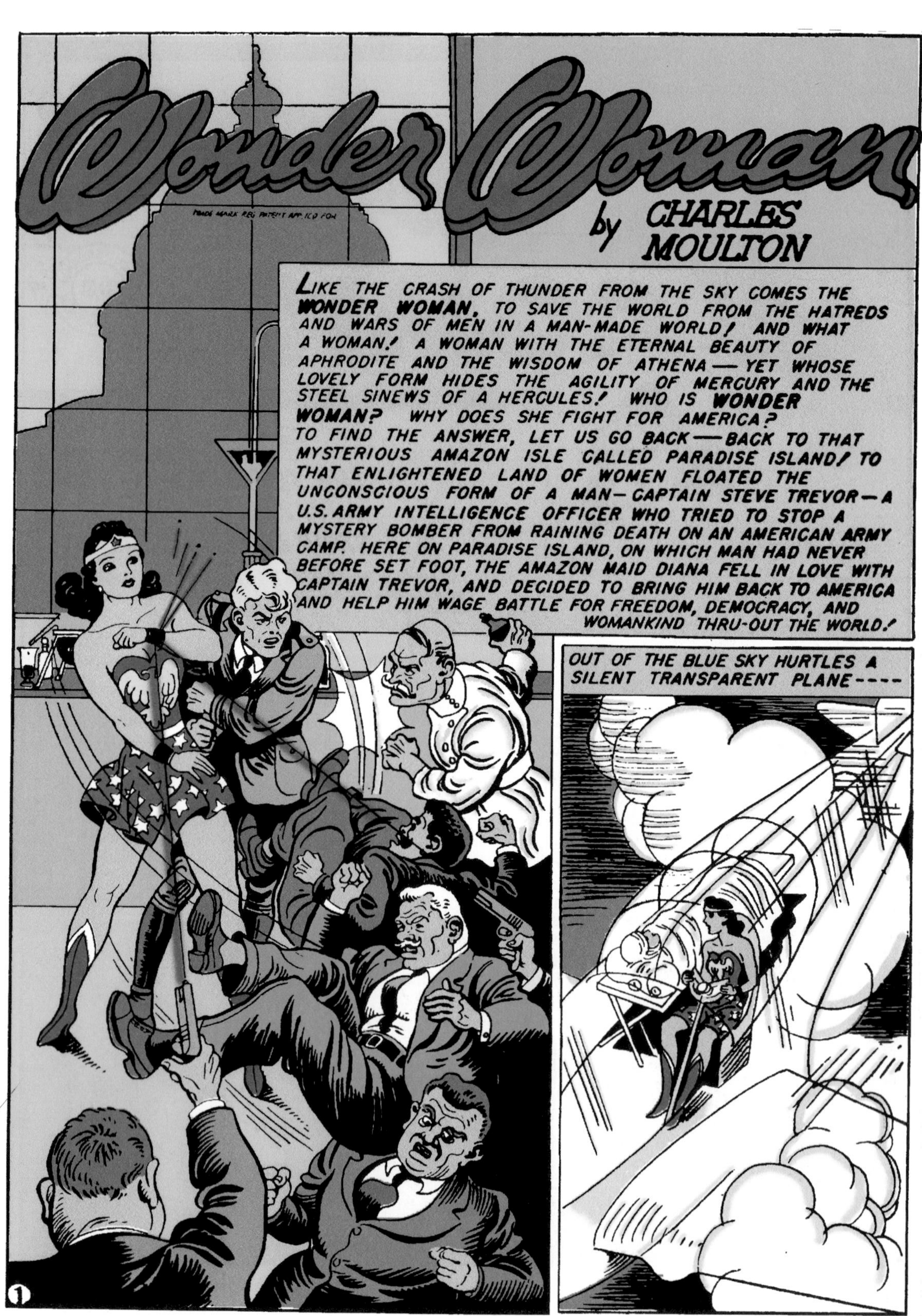
Wonder Woman
by CHARLES MOULTON
LIKE THE CRASH OF THUNDER FROM THE SKY COMES THE WONDER WOMAN, TO SAVE THE WORLD FROM THE HATREDS AND WARS OF MEN IN A MAN-MADE WORLD! AND WHAT A WOMAN! A WOMAN WITH THE ETERNAL BEAUTY OF APHRODITE AND THE WISDOM OF ATHENA — YET WHOSE LOVELY FORM HIDES THE AGILITY OF MERCURY AND THE STEEL SINEWS OF A HERCULES! WHO IS WONDER WOMAN? WHY DOES SHE FIGHT FOR AMERICA?
TO FIND THE ANSWER, LET US GO BACK — BACK TO THAT MYSTERIOUS AMAZON ISLE CALLED PARADISE ISLAND! TO THAT ENLIGHTENED LAND OF WOMEN FLOATED THE UNCONSCIOUS FORM OF A MAN — CAPTAIN STEVE TREVOR — A U.S. ARMY INTELLIGENCE OFFICER WHO TRIED TO STOP A MYSTERY BOMBER FROM RAINING DEATH ON AN AMERICAN ARMY CAMP. HERE ON PARADISE ISLAND, ON WHICH MAN HAD NEVER BEFORE SET FOOT, THE AMAZON MAID DIANA FELL IN LOVE WITH CAPTAIN TREVOR, AND DECIDED TO BRING HIM BACK TO AMERICA AND HELP HIM WAGE BATTLE FOR FREEDOM, DEMOCRACY, AND WOMANKIND THRU-OUT THE WORLD!
OUT OF THE BLUE SKY HURTLES A SILENT TRANSPARENT PLANE ----
1

AND AT THE CONTROLS IS AN AMAZON MAIDEN, NAMED DIANA BY HER MOTHER, QUEEN OF THE AMAZONS, AFTER HER GODMOTHER, GODDESS OF THE MOON!
HE'S STIRRING! PERHAPS I'D BETTER REMOVE HIS BANDAGES!
OH-H-H!

WHERE--? I'M IN HEAVEN! THERE'S AN ANGEL SMILING AT ME--- A BEAUTIFUL ANGEL!

HE'S FAINTED! HE'S STILL VERY WEAK. HE CALLED ME AN ANGEL--- A BEAUTIFUL ANGEL. THAT'S THE FIRST TIME A MAN EVER CALLED ME-- BEAUTIFUL!

ON--- ON SPEEDS THE PLANE UNTIL IT REACHES ITS DESTINATION — WASHINGTON, D.C.!
AT LAST I'M HERE — IN THE CAPITAL OF THE UNITED STATES!

DIANA BRINGS THE TRANS-PARENT PLANE DOWN ON AN ABANDONED FIELD ON THE OUTSKIRTS OF WASHINGTON.
THIS DESERTED BARN SHOULD DO NICELY AS A HIDEOUT FOR MY PLANE!

PICKING UP STEVE TREVOR, SHE RACES SWIFTLY TO THE WALTER REED HOSPITAL.
GOOD THING IT IS STILL VERY EARLY IN THE MORNING SO THE STREETS ARE DESER-TED.
2

AND INSIDE---
THIS IS CAPTAIN STEVE TREVOR OF THE ARMY INTELLIGENCE! HE'S HAD A BRAIN CONCUSSION! SEE THAT HE'S TAKEN CARE OF!
WHO-WHAT?

BUT-BUT WAIT! WHO ARE YOU?
I'LL SEND YOU A FULL REPORT SOMETIME! 'BYE!

NOW WHAT TO DO WITH MY TIME? HM-M! MOTHER TOLD ME SO MUCH ABOUT STYLES OF AMERICAN WOMEN THAT I'M DYING TO SEE THEM!
ALWAYS THE WOMAN, DIANA GOES WINDOW SHOPPING---
THERE'S SO MUCH MATERIAL TO THEIR DRESSES--- BUT THEY ARE CUTE! HM-M! THERE'S A NICE FROCK!
AND NOW AS PEOPLE BEGIN TO THRONG THE STREETS THEY ARE NO LITTLE AMAZED TO SEE THE SCANTILY CLAD GIRL WALKING ABOUT SO UNCONCERNED----
THE HUSSY! SHE HAS NO CLOTHES ON!
THE BRAZEN THING! HMPH! HMPH!
HA! SOUR GRAPES SISTER, DONT YOU WISH YOU LOOKED LIKE THAT!
BOY! WHATTA HONEY!
AW--- I'LL BET IT'S SOME SORT O' PUBLICITY STUNT FOR A NEW MOVIN' PITCHER.
IF IT IS, THEY CERTAINLY GO TO EXTREME LENGTHS TO ATTRACT THE PUBLIC EYE!
WELL, THEY CERTAINLY ATTRACTED MY EYE!
SUDDENLY ALL THOUGHTS OF DIANA ARE FORGOTTEN--- SCREAMS AND SHOTS CUT THROUGH THE AIR!
C'MON! LET'S GET TO THE CAR FAST!
BANK
IT'S A HOLD-UP!
AS IF OUT OF NOWHERE A FIGURE DARTS FORWARD AND BLOCKS THE BANDITS FROM THEIR CAR!
WHAT TH--? IT'S A DAME!
PLUG HER AND LET'S SCRAM OUT OF HERE!
LIKE ONE MAN, THE BANDITS LEVEL THEIR GUNS AND FIRE!
3
BUT WITH SPEED FASTER THAN THE EYE CAN FOLLOW, THE AMAZON MAIDEN CATCHES THE HURTLING BULLETS ON HER WRIST-BRACELETS!
IT'S FUN TO BE PLAYING "BULLETS AND BRACELETS" AGAIN!

SHE'S PLAYIN' WITH 'EM! SHE'S PLAYIN' CATCH WITH 'EM!
AND NOW I'M GOING TO PLAY CATCH WITH YOU!

DIANA'S HAND CLOSES LIKE A STEEL CLAMP ABOUT THE BANDIT'S WRIST---

WH-?

CATCH!

WHA - WHAT'S GOIN' ON AROUND HERE?
I DON'T KNOW. I HEARD SOMEONE SAY "IT'S A HOLD-UP." GOOD-BYE!

WAIT! WE WANT TO ASK YOU A FEW QUESTIONS!
SOME OTHER TIME, WHEN I'M ON THE "QUIZ KIDS" PROGRAM!
4

AS DIANA DARTS AWAY, ONE MAN SLIPS FROM THE EDGE OF THE CROWD---
DID YOU SEE HER SLAP THOSE BANDITS AROUND?
AND DID YOU SEE HER SLAP THOSE BULLETS AROUND? NOW THAT WAS SOMETHING!
WONDER WHO SHE IS?

HEY-- WAIT! SHE'S RUNNING FASTER! I'LL STEP ON THE GAS AND CATCH UP TO HER!

EVEN AS THE CAR WHIPS FORWARD, DIANA PUTS ON A GREAT BURST OF SPEED.
WHAT TH'—SHE'S GOING FASTER AND THE CAR'S DOING 35 MILES PER!

FASTER SPEEDS THE CAR, AND FASTER SPEEDS THE HUMAN METEOR AHEAD!
HOLY SMOKE! I'VE GOT THE CAR AT 50MILES PER HOUR—AND I STILL HAVEN'T CAUGHT UP WITH HER!

FASTER---FASTER---FASTER--FASTER- UNTIL DIANA COVERS GROUND AT A MILE A-MINUTE!
60 MILES AN HOUR--AND SHE'S STILL AHEAD! I'M GOING TO OPEN UP THIS BUGGY TO THE LIMIT!

FASTER AND STILL FASTER---UNTIL AT 80 MILES PER HOUR, THE CAR DRAWS ALONGSIDE THE MILE-A-MINUTE MAIDEN!
HEY--- WAIT-- I JUST WANT TO TALK TO YOU ABOUT A BUSINESS PROPOSITION!

SAY--WHAT ARE YOU? WHEW! YOU WERE BURNING UP THE ROAD!
WHAT'S THIS---BUSINESS PROPOSITION--YOU TALKED ABOUT?
5

MY NAME IS AL KALE! I BOOK ACTS FOR THEATRES! NOW I DON'T KNOW WHAT YOUR RACKET IS AND I DON'T CARE. ALL I KNOW IS THAT THOSE SPEEDY LEGS OF YOURS, OR THAT "BULLET" TRICK COULD NET US A FORTUNE!

YOU MEAN YOU WANT TO PUT ME ON A STAGE?
EITHER ON THE TRACK OR THE STAGE! RACING—OR THAT "BULLET" TRICK IN THE THEATRES. IT WOULD BRING YOU PLENTY OF MONEY!

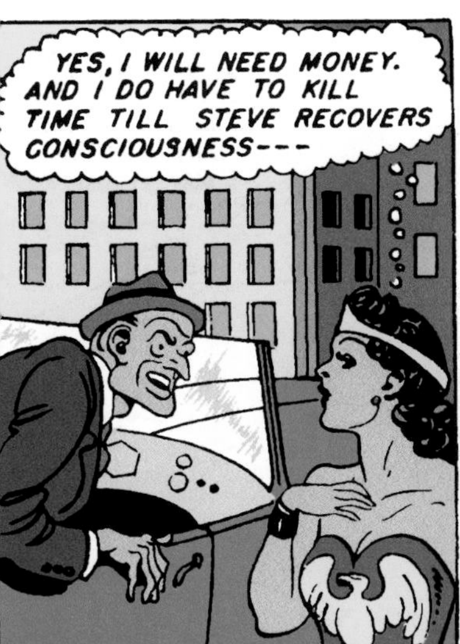
YES, I WILL NEED MONEY. AND I DO HAVE TO KILL TIME TILL STEVE RECOVERS CONSCIOUSNESS---

I'LL DO IT! I'LL PUT ON MY "BULLETS AND BRACELETS" ACT FOR YOU! BUT THE RACING IS OUT!
THAT'S O.K. WITH ME. WE'LL CLEAN UP WITH THAT "BULLETS" ACT ANYWAY! BOY-OH-BOY-OH-BOY-

AND "CLEAN UP" THEY DO---FOR THE "BULLETS AND BRACELETS" IS A GREAT ATTRACTION AND A SOURCE OF WONDER TO ALL!

THE PAPERS GIVE THE "WONDER WOMAN" PLENTY OF PUBLICITY----
DAILY BLADE
AMUSEMENT PAGE
BULLETS GO TO WASTE ON WONDER WOMAN
"WONDER WOMAN" BREAKS RECORDS AT BIJOU THEATRE

BUT AT LAST, ONE DAY THERE APPEARS AN ITEM THAT ATTRACTS WONDER WOMAN'S ATTENTION----
HOSPITAL AUTHORITIES REPORT THAT CAPTAIN TREVOR HAS AT LONG LAST RECOVERED CONSCIO A BRAIN CONCUSSION CAUSED THE COMA THAT LASTED THRE WEEKS. A MYSTERIOUS GIRL FIRST BROUGHT HI

BUT YOU CAN'T QUIT NOW! WE'RE KNOCKIN' 'EM DEAD! WE'RE MAKING MORE MONEY THAN---
MAKING MORE MONEY DOESN'T INTEREST ME ANY MORE! I'M SORRY, BUT I'M THROUGH WITH THE ACT!

I CAN'T HOLD HER. SHE DIDN'T SIGN ANY CONTRACT. WHEN I THINK OF ALL THE DOUGH WE COULD--- DOUGH ---SAY---I GOT HER DOUGH THAT SHE TOLD ME TO HOLD FOR HER! HMMM---
6

KALE---GONE--AND WITH ALL MY EARNINGS! I----- THERE HE IS — GETTING INTO HIS CAR!

WITHOUT A MOMENT'S HESITATION, WONDER WOMAN HURLS HER SLIM FORM THROUGH THE OPEN WINDOW-- AND PLUNGES TO THE STREET BELOW!
AND WONDER WOMAN LANDS ON THE BALLS OF HER FEET LIGHTLY AS A CAT!
MADE IT VERY NICELY!
WHAT'S THIS? I'M STEPPING ON THE GAS AND THE CAR DOESN'T MOVE! WHAT'S 'SMATTER
DON'T YOU THINK THIS IS A GOOD ENOUGH REASON?
YOU!
ULP! LET ME GO--- LET ME GO!
ALL RIGHT!
YI-I-I-II-II
AS LONG AS YOU INSIST!
DON'T LEAVE ME UP HERE!
NOW I'LL JUST TAKE MY OWN MONEY-AND BID YOU A FOND FAREWELL! GOOD-BYE, HIGH AND NOT SO MIGHTY!
THE NEXT DAY, WONDER WOMAN APPROACHES THE HOSPITAL----
STEVE... STEVE... I'VE GOT TO SEE HIM--BE NEAR HIM--BUT HOW?
7

AS SHE NEARS THE STEPS, WONDER WOMAN SEES A GIRL HUDDLED AND CRYING THERE---
I DON'T MEAN TO INTRUDE BUT CAN I HELP YOU?
NO ONE CAN HELP ME! BOO-HOO!

THE GIRL TELLS WONDER WOMAN THAT SHE IS AN ARMY NURSE JUST APPOINTED TO THIS HOSPITAL---
AND TODAY MY FIANCE JUST GOT A JOB IN SOUTH AMERICA, BUT HE CAN'T SEND FOR ME BECAUSE HIS SALARY IS TOO SMALL AT THE MOMENT!
THAT'S TERRIBLE, AND JUST THINK--IT ALL WOULD WORK OUT RIGHT IF ONLY YOU HAD A LITTLE MONEY!

I JUST NOTICED — WITH THESE GLASSES OFF, YOU LOOK A LOT LIKE ME! I HAVE AN IDEA! IF I GAVE YOU MONEY WOULD YOU SELL ME YOUR CREDENTIALS?
YOU--YOU MEAN YOU WANT TO TAKE MY PLACE HERE AT THE HOSPITAL? BUT-I CAN'T--- I MEAN--

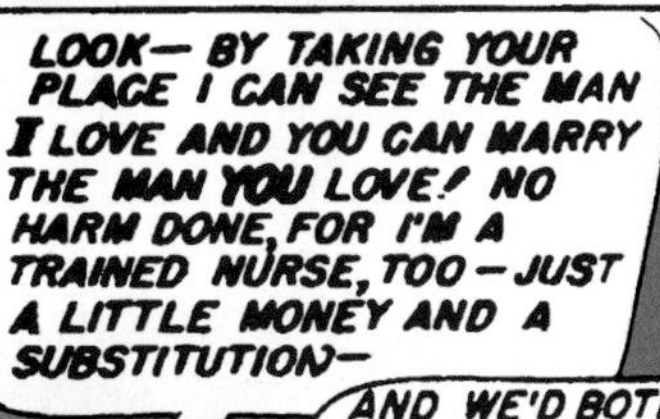
LOOK— BY TAKING YOUR PLACE I CAN SEE THE MAN I LOVE AND YOU CAN MARRY THE MAN YOU LOVE! NO HARM DONE, FOR I'M A TRAINED NURSE, TOO—JUST A LITTLE MONEY AND A SUBSTITUTION—

AND WE'D BOTH BE HAPPY! I'LL DO IT! OH—THIS IS WONDERFUL!

OH, BY THE WAY-MY NAME IS DIANA. WHAT'S YOURS?
WHY, THAT'S AN AMAZING COINCIDENCE—I'M DIANA TOO! DIANA PRINCE! AND YOU'D BETTER REMEMBER THAT LAST NAME— BECAUSE IT'LL BE YOURS FROM NOW ON.

AND SO THAT AFTERNOON----
AN ANGEL--- A BEAUTIFUL ANGEL!
OH, CAPTAIN TREVOR —YOU FLATTER ME I'M JUST DIANA PRINCE, YOUR SPECIAL NURSE!
HE REMEMBERED ME---HE REMEMBERED!

DAYS PASS AND STEVE TREVOR RECOVERS RAPIDLY UNDER HIS NEW NURSE'S TENDER CARE---

YOU'RE PRETTY SWELL TO ME, DIANA! BUT I'M JUST WASTING AWAY HERE. I SHOULD BE BACK ON MY JOB!
I DON'T BELIEVE IT'S YOUR JOB. YOU WANT TO FIND THAT "BEAUTIFUL ANGEL" YOU WERE TALKING ABOUT-THE ONE WHO BROUGHT YOU HERE! BE A GOOD BOY, NOW, AND KEEP QUIET---

GREAT GUNS! NOW I'VE GOT TO GO--- DOCTOR OR NO DOCTOR!

BY THE TIME THEY NOTICE I'M GONE, IT'LL BE TOO LATE TO STOP ME!

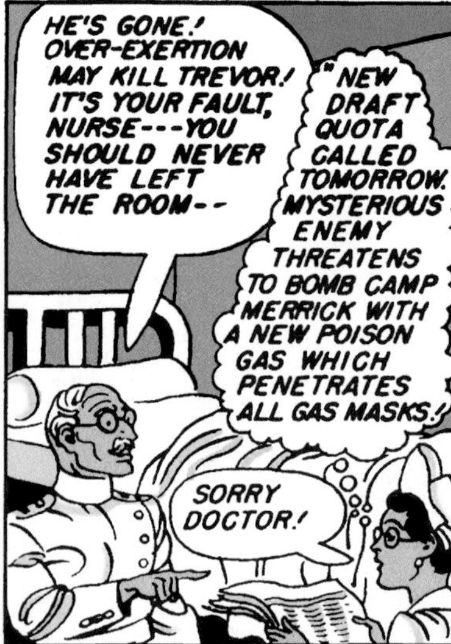
HE'S GONE! OVER-EXERTION MAY KILL TREVOR! IT'S YOUR FAULT, NURSE---YOU SHOULD NEVER HAVE LEFT THE ROOM--
"NEW DRAFT QUOTA CALLED TOMORROW. MYSTERIOUS ENEMY THREATENS TO BOMB CAMP MERRICK WITH A NEW POISON GAS WHICH PENETRATES ALL GAS MASKS!"
SORRY DOCTOR!

THAT NIGHT, NURSE DIANA PRINCE DARTS TOWARD AN OLD DESERTED BARN ON THE OUTSKIRTS OF WASHINGTON----
I HOPE NO ONE'S FOUND THIS HIDEOUT WHILE I'VE BEEN NURSING STEVE TREVOR!

INSIDE THE BARN, THE GIRL TRANSFORMS HERSELF FROM DRAB DIANA PRINCE TO THE EXCITING AMAZON MAIDEN... WONDER WOMAN!
IT FEELS GRAND TO BE MYSELF AGAIN! AND NOW FOR CLEVER STEVE TREVOR... THE IMPETUOUS DARLING!

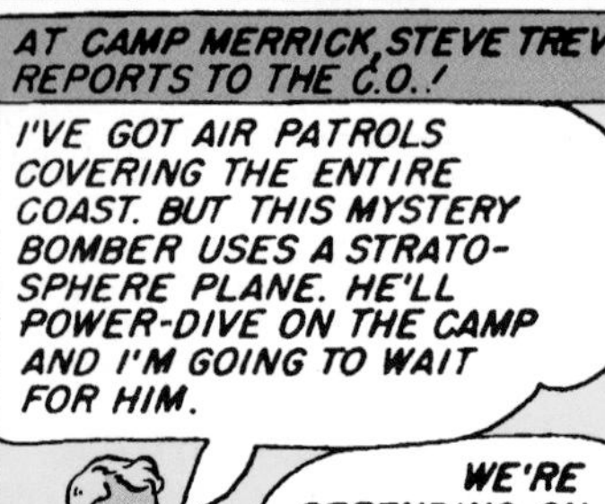
AT CAMP MERRICK, STEVE TREVOR REPORTS TO THE C.O.!
I'VE GOT AIR PATROLS COVERING THE ENTIRE COAST. BUT THIS MYSTERY BOMBER USES A STRATO-SPHERE PLANE. HE'LL POWER-DIVE ON THE CAMP AND I'M GOING TO WAIT FOR HIM.

WE'RE DEPENDING ON YOU, CAPTAIN!

HIGH OVER CAMP MERRICK, STEVE TREVOR CIRCLES LIKE A BIRD OF PREY--WAITING FOR THE ENEMY!

THEN--LIKE A DIVING, WINGED COMET--THE MYSTERY BOMBER!
WOW! HE MUST BE DOING 650 M.P.H.! I'VE GOT TO STOP HIM!

JUMPING BLUE BLAZES! THAT GUY'S GOT A FLYING FORT! I CAN'T EVEN DENT HIS POLISH!

THE AIR IS SUDDENLY DEAF-ENED BY A SHATTERING, THUNDEROUS EXPLOSION!

LIKE A STREAK OF LIGHT, A SILENT, TRANSPARENT PLANE HURTLES OUT OF THE BLUE WITH WONDER WOMAN AT THE CONTROLS!

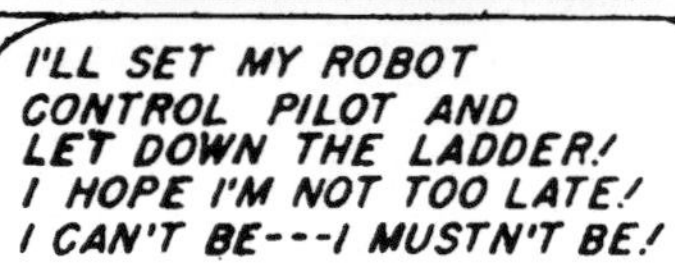

WONDER WOMAN'S RIGHT ARM GRASPS TREVOR'S FALLING BODY AND TIGHTENS AROUND HIS WAIST WITH THE UNFAILING GRIP OF A BOA CONSTRICTOR! THE SHOCK IS GREAT BUT HER LOVE AND STRENGTH ARE GREATER!

LOOK! THERE'S YOUR BOMB-SLINGER! WE'D BETTER COLLECT HIM AND ASK HIM A FEW QUESTIONS. TAKE THE CONTROLS.
DOWN THE SWAYING LADDER CLIMBS WONDER WOMAN AND THE PARACHUTIST FIRES POINT-BLANK!
STILL PLAYING HARD TO GET, EH?
NOTHING LIKE A GOOD RIGHT HOOK TO SETTLE AN ARGUMENT!
WHY, HE'S BEEN WOUNDED- I'D BETTER GET HIM UP TO MY PLANE.
THIS DEVIL IS DONE FOR! THAT CRASH—HE WON'T LIVE TO TALK.
THE CAPTAIN IS RIGHT--I DIE! BUT SOON MY COMRADES WILL COME IN MORE PLANES, MORE POISON GAS FROM THE SECRET BASE! YOU... YOU WILL NEVER FIND---
HE'S RIGHT! I LOCATED THEIR SECRET BASE ONCE, BUT THEY'VE MOVED IT AND I'LL NEVER FIND IT NOW!
BUT I CAN!
GOOD THING I ANTICIPATED THIS AND HAD MOTHER LOOK UP THIS SECRET BASE IN THE MAGIC SPHERE BEFORE I LEFT PARADISE ISLAND!
11
STRAIGHT AS AN ARROW, WONDER WOMAN'S PLANE FLIES TO THE SECRET BASE SHE HAD THUS LEARNED ABOUT.
WONDER WOMAN, IN HER SILENT, INVISIBLE PLANE, LANDS UNDETECTED ON THE ENEMY ISLAND!

AS TWO GUARDS PATROL THE GROUNDS, TWO SINISTER FIGURES CATAPULT OUT OF THE SHRUBBERY
WHAT ! ! ?
SINCE THESE DOORS ARE LOCKED·· WHY, WE'LL HAVE TO LET OURSELVES IN!
WELL I'LL BE.. LOOK AT HER!
HOW NICE TO MAKE YOUR ACQUAINTANCE!
HERE-PUT ON THIS MASK!
TREVOR FIRES AT A CONTAINER OF POISON GAS!
THE GAS GATHERS LIKE A MALIGNANT CLOUD ABOUT THE ENEMY BUT THE GAS MASKS PROTECT WONDER WOMAN AND TREVOR!
LOOK! THERE'S THEIR LEADER!
LOOK OUT! HE'S THROWING A SWITCH!
FOOLS! I'LL DIE- BUT YOU DIE WITH ME!
12
THERE IS ONE TERRIBLE, CATACLYSMIC BLAST... AN ETERNAL MOMENT OF SHATTERING RUIN...

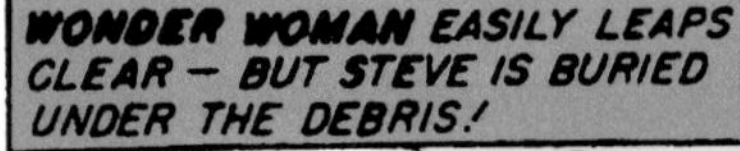

WONDER WOMAN EASILY LEAPS CLEAR — BUT STEVE IS BURIED UNDER THE DEBRIS!

WORKING AT A FEVERISH PACE WONDER WOMAN UNCOVERS STEVE TREVOR---
ARE YOU HURT, STEVE? WHY DIDN'T YOU JUMP LIKE I DID?
JUMP LIKE YOU? WHAT AM I — A KANGAROO?

YOUR LEG-- IT'S BROKEN!
MY LEG DOES SEEM BENT A BIT--BUT I'M GLAD OF IT. AT LEAST IT SHOWS YOU CARE!

YOUR LEG WILL BE RIGHT AS NEW IN A SHORT WHILE. ARUMPH... YOU DID MAGNIFICENT WORK, CAPTAIN.... MAGNIFICENT!
I DIDN'T DO IT!, A BEAUTIFUL ANGEL WAS RESPONSIBLE!

CONGRATULATIONS, CAPTAIN! YOU DID EXCELLENT WORK!
THANKS, CHIEF. BUT FOR HEAVEN'S SAKE, DON'T GIVE ME THE CREDIT. IT BELONGS TO THAT BEAUTIFUL GIRL— WONDER WOMAN!

LATER....
JUST SAW THE GENERAL OUTSIDE. THEY THINK YOU'RE DELIRIOUS, TALKING ABOUT A "BEAUTIFUL ANGEL"— A WONDER WOMAN WHO REALLY BROKE UP THAT NAZI GANG AND SAVED YOUR LIFE!
THAT'S RIGHT! YOU LAUGH, TOO.. BUT I'M NOT DELIRIOUS, YOU HEAR ME! THERE IS A WONDER WOMAN! I SAW HER!

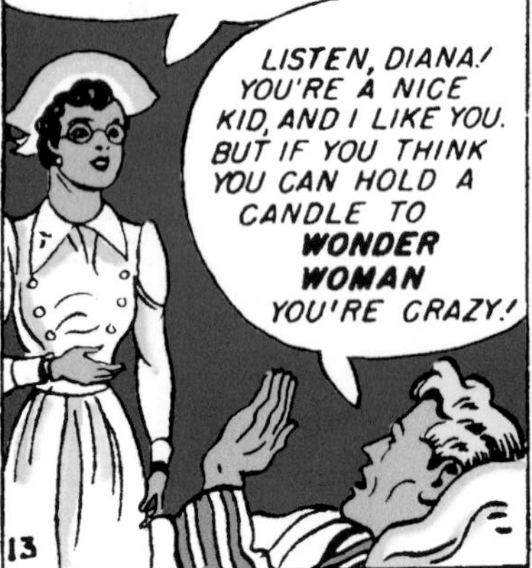

ALL RIGHT, I BELIEVE YOU! ANYWAY, CAPTAIN.... YOU DON'T NEED WONDER WOMAN NOW — YOU'VE GOT ME!
LISTEN, DIANA! YOU'RE A NICE KID, AND I LIKE YOU. BUT IF YOU THINK YOU CAN HOLD A CANDLE TO WONDER WOMAN YOU'RE CRAZY!
13

SO I'M MY OWN RIVAL, EH? THAT'S FUNNY... IF MOTHER COULD ONLY SEE ME NOW.... AS A VERY FEMININE WOMAN.. A NURSE, NO LESS, IN A WORLD FULL OF MEN, AND IN LOVE, TOO — WITH MYSELF FOR A RIVAL!

AND SO ENDS THE FIRST EPISODE OF **WONDER WOMAN** ALIAS ***DIANA PRINCE, ARMY NURSE!*** FOLLOW HER EXCITING ADVENTURES AS SHE BESTS THE WORLD'S MOST VILLAINOUS MEN AT THEIR OWN GAME EVERY MONTH IN **SENSATION COMICS**

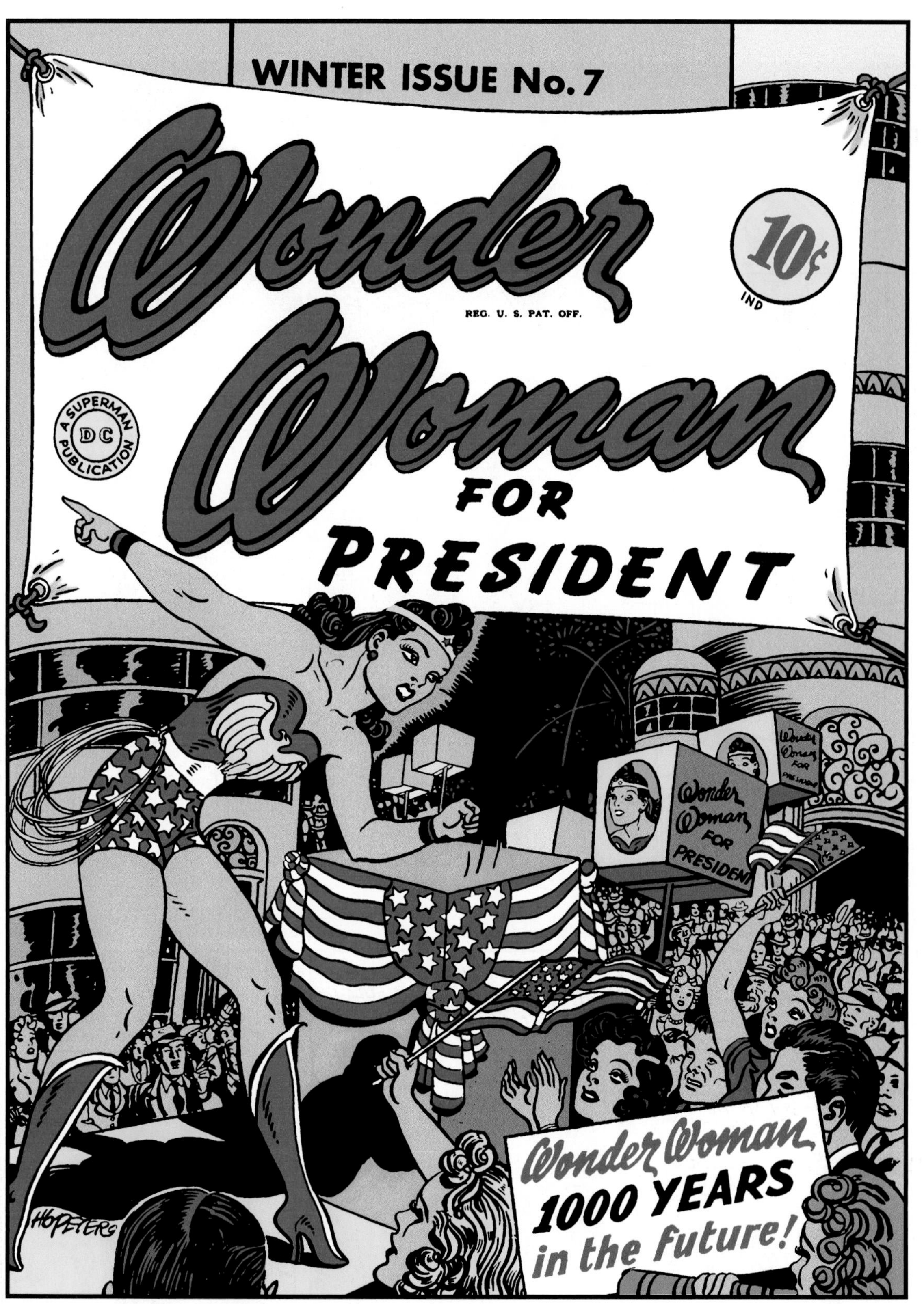
WINTER ISSUE No. 7
Wonder Woman
REG. U. S. PAT. OFF.
10¢
IND
A SUPERMAN DC PUBLICATION
FOR
PRESIDENT
Wonder Woman FOR PRESIDENT
Wonder Woman
1000 YEARS
in the future!
H.G. PETER

Wonder Woman

REG. U.S. PAT. OFF.

BY CHARLES MOULTON

WONDER WOMAN FROZEN ALIVE! THE PRESIDENT OF THE UNITED STATES KIDNAPED! WHAT HEADLINES SCREAM FROM THE FRONT PAGES OF A MILLION NEWSPAPERS IN 3004 A.D.! AND **WONDER WOMAN** HERSELF, THAT GORGEOUS, STUPENDOUS PERSONIFICATION OF ALL THAT IS GLORIOUS IN AMERICAN WOMANHOOD SHOWS YOU IN THIS EPISODE THE THRILLS THAT LIE AHEAD FOR **AMERICA'S WONDER WOMEN OF TOMORROW!**

US

H.G. PETER

ON THE MAGIC SPHERE AT PARADISE ISLAND THE QUEEN SHOWS **WONDER WOMAN** AMERICA'S FUTURE, 1000 YEARS HENCE.
YOU LOOK PLEASED, DAUGHTER, AND TRIUMPHANT!
I AM! A **WOMAN** WILL BE PRESIDENT OF THE UNITED STATES IN 3000 A.D.!
1B

BUT AMERICAN WOMEN WILL NOT RULE SUPREME AS WE AMAZONS DO. A **MAN** MIGHT RUN FOR PRESIDENT-HE MIGHT BEAT EVEN **YOU** AT THE POLLS!
I'D LIKE TO SEE HIM DO IT!
AMERICA 3000 A.D.

PERHAPS THE MAGIC SPHERE MAY GRANT YOUR WISH! ANYWAY LET'S SEE WHAT HAPPENS WHEN A MAN RUNS AGAINST A WOMAN FOR PRESIDENT IN 3004 A.D.!
OH, MOTHER-THIS IS EXCITING!
AMERICA 3000 A

THE MAGIC SPHERE SHOWS COLONEL TREVOR CALLING AT THE OFFICE OF GENERAL DARNELL
I NEED SOME CONFIDENTIAL ADVICE, GENERAL.
VERY WELL. DON'T GO, DIANA— WE COULDN'T KEEP SECRETS FROM YOU EVEN IF WE WANTED TO!
WHY, STEVE-THAT'S YOUR OLD 20TH CENTURY PIPE! YOU HAVEN'T SMOKED IT FOR DECADES!
HA HA! TRUST DI TO NOTICE! MEN ARE BACK NOWADAYS TO THE STYLES OF 1950!
AH- YOU MEAN THE MAN'S PARTY CROWD- MANLY'S PURPLE SHIRTS! BAH-
WELL-THOUSANDS OF MEN ARE JOINING PROFESSOR MANLY'S NEW POLITICAL PARTY. THEY'RE GOING TO ELECT A MAN PRESIDENT- HE'LL PUT MORE STRENGTH INTO THE GOVERNMENT!
"STRENGTH"- PHUI! YOU MEAN GRAFT! MANLY'S A SLICK HYPOCRITICAL CROOK!
PROFESSOR MANLY IS HONEST, GENEROUS, CLEVER - HIS THEORIES ARE WONDERFUL! AND- WELL- HE WANTS ME TO RUN FOR PRESIDENT!
DON'T DO IT, STEVE- HE'S USING YOU FOR A FRONT, TO COVER SOME CROOKED SCHEME. I DON'T TRUST MANLY!
DIANA, YOU'RE SIMPLY SORE BECAUSE MANLY CAN BEAT YOUR WOMAN'S PARTY! WHAT'S YOUR ADVICE, GENERAL?
WELL, MY OPERATIVES HAVE NEVER GOTTEN ANYTHING DEFINITE ON MANLY BUT- EXCUSE ME! HELLO- COMMISSIONER OF U.S. POLICE SPEAKING!
OPERATIVE X-7 REPORTING! NEW ERA LAW FORBIDDING MANUFACTURE OF ARMS IS BEING DEFIED! EXTERMINATOR RIFLES AND HAND GUNS ARE BEING MADE AND SOLD SECRETLY TO MEN!
THIS IS SERIOUS! REPORT PERSONALLY TO MISS PRINCE!
STEVE, I FEEL SURE THAT MANLY IS BEHIND THIS PLOT TO ARM MEN WITH KILLERS' WEAPONS! PLEASE DON'T JOIN HIS PARTY!
PROFESSOR MANLY WOULD NEVER BREAK THE LAW! I THINK YOU'RE JUST PREJUDICED, DIANA!
2B
LATER, AS POLICE OPERATIVE X-7 REPORTS TO DIANA —
THE MAN BEHIND THIS GUN PLOT IS - OHHH!
BANG

QUICKER THAN THOUGHT, DIANA LEAPS OVER HER DESK TO CATCH THE WOUNDED GIRL IN HER ARMS.
WHAT A HORRIBLE DEED! THERE HASN'T BEEN A MURDER LIKE THIS SINCE WOMEN CAME INTO POWER!

FINDING THE GIRL BEYOND HUMAN HELP, DIANA DASHES AFTER THE KILLER
I'VE GOT HIM NOW - THAT CORRIDOR HE TURNED INTO HAS NO OTHER OUTLET BUT THE PRESIDENT'S OFFICE.

BUT THE MURDERER'S HAND GUN, CLEVERLY THROWN, TRIPS DIANA AS SHE TURNS THE CORNER.
FAUGH! HOW CLUMSY OF ME!
CLANK!

RECOVERING QUICKLY, DIANA REACHES THE PRESIDENT'S OFFICE A SPLIT SECOND TOO LATE.
SORRY, MISTRESS PRINCE, WE CAN'T LET EVEN YOU ENTER WITHOUT YOUR PASS!
OH-H! WHO WENT IN THERE JUST NOW?

I DIDN'T SEE HIS FACE - HE WAS DRESSED IN THE ANCIENT MALE STYLE OF TROUSERS - HA HA! MEN LOOK SO COMICAL IN THOSE GARMENTS! HIS PASS WAS OKAY - SO IS YOURS, MISTRESS, SORRY TO DELAY YOU!

DIANA BURSTS INTO PRESIDENT ARDA'S PRIVATE OFFICE.
THERE'S THE MURDERER!
HAVE YOU GONE CRAZY, DI? THIS IS PROFESSOR MANLY!
US
3B

I DON'T CARE **WHO** HE IS! THAT MAN SHOT ONE OF MY GIRL OPERATIVES! I FOLLOWED HIM HERE AND -
THERE'S SOME MISTAKE - I'LL VOUCH FOR PROF MANLY'S HIGH CHARACTER!

NOW THAT YOU'RE HERE, DIANA, YOU MUST JOIN OUR CONFERENCE. COLONEL TREVOR WILL RUN FOR PRESIDENT AND PROF MANLY FOR VICE PRESIDENT ON THE MAN'S PARTY TICKET!
YOU CAN BEAT THEM EASILY, MISTRESS PRESIDENT!

BUT I WON'T RUN AGAINST STEVE!
THEN I WILL! I'D RATHER SEE STEVE BEATEN THAN LET HIM BE A STOOGE FOR MANLY'S CROOKED MOB!
YOU'LL MAKE A CHARMING CANDIDATE FOR THE WOMEN'S PARTY, MISS PRINCE- CONGRATULA-TIONS!

DIANA IS NOMINATED FOR PRESIDENT AND ETTA CANDY FOR VICE PRESIDENT AT THE WOMEN'S PARTY CONVENTION.
HOORAY! HOORAY! HOORAY! DI AND ETTA-HOORAY!
ETTA CANDY FOR VICE-PRESIDENT SHE'LL LEND WEIGHT TO OUR TICKET!
DIANA FOR PRESIDENT
DIANA FOR PRESIDENT SHE'LL EXPOSE MANLY

DIANA'S ABLE SPEECHES AND ETTA'S HUMOR APPEAL EQUALLY TO MEN AND WOMEN.
THREE CHEERS FOR PRINCE AND CANDY! HOORAY-HOORAY-HOORAY!
CLAP!
CLAP!
CLAP!

BUT STEVE MAKES A STRONG APPEAL TO THE YOUNGER WOMEN'S VOTE.
ISN'T HE CUTE- I'LL VOTE FOR TREVOR!
OH, HE'S HAND-SOME- I'M FOR STEVE!
HE LOOKS LIKE A FIGHTER- HE'S GOT MY VOTE!
THE DAILY TRUTH MAN'S CANDIDAT FOR PRESIDENT COL. STEVE TRE
48
I PLEDGE MYSELF TO WORK ESPECIALLY FOR WOMEN'S INTERESTS-
OH YOU GREAT, BIG WONDERFUL MAN! I WISH I COULD VOTE 10 TIMES FOR YOU!

ON ELECTION NIGHT OFFICIALS IN 48 STATE CAPITALS WORK FRANTICALLY TO COMPLETE THE COUNTING OF VOTES.
IT'S CLOSE BUT IT LOOKS LIKE ANOTHER VICTORY FOR THE WOMAN'S PARTY!
RIGHT! RADIO REPORTS ARE THE SAME EVERYWHERE!

SUDDENLY, IN 20 KEY STATES, PURPLE SHIRTS INVADE THE VOTE COUNTING ROOMS.
LIE DOWN ON THE FLOOR ON YOUR FACES AND NOT A WORD OUT OF YOU!
ELECTION OFFICIAL 1039

SWIFTLY THE HELPLESS OFFICIALS ARE BOUND AND GAGGED.
WORK FAST, PURPLE SHIRTS—A SINGLE SLIP WILL SPOIL OUR ENTIRE PLAN!

SUBSTITUTE OFFICIALS IN FAKE UNIFORMS CHANGE THE VOTE TOTALS IN FAVOR OF THE MAN'S PARTY.
DON'T CHANGE THE COUNT TOO MUCH, JUST ENOUGH TO ELECT TREVOR AND MANLY!
ELECTION OFFICIAL 1034

AT WOMAN'S PARTY HEADQUARTERS THE NEW TREND IS NOTED WITH AMAZEMENT.
I DON'T UNDERSTAND THIS- THE TOTALS IN ALL KEY STATES ARE SHIFTING TO THE MAN'S PARTY!
THERE'S SOME-THING QUEER ABOUT IT- WE'LL INVESTIGATE LATER!

BEFORE DAWN THE ELECTION IS CONCEDED TO THE MAN'S PARTY.
WELL, THEY'VE WON AND THAT'S THAT! BUT I STILL CAN'T SEE HOW THEY DID IT!
ELECTION OFFICIAL

AT MAN'S PARTY HEADQUARTERS TROOPS ARE CALLED TO PROTECT STEVE FROM HIS YOUNG ADMIRERS.
HOORAY FOR PRESIDENT STEVE! HE'S WONDERFUL! HANDSOME STEVE- LET ME AT HIM!
THANKS, LADIES- BUT TAKE IT EASY- WOO-OOF!
US
5B

BUT LATER BEHIND LOCKED DOORS—
I'VE ELECTED YOU, TREVOR- NOW YOU TAKE ORDERS FROM ME! SIGN THIS **DECREE** ORDERING ALL ELECTION BALLOTS DESTROYED!
I WILL **NOT**! ARE YOU CRAZY, MANLY?
US
DECREE

STEVE SLIPS AWAY FOR A SOLITARY HORSEBACK RIDE TO THINK OVER MANLY'S NEW ATTITUDE AND SUDDENLY FINDS HIMSELF SURROUNDED BY PURPLE SHIRTS.
HANDS UP!
WHAT GAME IS THIS?

I'LL PLAY THIS GAME **MY** WAY!
YOU'LL SOON FIND OUT WE'RE NOT **PLAYING**!

AH-UNH!
SEIZE HIM, MEN! YOU KNOW WHAT TO DO WITH HIM!

DIANA, MEANWHILE, RESIGNS HER POSITION AS GENERAL DARNELL'S SECRETARY AND ASSISTANT.
I HATE TO LEAVE THE GENERAL AFTER WORKING WITH HIM ALL THESE YEARS BUT WHAT ELSE CAN I DO?

Dear General:

I herewith tender my resignation as your secretary and aide. I do this because I want to investigate and prosecute Professor Manly without embarrassing your department.

I have proof that Manly murdered our Operative X-7 and I strongly suspect him of fraud in counting election returns.

Yours faithfully,

Diana Prince

AS SHE LEAVES POLICE HEADQUARTERS DIANA SEES A CROWD BUYING NEWSPAPERS WITH FEVERISH EXCITEMENT.
THE PRESIDENT DISAPPEARS! GUARDS ARRESTED! READ ALL ABOUT IT IN THE **DAILY TRUTH**!
WHAT! GIVE ME A PAPER **QUICK**!
6B

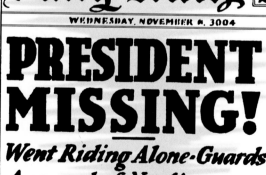

WEDNESDAY, NOVEMBER 4, 3004

PRESIDENT MISSING!

Went Riding Alone-Guards Accused of Negligence-Kidnaping Feared!

President-elect Steve Trevor eluded his body guards yesterday and was last seen riding

RUSHING BACK TO GENERAL DARNELL'S OFFICE, DIANA FINDS VICE PRESIDENT MANLY AT HIS DESK
THIS LETTER OF YOURS IS VERY INTERESTING! SO YOU HAVE EVIDENCE THAT I SHOT POLICE OPERATIVE X-7?
SHADES OF PLUTO! HOW DARE YOU READ THE GENERAL'S CORRESPONDENCE?

IN TREVOR'S ABSENCE I AM ACTING PRESIDENT– ADDRESS ME RESPECTFULLY!
I'LL ADDRESS YOU AS YOU DESERVE! AS A PRIVATE CITIZEN I'M FREE TO PROSECUTE YOU AND BY HERA, I'M GOING TO DO IT!

WE'LL SEE WHO DOES THE PROSECUTING! OFFICERS, ARREST THIS WOMAN!
BUT- ER- MR. PRESIDENT! MISTRESS PRINCE IS OUR SUPERIOR OFFICER—

I'M NO LONGER YOUR SUPERIOR OFFICER, GIRLS- YOU'LL HAVE TO OBEY THE ACTING PRESIDENT!
I CHARGE THIS PRISONER WITH PLOTTING AGAINST THE GOVERNMENT- GAG HER! SHE MUST NOT TALK TO ANYBODY!

ON MANLY'S ORDERS, DIANA IS PUT IN CLOSE CONFINEMENT.
WE HATE TO DO THIS TO YOU, MISTRESS PRINCE!
I BROUGHT YOUR HANDBAG- IF THEY EVER LET YOUR HANDS LOOSE YOU CAN POWDER YOUR NOSE!

LEFT ALONE IN HER SOLITARY CELL, DIANA WASTES NO TIME IN REMOVING HER STRAIGHTJACKET.
I'VE GOT TO FREE MYSELF AND FIND STEVE- NICE OF THAT GIRL GUARD TO BRING MY BAG! IT CONTAINS MY WONDER WOMAN COSTUME!
R-R-R-IP!-P!-P!
7B

I'LL BREAK OUT OF THIS PRISON QUIETLY. IF ANYONE SEES ME HERE HE MAY SUSPECT THAT I'M DIANA!

TO AVOID PRISON GUARDS I'LL SLIP OUT THIS WINDOW--

-AND CLIMB TO THE ROOF. THIS IS SO EASY I SHOULD THINK ALL PRISONERS WOULD ESCAPE THIS WAY!

IT'S NOT MORE THAN 50 FEET TO THE PRISON WALL - QUITE A SHORT JUMP - BUT I HOPE THE GUARDS DON'T SEE ME!

PSHAW! THAT GUARD SAW ME- I'LL HAVE TO DO SOMETHING ABOUT HER!
WONDER WOMAN! COME DOWN OR I'LL HAVE TO SHOOT!

LANDING ON THE WALL TOP, THE AMAZON PRINCESS THROWS HER MAGIC LASSO OVER THE PROTESTING GIRL GUARD.
I HAVEN'T TIME TO COME DOWN- YOU COME UP!
EEEK!

WRAPPING THE GUARD IN DIANA'S CAPE, WONDER WOMAN LEAPS FROM THE WALL.
IF THE WATCH TOWER GUARDS SEE ME NOW THEY'LL THINK I'VE GOT DIANA IN MY ARMS!
8B

LOOK- THERE'S WONDER WOMAN! SHE'S CARRYING OFF A PRISONER!
I'LL BET SHE'S RESCUING MISTRESS PRINCE! I WISH WE DIDN'T HAVE TO GIVE THE ALARM, BUT WE MUST!

STEVE, MEANWHILE, AFTER BEING KNOCKED OUT BY THE PURPLE SHIRTS, RECOVERS CONSCIOUSNESS AMID STRANGE SURROUNDINGS.
SOME-SOMETHING HIT ME-OUCH! WHO-HOW-WHAT'S THIS ALL ABOUT?
IT LOOKS LIKE WE'RE ALL PROF. MANLY'S PRISONERS— THIS VAULT'S HIS PRIVATE LABORATORY!

WE'RE ELECTION OFFICIALS! WE WERE COUNTING VOTES- THE WOMAN'S PARTY WAS AHEAD. SUDDENLY MANLY'S PURPLE SHIRTS APPEARED, TOOK US PRISONERS AND SUBSTITUTED FAKE OFFICIALS WHO CHANGED THE COUNT.
SO THAT'S WHY MANLY WANTS THE BALLOTS DESTROYED!

STEVE'S CONVERSATION IS INTERRUPTED BY THE APPEARANCE OF THE PURPLE SHIRT GUARDS.
COME ON, TREVOR, THE CHIEF WANTS TO SEE YUH!
GOOD! I YEARN FOR A LITTLE HEART-TO-HEART TALK WITH THE PROFESSOR!

SIT DOWN, PRESIDENT TREVOR!
I'M NO MORE PRESIDENT THAN YOU'RE A DECENT CITIZEN! DIANA PRINCE WON THE ELECTION- YOU KNOW THAT A RECOUNT OF BALLOTS WILL PROVE IT!

YES-THOSE BALLOTS MUST BE DESTROYED! I CAN ISSUE THE ORDER AS ACTING PRESIDENT BUT I'D RATHER YOU DID IT- LOOKS LESS SUSPICIOUS. I'LL GIVE YOU ONE MORE CHANCE!
NEVER! I'LL SEE YOU IN SIBERIA FIRST!

SIBERIA- HM- THAT GIVES ME AN IDEA! SIBERIA IS COLD- YOUR VIRTUOUS ARDOR NEEDS COOLING- HA HA! THIS WILL BE AN INTERESTING EXPERIMENT!

A HUGE BOTTLE IS BLOWN ABOUT STEVE AND LOWERED INTO A TANK OF LIQUID AIR.
FEEL CHILLY, TREVOR? THE LIQUID AIR OUTSIDE YOUR BOTTLE IS NEARLY 270° BELOW ZERO! YOU'LL FREEZE TO DEATH— BUT SLOWLY!

YOUR BOTTLE IS MADE OF CALCI-ATITE-IT PARTIALLY PROTECTS YOU FROM COLD. IF YOU BREAK IT HOPING TO ESCAPE, THE LIQUID AIR WILL FREEZE YOU SOLID INSTANTLY. OBEY ME AND I'LL RE-LEASE YOU!
FREEZING'S MY FAVORITE DEATH!

WHILE THE UNFORTUNATE STEVE WAITS STOICALLY FOR THE CREEPING COLD OF DISSOLUTION, WONDER WOMAN RACES BACK TO WASHINGTON.
MANLY MUST HAVE KIDNAPED STEVE IN ORDER TO BECOME ACTING PRESIDENT- BUT WHERE WOULD HE HIDE HIS PRISONER?

THE AMAZON SEEKS THE SECRET HEADQUARTERS OF THE PURPLE SHIRTS WHICH SHE HAS LOCATED DURING POLICE INVESTIGATION AS DIANA PRINCE.
WHO COMES? GIVE THE PASSWORD!
I'M WONDER WOMAN AND MY PASSWORD IS A STRONG RIGHT ARM!

THE BEAUTIFUL VISITOR IS GREETED CORDIAL-LY.
WELCOME, WONDER WOMAN! WE HAVE JUST HEARD BY RADIO THAT YOU RESCUED DIANA PRINCE FROM PRISON- OUR CHIEF WANTS TO SEE YOU!
WHAMM!

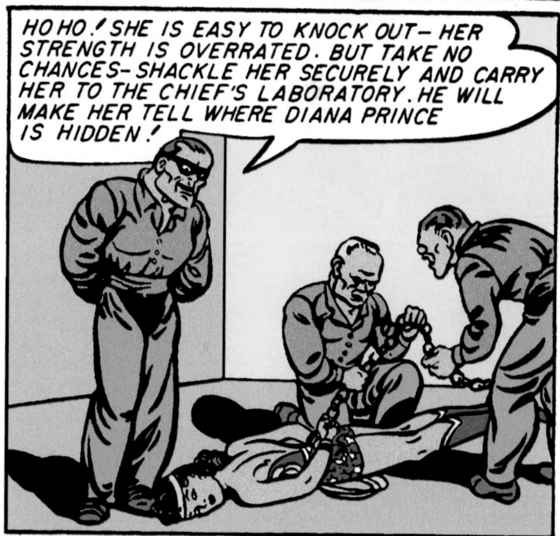
HO HO! SHE IS EASY TO KNOCK OUT- HER STRENGTH IS OVERRATED. BUT TAKE NO CHANCES- SHACKLE HER SECURELY AND CARRY HER TO THE CHIEF'S LABORATORY. HE WILL MAKE HER TELL WHERE DIANA PRINCE IS HIDDEN!

I'LL ACCOMPLISH MORE IF I LET THEM THINK THEY KNOCKED ME OUT WITH THAT LITTLE TAP ON THE HEAD! HAH! SO MAN-LY USES HIS LAB FOR A PRISON- HM- I'LL SEND A MENTAL RADIO MESSAGE TO ETTA CANDY—
CALLING ETTA CANDY CALLING ETTA----
10B

AS THEY REACH MANLY'S LABORATORY WONDER WOMAN APPEARS TO REVIVE.
I CAN WALK BY MYSELF! WHAT DEVIL'S CONTRAPTION IS THIS?
AH, MY DEAR LADY, THIS WILL INTER-EST YOU- A LIQUID AIR EXPERI-MENT IN HUMAN PSYCHOLOGY!

I AM USING THE COLDEST SUBSTANCE KNOWN TO COOL PRESIDENT TREVOR'S FIERY TEMPER! IF HE DOESN'T YIELD-WELL, WOULD YOU LIKE TO TALK TO HIM?
STEVE! SPEAK TO ME!
H'LO AN-GEL! FEEL N-NUMB-C-CAN'T-TALK-

LATER I'LL TRY THIS EXPERIMENT ON **YOU**! DON'T ATTEMPT TO RESCUE TREVOR-IF YOU BREAK THIS TANK A FLOOD OF LIQUID AIR WILL GUSH OVER ALL OF US, FREEZING OUR BODIES INSTANTLY!
I'VE **GOT** TO DO IT!

AS **WONDER WOMAN** SHOUTS A WARNING EVERY GUARD IN THE ROOM RUSHES TO SEIZE HER.
LOOK OUT! I'M GOING TO ESCAPE!

THE COURAGEOUS AMAZON, UNFLINCHING, SMASHES THE TANK RELEASING A DELUGE OF LETHAL LIQUID AIR.
CRASH
CRASH!
HISS-SS
S-S-S

THE DEADLY FLOOD OF FUMING FLUID ENGULFS **WONDER WOMAN** AND HER FOES ALIKE, FREEZING THEM IN A SPLIT SECOND INTO HUMAN ICICLES!
11B
MINUTES LATER STEVE, REALIZING THAT THE TANK IS NO LONGER FILLED WITH SUBZERO LIQUID SHAKES OFF HIS NUMBNESS AND BREAKS THE BOTTLE.
W-WHAT HAPPENED? TANK'S BROKEN-LIQUID AIR GONE - ALL EVAPORATED—

WONDER WOMAN - ANGEL - WAKE UP! WHAT'S MATTER - I CAN'T UN'STAND - MIND'S STILL GROGGY! YE GODS - SHE'S FROZEN STIFF! OH-H NO- NO, NO- IT CAN'T BE TRUE!

I CAN'T BELIEVE IT-MY WONDER WOMAN GONE-DEAD-SHE GAVE HER LIFE FOR ME! SHE BROKE THE TANK AND THE LIQUID AIR FROZE THEM ALL, THEN EVAPORATED! I-I WISH IT HAD KILLED ME TOO!

AT THIS MOMENT ETTA CANDY ARRIVES ON THE SCENE WITH HER COLLEGE TROOPERS.
WOO WOO! WHAT GOES, BROTHER? BR-RR- THIS ROOM IS FREEZING COLD!
WONDER WOMAN'S FROZEN — LIQUID AIR—

LET HER ALONE, ETTA! NOTHING WE CAN DO—
THE HECK THERE ISN'T! WONDER WOMAN'S NO FOOL- SHE LET HERSELF BE FROZEN BECAUSE SHE KNEW I COULD THAW HER OUT! COME ON, GIRLS, HELP ME CARRY HER!

WE'LL PUT HER IN HERE AND RAISE THE TEMPERATURE VERY SLOWLY- I'LL EXPLAIN-
TEMPERATURE CONTROL ROOM
12B

ETTA EXPLAINS: "WHEN A LIVING BODY IS FROZEN VERY QUICKLY IT DOES NOT DIE IMMEDIATELY BUT REMAINS IN A STATE OF SUSPENDED ANIMATION. HOW LONG IT'LL LIVE DEPENDS ON THE STRENGTH AND VIGOR OF THE PERSON FROZEN. WONDER WOMAN'D LIVE FOR A YEAR, I BETCHA! D'JA EVER SEE A COLLEGE PROF. TAKE A LIVE GOLDFISH, PLUNGE IT INTO LIQUID AIR, AN' PULL IT OUT FROZEN STIFF? THEN HE DROPS IT INTO WARM WATER AND OFF SWIMS MR. FISH AGAIN. YOU JUST WATCH WONDER WOMAN COME TO LIFE!"

SHE-SHE ISN'T MOVING!
WAIT- WE HAFTA THAW HER VERY SLOWLY!
REGULATOR

SUDDENLY **WONDER WOMAN** COMES TO LIFE!
YOU DID IT! ETTA- SHE'S ALIVE- **WONDER WOMAN'S WAVING** AT US!

ETTA, YOU'RE THE BEST PAL A GIRL EVER HAD! I **KNEW** I COULD COUNT ON YOU!
YEAH- BUT DON'T TRY IT AGAIN UNLESS I'VE HAD PLENTY OF CANDY - MY BRAIN MIGHT JAM!
HOORAY! YAYAYAY! **WONDER WOMAN'S** SAVED!

YOU'D BETTER THAW OUT MANLY AND HIS GANG AND HAVE THE GIRLS TAKE THEM TO JAIL!
AW- LET 'EM STAY FROZEN!
NO, SIR! MANLY'S GOTTA CONFESS HE MONKEY-WRENCHED THE ELECTION! DI AND I WANTA BE PRESIDENT!

WHILE **WONDER WOMAN** AND STEVE FREE THE PRISONERS.
I SHOULD GO TO PRISON WITH MANLY FOR THIS DESPICABLE ELECTION FRAUD!
NO, NO, COLONEL TREVOR! NOBODY BLAMES YOU! AND BESIDES, YOU AND **WONDER WOMAN** SAVED US ALL!

INFORMED BY POLICE FOURTH DIMENSIONAL RADIO, GENERAL DARNELL HURRIES TO THE SCENE---- **WONDER WOMAN** MAKES A LIGHTNING CHANGE!
GLAD YOU'RE OKAY, STEVE, BUT WHERE **IS** - OH! **THERE** YOU ARE, MISTRESS PRESIDENT! BY GEORGE- YOU **DO** MOVE AROUND QUICKLY-- ER- WHERE'S **WONDER WOMAN?**
I GUESS SHE LEFT- **SHE** MOVES MUCH MORE QUICKLY THAN I ----

AND SO, DIANA PRINCE, AFTER MANY YEARS OF FAITHFUL SERVICE TO HER COUNTRY, FINALLY HOLDS ITS HIGHEST OFFICE ----
I SOLEMNLY SWEAR TO PERFORM MY DUTIES FAITHFULLY AS PRESIDENT OF THE UNITED STATES.
13B.

WHILE BACK IN 1943 ON PARADISE ISLAND----
OH MOTHER, HE **DIDN'T** BEAT ME AFTER ALL - I ALMOST WISH HE HAD, POOR STEVE!
SILLY GIRL - STEVE AND ALL MEN ARE MUCH HAPPIER WHEN THEIR STRONG AGGRESSIVE NATURES ARE CONTROLLED BY A WISE AND LOVING WOMAN!
The End

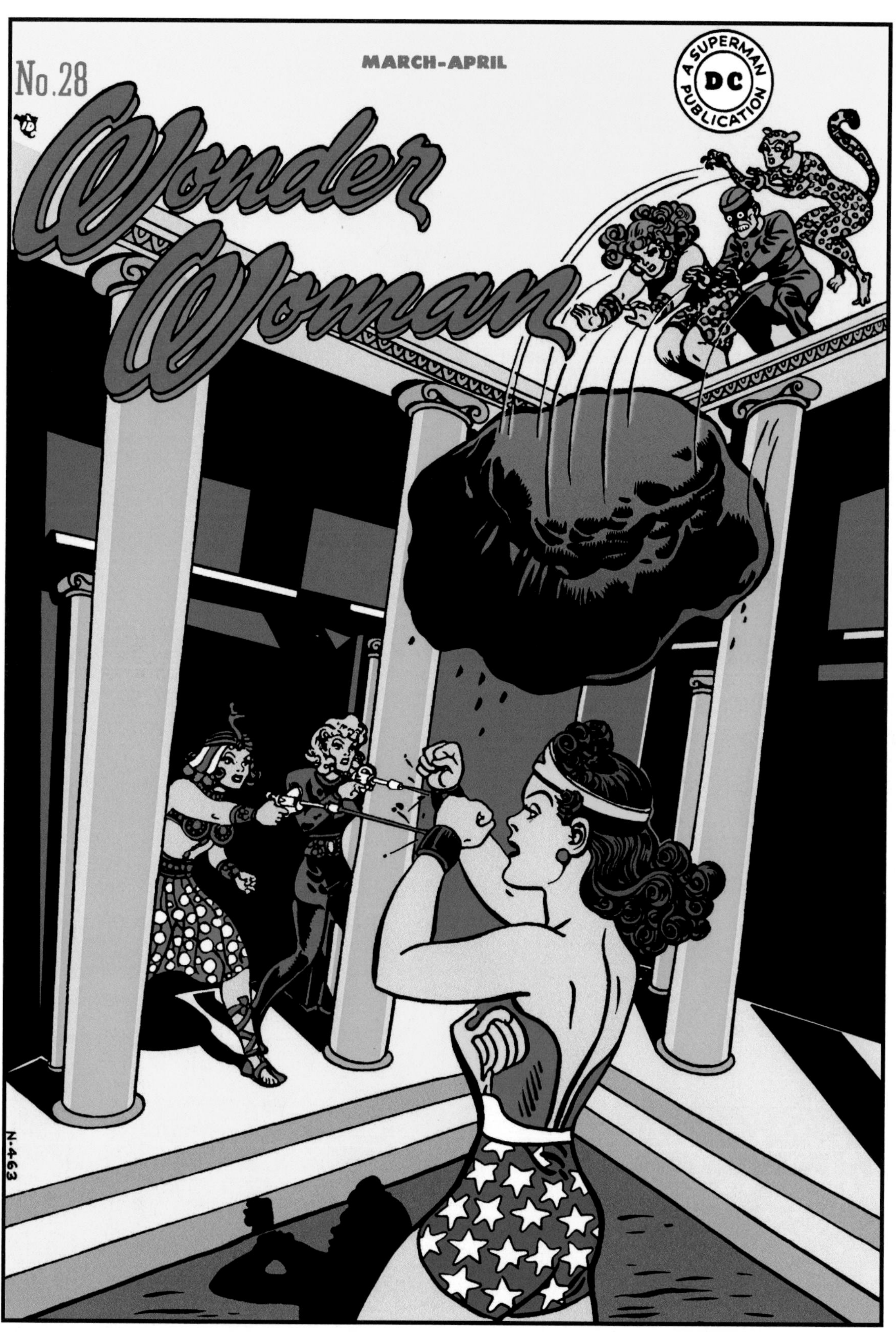
No. 28
MARCH-APRIL
A SUPERMAN PUBLICATION
DC
Wonder Woman
N-4-63

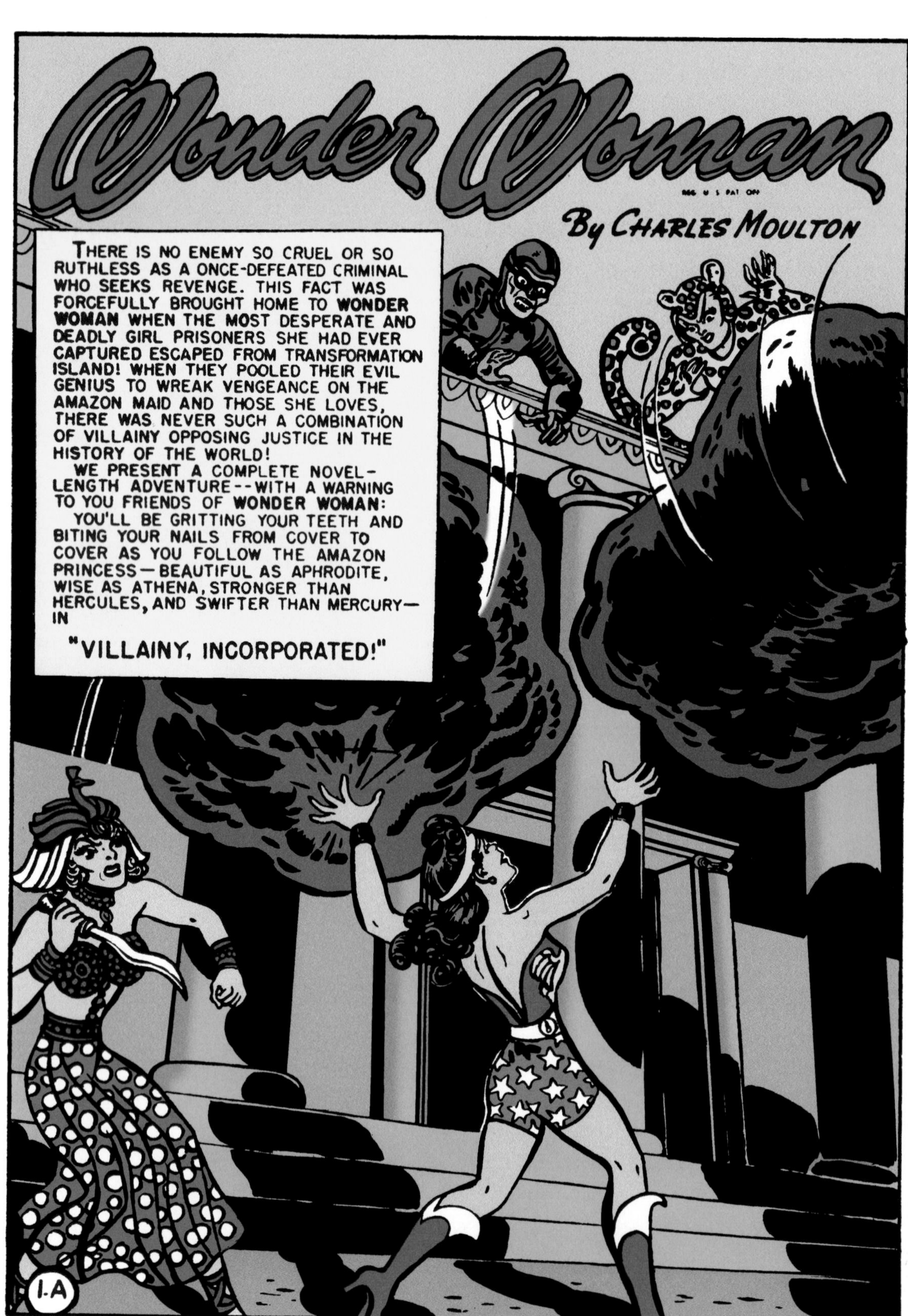
Wonder Woman
REG. U.S. PAT. OFF.
By CHARLES MOULTON
THERE IS NO ENEMY SO CRUEL OR SO RUTHLESS AS A ONCE-DEFEATED CRIMINAL WHO SEEKS REVENGE. THIS FACT WAS FORCEFULLY BROUGHT HOME TO WONDER WOMAN WHEN THE MOST DESPERATE AND DEADLY GIRL PRISONERS SHE HAD EVER CAPTURED ESCAPED FROM TRANSFORMATION ISLAND! WHEN THEY POOLED THEIR EVIL GENIUS TO WREAK VENGEANCE ON THE AMAZON MAID AND THOSE SHE LOVES, THERE WAS NEVER SUCH A COMBINATION OF VILLAINY OPPOSING JUSTICE IN THE HISTORY OF THE WORLD!
WE PRESENT A COMPLETE NOVEL-LENGTH ADVENTURE--WITH A WARNING TO YOU FRIENDS OF WONDER WOMAN:
YOU'LL BE GRITTING YOUR TEETH AND BITING YOUR NAILS FROM COVER TO COVER AS YOU FOLLOW THE AMAZON PRINCESS—BEAUTIFUL AS APHRODITE, WISE AS ATHENA, STRONGER THAN HERCULES, AND SWIFTER THAN MERCURY—IN
"VILLAINY, INCORPORATED!"
1-A

YOU REMEMBER WHEN **WONDER WOMAN** CONQUERED THE INVADING SATURNITES ON EVIL ISLAND, THE MIGHTY AMAZON CAPTURED EVERY MAN AND WOMAN MARAUDER. SHE HAD PLANNED TO SEND THEM BACK AS PRISONERS TO SATURN WHERE THEY WOULD MEET STERN JUSTICE.

WE'LL BIND THESE PRISONERS AND PUT THEM ON BOARD THEIR SATURNIC SPACE SHIP.
OH MEPHISTO HELP US! THE EMPEROR WILL PUT US IN CHAINS FOR LIFE--TO BE DEFEATED IS THE WORST CRIME ON SATURN!

WONDER WOMAN BINDS THE SATURNIC GIRLS IN CAPTIVE LINE WITH HER MAGIC LASSO.
OH, WONDER WOMAN, PLEASE KEEP US SATURNIC GIRLS PRISONERS HERE ON EARTH!

OUR FATE ON SATURN WILL BE HORRIBLE! YOU'VE NO IDEA HOW SATURNIC PRISONERS ARE TREATED--
OH, YES I HAVE-- I'VE BEEN A CAPTIVE THERE MYSELF. VERY WELL-- I'LL TAKE YOU GIRLS TO TRANSFORMATION ISLAND.

ON TRANSFORMATION ISLAND WONDER WOMAN DELIVERS HER PRISONERS TO MALA, AMAZON PRISON CHIEF.
THESE SATURNIC CAPTIVES ARE DANGEROUS GIRLS! YOU'D BETTER PUT VENUS GIRDLES ON THEM BEFORE UNTYING THEIR HANDS.
THEY LOOK SUBMISSIVE-- BUT YOU KNOW BEST, PRINCESS.
2-A

WHAT DOES THAT BEAUTIFUL GOLD GIRDLE DO TO A PRISONER?
IT IS MAGIC METAL FROM VENUS-- IT REMOVES ALL DESIRE TO DO EVIL AND COMPELS COMPLETE OBEDIENCE TO LOVING AUTHORITY.

SOON ALL THE SATURNITES WEAR GIRDLES EXCEPT EVILESS.

I HAVE A PLAN-- BY CONTROLLED BREATHING, I CAN STOP MY HEART, MAKE MY BODY COLD--AND THEN-- HA HA!

MM-- I'LL HAVE TO GET A LARGER GIRDLE--

BEFORE MALA CAN RETURN WITH THE NEW GIRDLE, EVILESS FALLS, APPARENTLY UNCONSCIOUS.

WHAT'S THE MATTER, EVILESS? GREAT HERA, THE GIRL'S FAINTED!

"FAINTED"-- SHE'S **DEAD**! HER HEART'S STOPPED BEATING!

AND HER FLESH IS STONE COLD! SHE MUST HAVE TAKEN POISON, BUT HOW **COULD** SHE, WITH HER HANDS TIED?

I'LL GET MY PURPLE RAY MACHINE FROM PARADISE ISLAND. IT WILL BRING EVILESS BACK TO LIFE!
3-A

I'LL PUT HER ON THIS COT AND UNTIE HER HANDS--

THESE HEAVY BLANKETS MAY BRING WARMTH TO HER BODY TILL **WONDER WOMAN** RETURNS! I'LL PREPARE THE ELECTRIC CONNECTIONS FOR **WONDER WOMAN'S** PURPLE RAY.

WHILE MALA'S BACK IS TURNED, EVILESS' "DEAD" HAND COMES TO LIFE.

UNDER THE BLANKETS A LONG, SATURNIAN SLEEVE IS PUSHED UP AND **WONDER WOMAN'S** LASSO IS WOUND CLEVERLY AROUND EVILESS' ARM.
WHEN I PULL MY SLEEVE DOWN AGAIN, THE MAGIC LASSO WILL BE HIDDEN--

THE SEEMINGLY DEAD PRISONER SUDDENLY REVIVES.
OH--WHAT HAPPENED? I-I MUST HAVE FAINTED! I HAVE THESE QUEER HEART ATTACKS FREQUENTLY--
MERCIFUL MINERVA--WE THOUGHT YOU WERE DEAD! IF YOU'VE RECOVERED, I MUST PUT ON YOUR VENUS GIRDLE--

I'LL **GLADLY** PUT THIS PRISONER'S GIRDLE ON MYSELF!

UNSEEN BY MALA, THE CLEVER SATURNIAN SLIPS A SPLINTER INTO THE GIRDLE LOCK.
THIS WILL PREVENT THE LOCK FROM ENGAGING. BUT THEY'LL **THINK** IT IS LOCKED--HA HA!
4-A

WHAT! EVILESS **ALIVE** AGAIN?
SHE WASN'T DEAD--WE WERE MISTAKEN. SHE HAD SOME QUEER SEIZURE, BUT NOW THAT SHE'S LOCKED SECURELY IN HER VENUS GIRDLE, SHE'LL BE OKAY.

WITH THE PRISONERS SAFELY LOCKED IN THEIR CELLS, WONDER WOMAN PREPARES TO TAKE OFF.
SORRY I MUST GO-- GREAT GODDESSES! I FORGOT MY LASSO--
I UNTIED IT FROM EVILESS' WRISTS-- WHERE DID I PUT IT?

THE ENTIRE PRISON AND ALL PRISONERS ARE SEARCHED.
WHAT ARE YOU LOOKING FOR, MISTRESS? I--
NEVER MIND-- I DON'T SEE HOW YOU COULD HIDE ANYTHING UNDER THOSE CLOTHES!
IT'S NOT HIDDEN HERE.

WHERE CAN YOUR LASSO BE? PERHAPS A GUARD FOUND IT AND TOOK IT TO PARADISE ISLAND. I'LL SURELY FIND IT--
MENTAL-RADIO ME AND I'LL COME BACK FOR IT-- I MUST HURRY NOW!

MEANWHILE, EVILESS IS TORN BY MENTAL CONFLICT.
THIS GIRDLE MAKES ME SUCH A SOFTIE! I WANTED TO TELL MALA THAT I HAVE WONDER WOMAN'S LASSO. BUT SHE FORBADE ME TO SPEAK AND I HAD TO OBEY HER!

NOW TO REMOVE THIS GIRDLE-- I FIXED THE LOCK SO IT'LL OPEN. BUT-- BUT I WANT TO WEAR IT-- I FEEL SO PEACEFUL AND HAPPY! YET IF I DON'T DEFEAT MY CAPTORS, I CAN NEVER RETURN TO SATURN--

I MUST ESCAPE-- I WON'T WEAR THE GIRDLE--
MALA! OH, MALA, COME QUICKLY! I HAVE ANOTHER SEIZURE-- HELP!
5.A

BUT AS MALA RUSHES TO HELP THE PRISONER--
HA! NOW I'VE GOT YOU, "MISTRESS" MALA-- HA HA HA!
BAH! D'YOU THINK A ROPE WILL HOLD AN AMAZON?-- BLACK PLUTO! IT'S WONDER WOMAN'S LASSO-- I CAN'T BREAK THAT!

GIVE ME THE KEYS TO ALL CELLS AND PRISONERS' CHAINS!
I'M COMPELLED TO OBEY. OUR PRISONERS WEAR NO CHAINS, BUT HERE IS THE KEY TO THEIR VENUS GIRDLES. THE OTHER IS A MISTRESS KEY TO ALL PRISON DOORS.

EVILESS LOCKS HER OWN VENUS GIRDLE ON MALA.
YOU DON'T NEED TO TIE MY HANDS SO TIGHT-- I CAN'T BREAK EVEN THE WEAKEST ROPE YOU BIND ME WITH WHILE I WEAR THIS VENUS GIRDLE!

EVILESS RELEASES HER SATURNIC GIRLS, WHO SURPRISE THEIR GUARDS.
PUT VENUS GIRDLES ON ALL AMAZON GUARDS, GIRLS-- THEN THEY'LL BE COMPELLED TO OBEY US!

GO, CAPTIVE GUARDS, AND RELEASE ALL PRISONERS FROM THEIR CELLS! BRING THEM TO THE PRISON ASSEMBLY ROOM QUICKLY.
YES, MISTRESS!
6-A

THE PRISONERS, STILL WEARING VENUS GIRDLES, ARE QUICKLY ASSEMBLED.
SISTERS, WE HAVE CONQUERED ALL GUARDS--TRANSFORMATION ISLAND IS OURS! I'LL UNLOCK YOUR GIRDLES--
NO, NO! WE DON'T WANT OUR GIRDLES REMOVED!

YOU FOOLS! YOU'VE LET THESE AMAZONS BREAK YOUR SPIRIT --YOU'VE LEARNED TO BE PEACEFUL AND OBEDIENT. OKAY, YOU CAN KEEP YOUR GIRDLES ON AND OBEY US AS OUR SLAVES!

BUT SOME PRISONERS ARE NOT YET REFORMED.
WE'LL JOIN YOU--WE WANT FREEDOM AND REVENGE ON THE AMAZONS!
YOU'RE WISE, GIRLS--I'LL REMOVE YOUR GIRDLES--YOU PUT ON YOUR OWN CLOTHES AGAIN.

I'M GIGANTA, FORMERLY A FEMALE GORILLA!
I'M QUEEN CLEA OF SUNKEN ATLANTIS.
I'M BYRNA BRILYANT, THE BLUE SNOW MAN.
I'M PRINCESS MARU, ALIAS DR. POISON.
I'M HYPNOTA, MAGICIAN OF THE BLUE RAY.
I'M ZARA, PRIESTESS OF CRIMSON FLAME.
I'M THE CHEETAH--REALLY, PRISCILLA RICH.
GOOD--NOT A SISSY IN THE LOT--THIS IS WHAT I CALL VILLAINY INCORPORATED!

WE WILL CONQUER THE AMAZONS ON PARADISE ISLAND AND USE IT FOR A BASE TO RAID EARTH COUNTRIES. FIRST WE'LL CAPTURE AMAZON QUEEN HIPPOLYTE. I MADE THE CAPTIVE GUARDS GIVE ME INFORMATION--
7-A

EVERY NIGHT THE QUEEN WALKS ALONE IN THIS PALACE GARDEN. YOU THREE WILL APPEAR THERE. SHE'LL THINK YOU'RE MEN, STRICTLY FORBIDDEN ON PARADISE ISLAND. SHE'LL PURSUE YOU, OF COURSE, AND THE REST IS UP TO US!

THAT NIGHT, AS QUEEN HIPPOLYTE WALKS IN HER GARDEN--
WHAT DO I HEAR--MEN'S WORLD VOICES? IMPOSSIBLE! AND YET--WELL, I'LL SOON SEE!

GREAT MINERVA--MEN ON PARADISE ISLAND! HOW COULD THIS HAVE HAPPENED? I MUST CATCH THEM MYSELF AND SEEK APHRODITE'S FORGIVENESS FOR THIS OVERSIGHT!

AS THE QUEEN PURSUES THE INVADERS--
8-A

GRAB HER, GIRLS! QUEEN HIPPOLYTE, I COMMAND YOU TO SURRENDER!
ULP--OH! SOMETHING COMPELS ME TO OBEY YOU!

THE QUEEN, BOUND WITH THE MAGIC LASSO, IS CARRIED TO THE SHORE.
HURRY, GIRLS! WE MUST GET HER TO TRANSFORMATION ISLAND BEFORE THE AMAZONS KNOW SHE'S CAPTURED.

QUEEN HIPPOLYTE IS COMPELLED TO BROADCAST RADIO ORDERS.
ALL AMAZONS WILL ASSEMBLE HERE IN PRISON ASSEMBLY HALL, TRANSFORMATION ISLAND, TOMORROW AT SUNRISE!

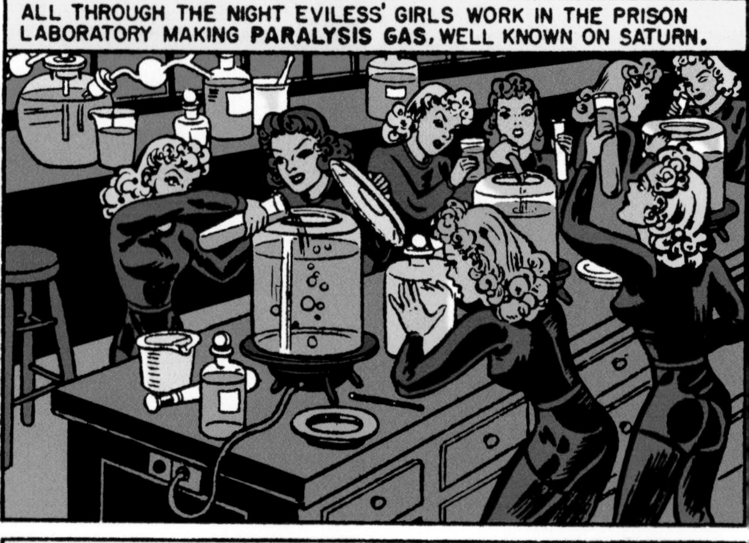
ALL THROUGH THE NIGHT EVILESS' GIRLS WORK IN THE PRISON LABORATORY MAKING **PARALYSIS GAS**, WELL KNOWN ON SATURN.

AT SUNRISE, THE ASSEMBLY HALL IS PACKED WITH AMAZONS.
YOUR QUEEN HAS BROUGHT YOU HERE TO MAKE YOU PRISONERS!
WHO'S CRAZY NOW?
HUH?
WHAT'S THE JOKE?

SATURNIANS OVERCOME THE AMAZONS WITH PARALYSIS GAS WHILE PRISONERS PUT VENUS GIRDLES ON THE PARALYZED GIRLS.
9-A

FROM NOW ON, YOU WON'T BE LONESOME IN PRISON, HIPPOLYTE-- HA HA! WE'VE CAPTURED EVERY LAST AMAZON ON PARADISE ISLAND!
OH-H-H-- HOW TERRIBLE! WHAT ARE YOU GOING TO DO WITH US?
SMACK!

WE'LL USE YOU AS SLAVES. YOU'RE LUCKY-- YOU WON'T HAVE TO WEAR CHAINS LIKE SATURNIAN PRISONERS-- VENUS GIRDLES WILL HOLD YOU HELPLESS. WE NEED ONE MORE CAPTIVE-- **WONDER WOMAN!** YOU MUST RADIO FOR HER.
OH, NO! **PLEASE--**

BUT HIPPOLYTE IS COMPELLED TO SEND HER DAUGHTER A MENTAL RADIO MESSAGE.
CALLING PRINCESS DIANA OF THE AMAZONS-- COME TO PARADISE ISLAND IMMEDIATELY!

DIANA (**WONDER WOMAN**) PRINCE RECEIVES THE QUEEN'S MESSAGE AT HER OFFICE.
BLAZES! HOW CAN **YOU** TAKE A MENTAL MESSAGE SENT TO **WONDER WOMAN?**
WHY--ER--**WONDER WOMAN** INVENTED A NEW ATTACHMENT SO I CAN TAKE MESSAGES FOR HER.
COME TO PARADISE ISLAND IMMEDIATELY!

STEVE, WILL YOU TELL GEN. DARNELL THAT I MUST FIND **WONDER WOMAN** AND GIVE HER THIS MESSAGE?
OH I SUPPOSE SO-- BUT THE GENERAL WON'T LIKE IT. HE'S ALWAYS AFRAID SHE'LL GET YOU INTO DANGER.

TRANSFORMING HERSELF QUICKLY TO **WONDER WOMAN**, DIANA FLIES TO PARADISE ISLAND
HM-- THAT'S ODD! I CAN'T SEE A SINGLE AMAZON ON PARADISE ISLAND! WHERE CAN THE GIRLS BE?
10-A

AS **WONDER WOMAN** DESCENDS, A SUDDEN STORM OF **BLUE SNOW** SURROUNDS HER PLANE.
BY ATHENA'S SPEAR, THAT'S **BLUE SNOW**-- IT'LL CRASH MY PLANE! WHO'S DOING THIS? HAS BYRNA BRILYANT, THE **SNOW MAN**, ESCAPED AMAZON PRISON?

WONDER WOMAN'S PLANE IS FORCED DOWN UNDER AN AVALANCHE OF BLUE SNOW.
HA! MY TELESCOPIC SNOW RAY HAS CAUGHT WONDER WOMAN! EVEN IF SHE CAN GET OUT OF HER PLANE, SHE'LL FREEZE TO DEATH INSTANTLY!

SURRENDER, WONDER WOMAN, BEFORE YOU FREEZE TO DEATH! MY SNOW RAY IS LOWERING THE TEMPERATURE EVERY SECOND!

BUT THE DAUNTLESS AMAZON BURSTS HER WAY THROUGH FROZEN SNOW AND FREEZING RAYS COLD ENOUGH TO KILL ANY MAN.

WITH ONE SWING OF HER MIGHTY FIST WONDER WOMAN DEMOLISHES THE SNOW RAY TELESCOPE GUN.
SMASH!

AS WONDER WOMAN PURSUES THE FLEEING SNOW MAN INTO THE PALACE, DR. POISON AND THE CHEETAH PUSH HUGE STONES OFF THE ROOF.
11-A

THE POWERFUL PRINCESS, THOUGH CAUGHT UNAWARE, ACTS WITH THE SPEED OF LIGHT.
WELL, WELL -- SO POISON AND THE CHEETAH ALSO ESCAPED AND PLANNED A LITTLE SURPRISE PARTY!

INSIDE THE PALACE, TWO GIGANTIC FORMS HURL THEMSELVES AT WONDER WOMAN.
UNF--GIGANTA AND QUEEN CLEA--I AM GETTING A RECEPTION!

SORRY, BUT IF YOU INSIST--
ARR-RRGH!
UG--ULP--

AS WONDER WOMAN TURNS, HYPNOTA'S BLUE HYPNOTIC RAY STRIKES HER FULL IN THE EYES
OHH-H-H--H-HYPNOTA! IT'S MY WILL AGAINST YOURS--

THAT FOR YOUR BLUE RAYS, MAGIC MONGER! I'LL--
W-WAIT--BEFORE YOU D-DO ANYTHING TO ME, LISTEN TO YOUR MOTHER, ON THE MENTAL RADIO!

WONDER WOMAN RUSHES TO THE RADIO ROOM—
WE AMAZONS ARE ALL CAPTIVES OF ESCAPED PRISONERS--UNLESS YOU SURRENDER, THEY WILL KILL ME--
OH--WHAT SHALL I DO?
12 A

IT DOESN'T MATTER WHAT YOU DO NOW--WE SHALL EXECUTE YOU AND THE QUEEN--HA HA! THE LONG, HARD WAY!
EVILESS! SO YOU STOLE MY MAGIC LASSO--WELL, THIS LOOKS LIKE THE END!
DON'T GO AWAY, READER--AS YOU CAN SEE--THERE IS MORE TO THIS STORY--READ ON--BECAUSE WONDER WOMAN HASN'T EVEN BEGUN TO FIGHT!

Wonder Woman
REG. U. S. PAT. OFF.
By Charles Moulton
FIERCE AND IMPLACABLE IS THE HATRED OF THE ESCAPED PRISONERS FOR WONDER WOMAN. AND CLEVER BEYOND BELIEF ARE THE EVIL DEVICES OF TWO BEAUTIFUL AND REVENGEFUL GIRLS WHO MADE GOOD THEIR ESCAPE FROM TRANSFORMATION ISLAND TO THE MAN'S WORLD!
ARMED WITH VAST, STOLEN WEALTH, THESE RUTHLESS SIRENS PLAY HAVOC WITH THEIR HELPLESS VICTIMS. AND WHEN THE MIGHTY AMAZON MAID TRACKS THEM TO THEIR LAIR, THIS RELENTLESS CRIME TEAM SETS FOR WONDER WOMAN A TERRIFYING
"TRAP OF CRIMSON FLAME."
1-B
HG PETER

WONDER WOMAN, CAPTURED BY EVILESS ON PARADISE ISLAND, IS BOUND WITH THE MAGIC LASSO.
NOW, WE'LL TAKE YOU TO YOUR OWN AMAZON PRISON ON TRANSFORMATION ISLAND --HA HA!

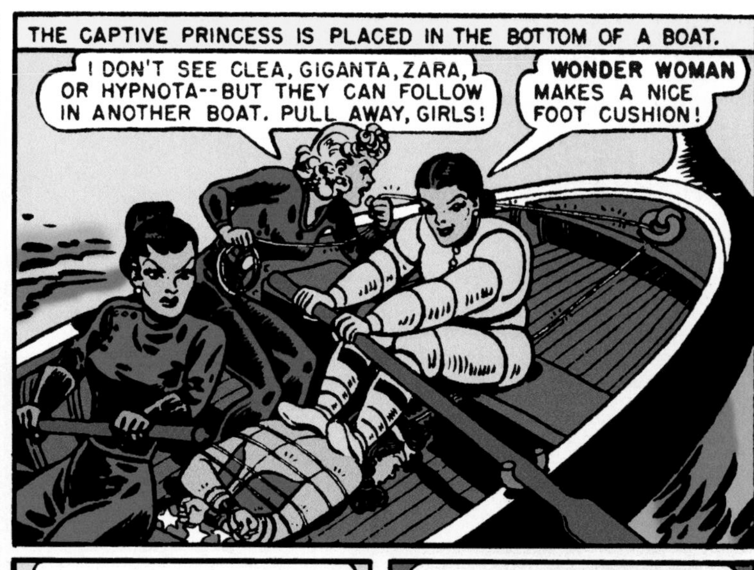
THE CAPTIVE PRINCESS IS PLACED IN THE BOTTOM OF A BOAT.
I DON'T SEE CLEA, GIGANTA, ZARA, OR HYPNOTA--BUT THEY CAN FOLLOW IN ANOTHER BOAT. PULL AWAY, GIRLS!
WONDER WOMAN MAKES A NICE FOOT CUSHION!

NOW, MY PRISONER, YOU ARE SECURELY TIED. I COMMAND YOU TO MAKE NO ATTEMPT TO ESCAPE!

EVILESS WASN'T HOLDING THE LASSO WHEN SHE COMMANDED ME NOT TO ESCAPE SO I'M NOT COMPELLED TO OBEY HER! THEY BOUND ME VERY TIGHT BUT IF I CAN BEND MY LEGS A LITTLE--

SUDDENLY THE TIGHTLY BOUND AMAZON SPRINGS TO HER FEET.
AY-EE! HELP--SEIZE THE CAPTIVE!
EEE-EEEK!
2-B

GREAT MEPHISTO--THAT AMAZON'S STRENGTH IS INCREDIBLE! BUT SHE'S STILL TIED TO THE BOAT--

UNFORTUNATELY FOR EVILESS, THE LASSO TYING WONDER WOMAN TO THE BOAT CANNOT BE BROKEN.

I HATE TO PULL EVILESS UNDER WATER--I WONDER --CAN SATURNIANS SWIM?

EVILESS CAN'T SWIM-- SHE'S DROWNING! I MUST SAVE HER--APHRODITE'S LAW COMMANDS US TO SAVE LIVES ALWAYS--ENEMIES OR NOT!

GOOD--THE GIRL'S STILL ALIVE!
3-B

WONDER WOMAN SAVES EVILESS--BUT SATURNIANS KNOW NO GRATITUDE.
SHE HOLDS THE LASSO THIS TIME-- I MUST OBEY HER!

WONDER WOMAN IS COMPELLED TO CARRY HER CAPTOR TO TRANSFORMATION ISLAND.
DO ME ONE FAVOR--SPARE MY MOTHER, QUEEN HIPPOLYTE!
CERTAINLY NOT! YOU TWO ARE DANGEROUS AND MUST DIE. WE SATURNIANS HAVE NO SENTIMENTAL FEELINGS.

MOTHER AND DAUGHTER MEET IN CAPTIVITY.
OH MOTHER! I LOST MY LASSO--
THEY CAUGHT ME WITH IT, THEN MADE ME OBEY WITH THIS VENUS GIRDLE!

YOU MAY BE SURPRISED TO NOTE THAT THESE FLAMING CHAINS DO NOT BURN YOU! CLEVER INVENTION OF ZARA'S! THE FLAME IS HARMLESS TO YOU— BUT NOT TO THE CHAIN— AS IT BURNS, IT GETS TIGHTER AND TIGHTER---

WHAT SWEET GIRLS YOU ARE!

4.B

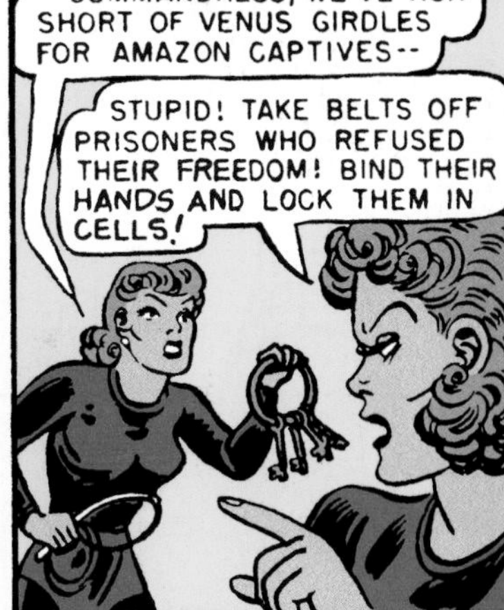

A SATURNIAN GUARD GIRL INTERRUPTS EVILESS' SPORT.
COMMANDRESS, WE'VE RUN SHORT OF VENUS GIRDLES FOR AMAZON CAPTIVES--
STUPID! TAKE BELTS OFF PRISONERS WHO REFUSED THEIR FREEDOM! BIND THEIR HANDS AND LOCK THEM IN CELLS!

DON'T WORRY--TAKING YOUR GIRDLE WON'T DEPRIVE YOU OF THE CAPTIVITY YOU'RE SO UNWILLING TO GIVE UP! YOU'LL STILL BE HELPLESS AND BEHIND BARS WHILE WE KILL THE AMAZON QUEEN AND PRINCESS!

LEFT ALONE, PRISONER IRENE FEELS A VAST SURGE OF ENERGY AND POWER WITHIN HERSELF.
WITHOUT THE GIRDLE I FEEL DOMINANT-- INVINCIBLE!

BUT I DON'T FEEL CRUEL AND WICKED AS I USED TO-- THE AMAZONS HAVE TRANSFORMED ME! I LOVE WONDER WOMAN AND QUEEN HIPPOLYTE-- I CAN'T BEAR TO HAVE THEM HURT-- I MUST SAVE THEM!

WHAT GOOD IS MY AMAZON TRAINING IF I CAN'T BREAK LITTLE ROPES LIKE THESE? I WILL BREAK THEM!
SNAP

AND THESE WEAK BARS-- WONDER WOMAN WOULD BEND THEM WITH ONE FINGER. BY HERCULES, I CAN BEND THEM!

COME ON, GIRLS, BREAK YOUR ROPES AND CELL BARS-- YOU CAN DO IT! WE'VE GOT TO SAVE WONDER WOMAN AND THE QUEEN!

INSPIRED BY IRENE'S EXAMPLE, THE PRISONERS, TRANSFORMED BY AMAZON TRAINING, BREAK THEIR BONDS AND CELL BARS.
WHOOPEE! LET'S GO, GIRLS!
HOLA--I'M FREE!
5-8

MEANWHILE, THE FLAMING CHAINS BEGIN TO TIGHTEN--
RELAX YOUR MUSCLES, DAUGHTER--
RIGHT, MOTHER--BUT IF ONLY THIS LASSO WERE UNTIED, I COULD BREAK THESE CHAINS DESPITE THEIR FLAMES!

SUDDENLY, THE MASSIVE LOCKED DOORS OF THE PRISON HALL BURST INWARD.
HOLA! WE'LL SAVE OUR MISTRESSES!
DOWN WITH THE REBELS--AT THEM, SISTERS!

THE LOYAL PRISONERS ATTACK FIERCELY, BUT THE REBEL LEADERS SWING FLAMING CHAINS.
ULP
UG
ARRR-RRGH!
POW

MEANWHILE, THE FLAME CHAINS DRAW EVER TIGHTER AROUND THE CAPTIVES.
COME QUICK, IRENE-- UNTIE MY LASSO!
COMING, BELOVED MISTRESS!
6-B

IRENE UNTIES THE LASSO AND--
OH WHAT STRENGTH--PRINCESS, YOU ARE WONDERFUL!
SNAPP!

WONDER WOMAN FREES THE QUEEN AND--
YOU LOYAL PRISONERS HAVE PROVED YOU'RE TRANSFORMED AND FIT TO BE FREE!
BIND THESE REBELS TIGHT, GIRLS--THEN PUT ON THEIR VENUS GIRDLES!

ALL CAPTIVE AMAZONS ARE FREED AND THE RE-CAPTURED PRISONERS COUNTED.
FOUR PRISONERS ARE MISSING! CLEA, GIGANTA, HYPNOTA, AND ZARA. WHERE ARE THEY HIDING?
I DON'T KNOW, MISTRESS--THOSE FOUR NEVER RE-TURNED HERE FROM PARADISE ISLAND.

RETURNING TO THE ROYAL PALACE, QUEEN HIPPOL-YTE ORDERS A SEARCH OF PARADISE ISLAND.
YOUR CROWN JEWELS ARE GONE, MAJESTY, ALSO OUR STRATOSPHERE JET PLANE. THE MISSING PRISONERS MUST HAVE LOOTED YOUR PALACE AND ESCAPED TO THE MAN'S WORLD!

THE QUEEN FOLLOWS THE FUGITIVES' COURSE ON ATHENA'S MAGIC SPHERE.
WELL, WE KNOW THEY STOLE YOUR PRICELESS JEWELS--
BUT LOOK--GREAT HERA! THEY'RE DISAPPEARING INTO THE STRATOSPHERE--THE MAGIC SPHERE CAN'T FOLLOW THEM BEYOND THIS EARTH'S ATMOS-PHERE!
TIME
PRESENT
1492
FRANCE
1948
CHINA
7-B

I'LL FIND THOSE FOUR MISCHIEF MAKERS IN THE MAN'S WORLD--DON'T WORRY, MOTHER!
I'VE A FEELING YOU WILL HAVE TROUBLE--APHRODITE WITH YOU, MY CHILD!

FROM WASHINGTON INTELLIGENCE HEADQUARTERS, DIANA (**WONDER WOMAN**) PRINCE WARNS ALL PAWN-SHOPS AND JEWEL BROKERS IN THE UNITED STATES TO WATCH FOR QUEEN HIPPOLYTE'S JEWELS. BUT FOR MANY MONTHS, NO AMAZON GEMS APPEAR IN THE JEWEL MARKET. THEN, SUDDENLY--

YES, YES--YOU'RE MR. STALUS, THE WELL-KNOWN JEWEL BROKER--
A REMARKABLE DIAMOND WAS OFFERED ME TODAY-- "BOBBY DAZZLER" TYPE. IT'S WORTH AROUND $250,000 AND ANSWERS THE DESCRIPTION OF ONE OF THE AMAZON QUEEN'S STOLEN JEWELS--

NO, I DIDN'T BUY IT. THE SELLER WAS A YOUNG GIRL--LOOKED LIKE AN OFFICE WORKER-- FIVE FEET FIVE--BRUNETTE--VERY PRETTY. BUT SHE HAD ODD EYES-- ONE BLUE, THE OTHER BROWN--

HM-- THE ONLY REAL CLUE IN THAT DESCRIPTION IS THE ODD COLORED EYES. BUT THAT DOESN'T HELP MUCH--I CAN'T GO ALL OVER WASHINGTON STOPPING EVERY PRETTY BRUNETTE AND INSPECTING HER EYE COLORS!

BUT AS DIANA ENTERS STEVE'S OFFICE--
BY HERA! THERE'S A BRUNETTE WITH ONE BLUE EYE AND ONE BROWN-- CLARICE MYSTIK! I'LL QUESTION HER.
CLARICE--I HEAR YOU HAVE A RARE DIAMOND FOR SALE.

DIAMOND? OH, NO, LT. PRINCE! WHERE WOULD A POOR GIRL LIKE ME GET A VALUABLE DIAMOND?
I BELIEVE SHE'S LYING--I MUST WATCH HER-- BUT HOW CAN I KEEP NEAR CLARICE WITHOUT HER SPOTTING ME? HA--I'VE AN IDEA!
8-B

CHANGING SWIFTLY TO WONDER WOMAN, DIANA RACES TO THE ROOF--
I'LL LET MYSELF DOWN ON THE LASSO AND WATCH CLARICE THROUGH HER OFFICE WINDOW.

HA! SHE'S HIDING SOMETHING-- I'LL BET THAT'S THE DIAMOND!

CLARICE OPENS HER PURSE TO GET A COMPACT AND--

EEE-EEKK! THE **CRIMSON FLAME!**

TREMBLING WITH FEAR, CLARICE TURNS TO HER TYPEWRITER, BUT AS HER FINGERS TOUCH THE KEYS--

OH--**OH!** I--I CAN'T ENDURE THIS--WH-WHAT DOES THE HIGH PRIESTESS **WANT--**

SUDDENLY, ON THE GIRL'S BARE ARM, A BLOOD-RED MESSAGE APPEARS.
YOUR SLAVE OBEYS, PRIESTESS! I--I'M COMING!
COME TO THE TEMPLE OF FLAME IMMEDIATELY
9-B

THIS IS ZARA'S OLD GAME-- SHE HAS STARTED HER PHONEY CULT OF THE **CRIMSON FLAME!**

WONDER WOMAN FOLLOWS HER SUSPECT VIA THE TREE TRAIL.
LUCKY THERE ARE PLENTY OF TREES ON THIS STREET--

SUFFERING SAPPHO-- WHY IS THAT GIRL KICKING A MANHOLE COVER?
TAP! TAP! TAP!! TAP-TAP-TAP!

WHILE WONDER WOMAN HESITATES, THE MANHOLE COVER BEGINS TO SINK.
THAT COVER MUST BE THE ENTRANCE TO ZARA'S HIDEAWAY! SHALL I LASSO CLARICE OR JUMP DOWN--

WONDER WOMAN DECIDES TO JUMP, BUT TOO LATE.
OH-OH! THIS TRICK GADGET WAS TOO FAST FOR ME--I'LL HAVE TO DISCOVER HOW TO OPEN IT AGAIN.

TWO TAPS--ONE--THEN THREE--THAT'S THE WAY CLARICE KICKED IT. BUT IT DOESN'T OPEN--
TAP! TAP! TAP! TAP-TAP-TAP!
10-B

WHOOSH! I SPOKE TOO SOON--HERE WE GO--

DOWN, DOWN SHOOTS THE DARING AMAZON--
THE MANHOLE COVER DUMPED ME INTO THIS ELEVATOR CAR--NOW WHERE AM I GOING? I HOPE I'M HEADED FOR ZARA'S "TEMPLE OF CRIMSON FLAME"!

DEEP UNDERGROUND, THE ELEVATOR CAGE STOPS IN A CIRCLE OF FLAME.
SPEAK, O VISITOR FROM WITHOUT, AND GIVE THE SACRED PASSWORD!
I'M STUCK--I DON'T KNOW THEIR PASSWORD!

THE PASSWORD MUST REFER TO ZARA'S FLAME CULT--I'LL TRY THIS--
I SEEK THE PRIESTESS OF CRIMSON FLAME!
THAT IS NOT THE PASSWORD--YOU ARE A SPY! REVEAL YOUR TRUE IDENTITY OR THE FLAME SHALL CONSUME YOU!

NO USE ARGUING WITH A LOUDSPEAKER--I'LL SEE WHO'S BEHIND THIS WALL OF FLAME!
11-B.

BUT AS THE MIGHTY AMAZON FIGHTS HER WAY THROUGH THE SEETHING INFERNO, A DEADLY BLUE RAY ASSAULTS HER SENSES.
GREAT VULCAN--THERE'S SOMETHING **BESIDES** FIRE TO CONTEND WITH HERE!

AS **WONDER WOMAN** EMERGES FROM THE FLAME, SHE FALLS UNCONSCIOUS.
EET **EES WONDAIR WOMAN**--SHE ESCAPED FROM OUR SEESTER PRISONAIRS ON TRANSFORMATION ISLAND!
YOUR FLAME CONFUSED HER AND MY BLUE HYPNOTIC RAY CONQUERED HER BRAIN COMPLETELY! HA HA!

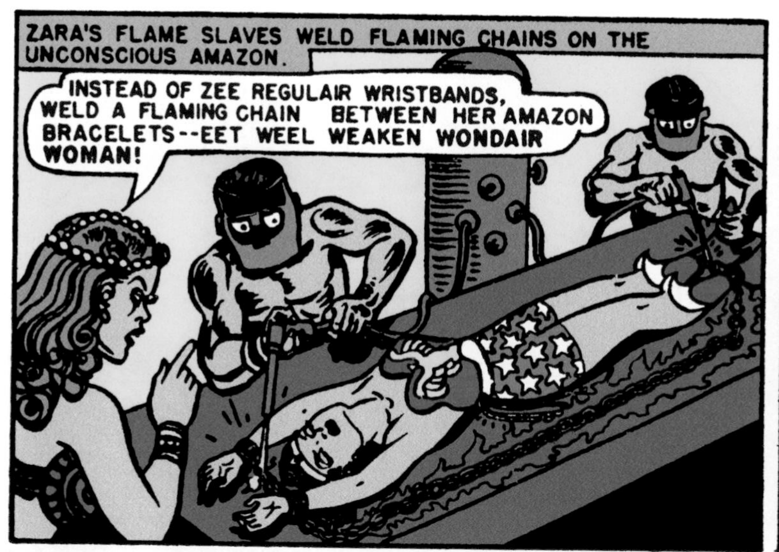
ZARA'S FLAME SLAVES WELD FLAMING CHAINS ON THE UNCONSCIOUS AMAZON.
INSTEAD OF ZEE REGULAIR WRISTBANDS, WELD A FLAMING CHAIN BETWEEN HER AMAZON BRACELETS--EET WEEL WEAKEN WONDAIR WOMAN!

WONDER WOMAN RECOVERS CONSCIOUSNESS A CAPTIVE.
SO--YOU'VE CHAINED MY BRACELETS! WHO DID THIS?
WHAT DOES EET MATTAIR? I WARN YOU--DO NOT TRY TO BREAK ZOZE FLAMING CHAINS, OR ZAY WEEL PARALYZE YOU UNTEEL YOU DIE!

THESE FLAME CHAINS DO PARALYZE ME, BUT I'LL BREAK THEM—ULP--OH! I CAN'T--MEN MUST HAVE CHAINED MY AMAZON BRACELETS TOGETHER!
YOU ARE HELPLESS AND YOU WEEL BE MY SLAVE--COME, I SHOW YOU WHY!
12-B

GREAT GODDESSES--YOU'VE CAPTURED THE HOLLIDAY GIRLS!
I TELEPHONED ZEE GIRLS YOU NEED HELP AND ZEY COME QUEEK --HA HA! ZEE GOD OF FLAME CAPTURE ZAIR MINDS WIZ ZEE BLUE HYPNOTIC RAY.

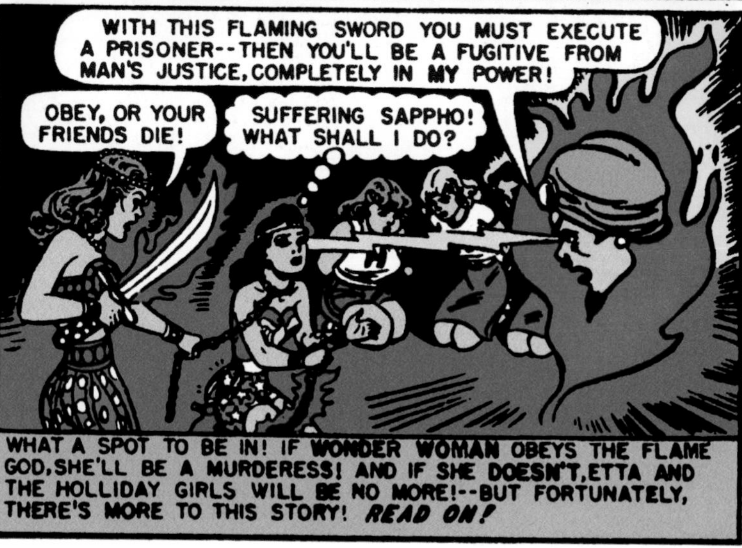
WITH THIS FLAMING SWORD YOU MUST EXECUTE A PRISONER--THEN YOU'LL BE A FUGITIVE FROM MAN'S JUSTICE, COMPLETELY IN MY POWER!
OBEY, OR YOUR FRIENDS DIE!
SUFFERING SAPPHO! WHAT SHALL I DO?
WHAT A SPOT TO BE IN! IF WONDER WOMAN OBEYS THE FLAME GOD, SHE'LL BE A MURDERESS! AND IF SHE DOESN'T, ETTA AND THE HOLLIDAY GIRLS WILL BE NO MORE!--BUT FORTUNATELY, THERE'S MORE TO THIS STORY! READ ON!

Wonder Woman
REG. U. S. PAT. OFF.
By CHARLES MOULTON
"IN THE HANDS OF THE MERCILESS!"
FROM FIERCE FLAMES TO THE BITTER DEPTHS OF AN ICY OCEAN THE GLAMOROUS AMAZON IS HURLED! EVEN WONDER WOMAN IS NOT INDESTRUCTIBLE. AND WHEN TWO VENGEFUL GIANTESSES DEVOTE THEIR INCREDIBLE STRENGTH AND FIENDISH INGENUITY TO DESTROYING THE MIGHTY MAID FROM PARADISE ISLAND, IT LOOKS AS IF HER END HAS COME.
WONDER WOMAN IS FORCED TO FIGHT TO THE LAST OUNCE OF HER MARVELOUS POWER AND INVINCIBLE COURAGE TO SAVE HER FRIENDS FROM A FRIGHTFUL FATE!
HG PETER
1-C

DAZED BY "HIGH PRIESTESS" ZARA'S ORDEAL OF CRIMSON FLAME AND THE BLUE HYPNOTIC RAY OF "FLAME GOD" HYPNOTA, **WONDER WOMAN** KNEELS BEFORE THE WEIRD FLAME ALTAR, HER AMAZON STRENGTH OF MIND AND BODY LOST BY APHRODITE'S LAW BECAUSE MEN WELDED CHAINS BETWEEN HER BRACELETS.

THE CAPTIVE HOLLIDAY GIRLS WILL BE KILLED UNLESS **WONDER WOMAN** OBEYS.
TAKE ZIS FLAMING SWORD AND PREPARE TO EXECUTE A PRISONER!
I'LL PRETEND TO OBEY AND STALL FOR TIME -- MAYBE I CAN THINK OF SOME PLAN --

TO BIND MY NEW SLAVE **WONDER WOMAN** FOREVER TO MY SERVICE, I SHALL COMPEL HER TO SLAY WITH THE FLAMING SWORD A DISCIPLE WHO HAS DISOBEYED ME. BRING BEFORE ME THE PRISONER CLARICE MYSTIK!

PRISONAIR CLARICE, YOU FAILED TO SELL ZEE AMAZON DIAMOND AS ZEE GOD COMMANDED!
I-I T-TRIED-- M-MERCY, O GOD OF FLAME!
FAILURE IS DISOBEDIENCE -- YOU MUST DIE. AMAZON SLAVE, EXECUTE THE PRISONER!

NEVER BEFORE HAVE I KILLED A HUMAN BEING--
--AND I DON'T INTEND TO NOW!
2-C

O **PLEASE**--**DON'T** MAKE ME KILL CLARICE!
ZEE GOD OF FLAME COMMANDS EET--OBEY, FLAME SLAVE, OR YOUR FRIENDS ALSO SHALL BE EXECUTED!

WONDER WOMAN APPEARS TO STUMBLE OVER HER ANKLE CHAINS.

QUICK, ETTA, GRAB THIS SWORD AND CUT THE CHAIN BETWEEN MY BRACELETS!
AWKWARD SLAVE --FOR ZEES YOU SHALL BE PUNEESHED!
RIGHT, KEED--

WOO WOO! THIS IS EASY AS CUTTIN' CHOCOLATE FUDGE!
SWOOSH!

IN THE FLASH OF AN EYE THE MIGHTY AMAZON, HER STRENGTH RESTORED, BREAKS HER CHAINS.
SNAP!
SNAP!

WHILE ETTA FREES THE GIRLS, WONDER WOMAN INDULGES IN A LITTLE SWORD PLAY.
I ALWAYS LIKED FENCING--
3-C

THE FLAME CULT RACKETEERS ARE QUICKLY CAPTURED.
YOU ESCAPED PRISONERS WILL HAVE TWO NEW COMPANIONS ON YOUR RETURN TO TRANSFORMATION ISLAND!
WE WEEL YET GET OUR REVENGE ON YOU, WONDER WOMAN!

ZARA, EXPLAIN YOUR FLAME CULT TRICKS TO CLARICE.
I MUS' OBEY. ZEE TONGUES OF FLAME ARE HYDROGEN GAS CAPSULES ZAT EXPLODE AND BURN UP. ZEE WRITING ON YOUR ARM WAS INVISIBLE INK ZAT APPEARS LATER.

ZEE FLAME GOD WHOM YOU WORSHIP EES HYPNOTA--I PUT HIS FACE IN ZEE FLAME WITH TELEVISION PROJECTOR.
WHAT A FOOL I WAS!
YOU CAN HELP OTHER GIRLS NOT TO BE FOOLS BY EXPLAINING THESE CULT TRICKS.

HERE Y'ARE, PRINCESS-- PUFF, PUFF! HERE'S YOUR MOM'S JOOLS!
THAT'S LESS THAN HALF-- WHERE ARE THE REST?
CLEA AND GIGANTA TOOK THEM-- WE DON'T KNOW WHERE THEY ARE!

WHILE WONDER WOMAN FLIES THE PRISONERS TO TRANSFORMATION ISLAND, STEVE HAS AN UNUSUAL VISITOR.
AH--THOU ART THE HANDSOME COL. TREVOR WHOM I HAVE MET BEFORE!
ER--AH-- IF YOU'D SHOW ME YOUR FACE--

NEVER MIND MY FACE-- I'M GLAD THOU DOST NOT REMEMBER ME! I HAVE COME TO SEE THEE BECAUSE I KNOW THOU ART VERY INFLUENTIAL WITH THY GOVERNMENT. I WISH TO BUY A SUBMARINE.
4.C

A SUBMARINE?
NOW I KNOW THIS DAME-- SHE'S QUEEN CLEA, THE ESCAPED AMAZON PRISONER! SHE WANTS A SUB TO REACH HER SUNKEN CONTINENT, ATLANTIS. I'LL PLAY INNOCENT AND GET A LEAD TO THE AMAZON JEWELS SHE STOLE.

THE GOVERNMENT IS SELLING SURPLUS SUBMARINES. BUT THEY COST PLENTY--
POOF! I HAVE ENOUGH TO BUY 20 SUBS--COME WITH ME AND I WILL SHOW THEE.
SNAP

CLEA LEADS STEVE TO A CAVE NEAR THE SHORE.
THIS WAS A PIRATES' CAVE-- I FOUND THEIR BURIED TREASURE! FOLLOW ME--

BEHOLD MY TREASURE! ONE TENTH OF THESE JEWELS WILL PAY FOR A SUBMARINE.
RIGHT--EXCEPT FOR ONE FACT. THESE JEWELS BELONG TO AMAZON QUEEN HIPPOLYTE!

HANDS UP! YOU ARE THE ESCAPED PRISONER, QUEEN **CLEA** OF ATLANTIS!
YOU-- YOU MISERABLE **MANLING**--YOU--
5.C

AT THIS MOMENT, A HUGE CLUB DESCENDS.
ARRR-RRGH!
GOT HIM!
BANG
WHAM
UG-ULP!

STEVE RECOVERS CONSCIOUSNESS IN AN AWKWARD SITUATION.
THOU'LT BUY THAT SUBMARINE, OR I'LL CUT THEE--**SLOWLY**--TO RIBBONS!
WHILE I BURN YOUR EYES OUT!
YOU'RE CERTAINLY PLAYFUL GIRLS! GO AHEAD AND HAVE YOUR FUN.

THE MANLING IS BRAVE -- TORTURE WILL NEVER PERSUADE HIM!
HE'LL YIELD IF WE CAPTURE THE HOLLIDAY GIRLS -- AND WE MIGHT CATCH WONDER WOMAN!

WE HATE TO LEAVE YOU ALONE, BUT SOON WE'LL BRING YOU CAPTIVE COMPANIONS!
LATER, THOU SHALT BECOME A SLAVE IN ATLANTIS!

DIANA, MEANWHILE, GETS A CALL FROM PROF. ZOOL OF HOLLIDAY COLLEGE.
I'M HAVING TROUBLE WITH MY EVOLUTION MACHINE -- ONLY THE DEVOLUTION CURRENT WORKS. CAN YOU LOCATE WONDER WOMAN?
SHE'S BUSY NOW, PROFESSOR -- LATER, PERHAPS!

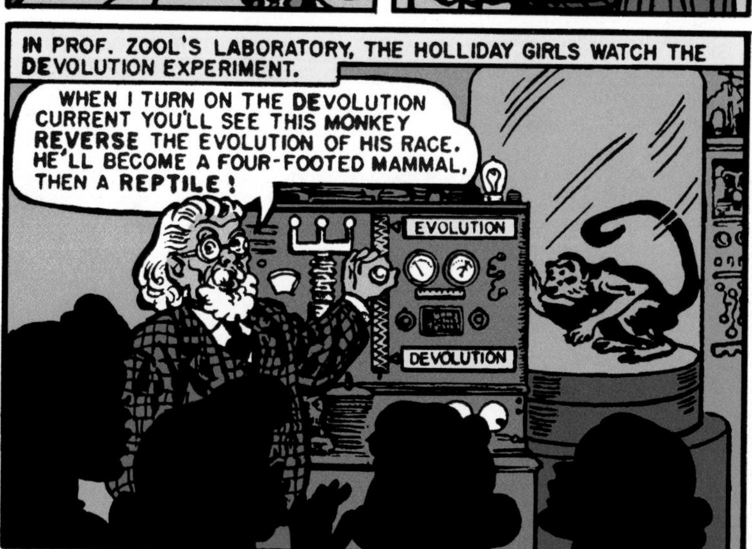
IN PROF. ZOOL'S LABORATORY, THE HOLLIDAY GIRLS WATCH THE DEVOLUTION EXPERIMENT.
WHEN I TURN ON THE DEVOLUTION CURRENT YOU'LL SEE THIS MONKEY REVERSE THE EVOLUTION OF HIS RACE. HE'LL BECOME A FOUR-FOOTED MAMMAL, THEN A REPTILE!
EVOLUTION
DEVOLUTION

AS THE BELL GLASS BECOMES SUPERCHARGED WITH REVERSED ELECTRONIC CURRENT, BLUE FLAMES APPEAR AND THE MONKEY BEGINS TO CHANGE BACK TO A PREHISTORIC TREE FOX.

DEVOLUTION CONTINUES.
WOO WOO! YOU DOOD IT AGAIN, PROFESSOR! THAT FOX IS A SURE 'NUFF CONKERNILE --
CAN'T YOU GIRLS TAKE ANYTHING SERIOUSLY? I SHOULD CHANGE YOU ALL BACK TO MONKEYS!
6-C

SUDDENLY, THERE APPEARS THE GORILLA THAT ZOOL'S MACHINE ONCE CHANGED TO A GIRL.
ARRR--RGH! I'VE GOT THEM--QUICK, CLEA, THE NET!
H-HELP!
EE-EEK!
EEEEK!

IN THE TWINKLING OF AN EYE, CLEA'S ATLANTEAN HUNTING NET SURROUNDS ITS PREY.
HERE'S THE BAIT FOR OUR TRAP--WE'LL MAKE THESE GIRLS CALL WONDER WOMAN FOR HELP!

AT THIS MOMENT, DIANA, HAVING TRANSFORMED HERSELF TO WONDER WOMAN, ARRIVES TO HELP PROF. ZOOL REPAIR HIS MACHINE.
SORRY I'M LATE-- HESTIA! WHAT GOES ON HERE?

INSTANTLY GIGANTA SEIZES WONDER WOMAN.
SUFFERING SAPPHO--IT'S GIGANTA!
7-C

GIGANTA'S UNEXPECTED ATTACK CARRIES WONDER WOMAN TO THE FLOOR.

BUT THE SKILLED AMAZON WRESTLER DOES A HEAD STAND.

I'LL TIE YOU UP, GORILLA GIRL, AND THEN--
GRR-RRGH!

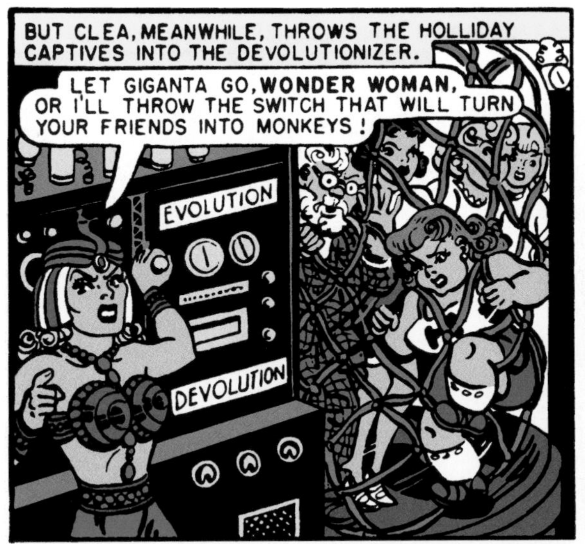
BUT CLEA, MEANWHILE, THROWS THE HOLLIDAY CAPTIVES INTO THE DEVOLUTIONIZER.
LET GIGANTA GO, WONDER WOMAN, OR I'LL THROW THE SWITCH THAT WILL TURN YOUR FRIENDS INTO MONKEYS!
EVOLUTION
DEVOLUTION

QUICKER THAN THOUGHT, WONDER WOMAN LEAPS AT CLEA--BUT THE ATLANTEAN'S HAND PULLS DOWN THE DEVOLUTION SWITCH.
DEVOLUTIO

THE MIGHTY AMAZON SNATCHES THE SWITCH FROM CLEA--TOO LATE.
GREAT PLUTO! ZOOL AND THE HOLLIDAY GIRLS ARE DEVOLVING INTO APES!
EVOLUTION
DEVOLUTION

WONDER WOMAN TURNS THE SWITCH TO "EVOLUTION" BUT NOTHING HAPPENS.
GREAT MINERVA! ZOOL HASN'T REPAIRED HIS POSITIVE EVOLUTION CURRENT, AND THEY'RE ALL TURNED TO GORILLAS EXCEPT THEIR HEADS!
QUICK, GIGANTA!
EVOLUTION
DEVOL
8c

EVEN AN AMAZON CAN'T WITH-STAND A CRUSHING BLOW ON THE BASE OF THE SKULL--
SWOOSH
WHAM

WONDER WOMAN, UNCONSCIOUS, IS BOUND WITH HER MAGIC LASSO.
I'LL MAKE THE AMAZON CAPTIVE STEAL A SUBMARINE -- IF SHE REBELS -- WELL, WE STILL HAVE THE HOLLIDAY GORILLAS AS HOSTAGES! SHE MUST DO OUR BIDDING!

WONDER WOMAN, RECOVERING CONSCIOUSNESS, FINDS HERSELF IN A ROWBOAT.
HA! THOU HAST RECOVERED-- EXCELLENT! I'M TAKING THEE TO AN ANCHORAGE OF SURPLUS SUBMARINES-- THOU WILT STEAL ONE FOR ME!
HERA HAVE MERCY --I MUST OBEY CLEA!

THOU MUST REMAIN BOUND, CAPTIVE, WHILE PERFORMING THY TASK. I BIND THY WRISTS IN FRONT OF THEE!
YOU'RE SO KIND, CLEA!

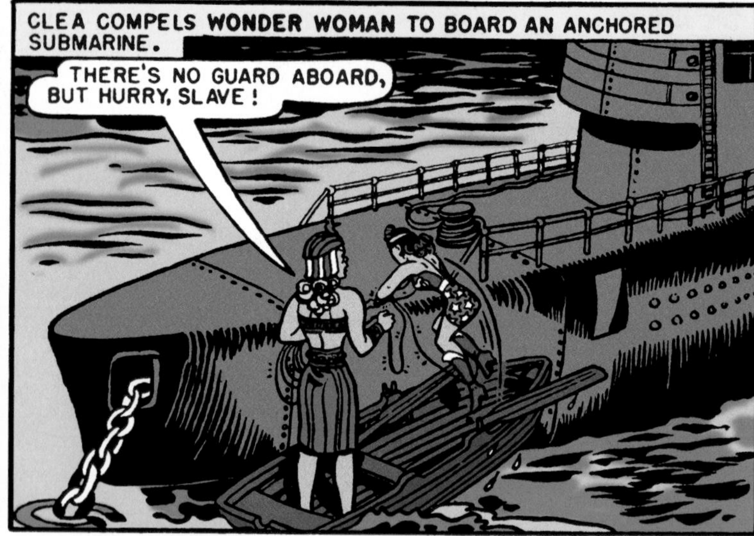
CLEA COMPELS WONDER WOMAN TO BOARD AN ANCHORED SUBMARINE.
THERE'S NO GUARD ABOARD, BUT HURRY, SLAVE!

BREAK THAT ANCHOR CHAIN QUICKLY!
SNA-P!
9-C.

THE CAPTIVE AMAZON, SWIMMING WITH BOUND HANDS, IS COMPELLED TO TOW THE HUGE SUBMARINE.
FASTER, CAPTIVE!

THE SUB IS DOCKED AT CLEA'S TREASURE COVE.
COME, MY BIG LITTLE SLAVE, I HAVE A SURPRISE WAITING FOR THEE IN MY CAVE OF JEWELS!

BUT IT IS CLEA WHO IS SURPRISED.
TREVOR'S ESCAPED! HE FRAYED HIS ROPES ON THAT POST AND BROKE LOOSE!
NOW WE MUST KILL THE PRISONERS AND RACE FOR ATLANTIS, LEAVING NO TRACE!

WONDER WOMAN IS FORCED TO CARRY THE AMAZON JEWELS TO THE SUBMARINE.
I'LL SEND STEVE A MENTAL RADIO BEAM JUST ON A CHANCE--
HELP, STEVE! FOLLOW THIS BEAM--

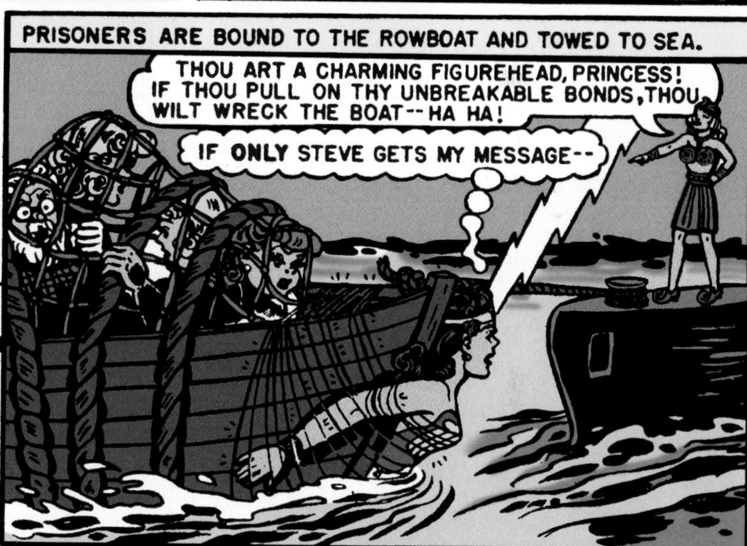
PRISONERS ARE BOUND TO THE ROWBOAT AND TOWED TO SEA.
THOU ART A CHARMING FIGUREHEAD, PRINCESS! IF THOU PULL ON THY UNBREAKABLE BONDS, THOU WILT WRECK THE BOAT--HA HA!
IF ONLY STEVE GETS MY MESSAGE--

BUT 10 MILES AT SEA, THE SUBMARINE SUBMERGES, PULLING THE ROWBOAT WITH IT.
OH I MUST SAVE THE HOLLIDAY CAPTIVES--
10-C

TWISTING IN HER BONDS, WONDER WOMAN SEIZES THE TOW CABLE IN HER TEETH.

WONDER WOMAN CUTS THE CABLE, BUT THE WATER-FILLED ROWBOAT SINKS.
BOAT'S SINKING ANYWAY, I MAY AS WELL SMASH IT--
CRAACK!

THE AMAZON MAID, FREE, QUICKLY BRINGS HER COMPANIONS TO THE SURFACE.
CAN YOU GIRLS SWIM NOW THAT YOU'RE GORILLAS ?
ARR-RRGH! WE'LL SHOW YA!

WITHOUT A SECOND'S DELAY, WONDER WOMAN, FOLLOWED BY THE HUMAN GORILLAS, SWIMS SWIFTLY DOWN TO PURSUE THE STOLEN SUBMARINE.
MY, MY! ONE DOES PECULIAR THINGS WHEN ONE IS A GORILLA!
BLUB
11-C

BEFORE THE SUB-SEA BOAT CAN COMPLETE ITS DIVE, IT IS CAPTURED AND BROUGHT TO THE SURFACE.
THERE'S STEVE COMING IN MY PLANE--THANK APHRODITE!

AS STEVE SWEEPS DOWN IN THE PRINCESS' PLANE, WONDER WOMAN GRABS THE LANDING LADDER.
SWOOSH
HOLD TIGHT, GORILLAS! THIS IS THE QUICKEST WAY TO GET BACK TO HOLLIDAY COLLEGE!

LANDING SAFELY ON THE HOLLIDAY CAMPUS, WONDER WOMAN SMASHES OPEN THE SUBMARINE.
MOTHER'LL HAVE TO PAY FOR THIS SUB, BUT I MUST GET THOSE ESCAPED PRISONERS BEFORE THEY HATCH MORE MISCHIEF!
CRACK

THE REBELS HAVE NO CHANCE AGAINST AN AROUSED WONDER WOMAN.
OW-W! I GIVE UP!
ARR-RRGH! I SURRENDER!

WONDER WOMAN SOON REPAIRS PROF. ZOOL'S EVOLUTION MACHINE AND—
WOO WOO! AM I GLAD YOU EVOLUTED US AGAIN-- WHILE I WAS A GORILLA, I DIDN'T LIKE CANDY!
12-C

LATER, ON PARADISE ISLAND--
HERE ARE THE PRISONERS, MOTHER, AND YOUR JEWELS-- THE GIRLS ARE ASHAMED AND GLAD TO BE BACK!
THE ONLY REAL HAPPINESS FOR ANYBODY IS TO BE FOUND IN OBEDIENCE TO LOVING AUTHORITY.
FOLLOW THE LATEST ADVENTURES OF WONDER WOMAN IN HER OWN MAGAZINE!

PART II: 1958-1986
THE PRINCESS

While almost all of her peers in the Justice Society faded from the newsstands by the mid-1950s, Wonder Woman (and Batman and Superman) survived the end of the Golden Age of comics and the campaign orchestrated against the medium by Fredric Wertham. In his 1954 book, *The Seduction of the Innocent,* Wertham accused comics of perverting the minds of children. But Wonder Woman was stronger than that. She even survived the loss of her creator, William Moulton Marston, who died in 1948. Robert Kanigher took over writing the series, continuing the legacy.

Despite a slight loss in sales, Wonder Woman continued to be a strong seller in the 1950s. When original artist H.G. Peter also died in 1958, the editor recruited a dynamic duo: Ross Andru on pencils and Mike Esposito on inks. The two would stay on the title for a decade. Their run with Kanigher would be revolutionary. Just like Mort Weisinger with Superman, Kanigher drastically expanded Wonder Woman's universe. We learned about the hero's childhood and her teenage years. During this Silver Age, Wonder Woman encountered numerous enemies, some serious and others goofy, as the series adopted a lighter science fiction tone. (Some classic examples include Angle Man, Egg-Fu and the Glop.)

Still, at the tail end of the 1960s, Wonder Woman, just like Batman before her, needed a makeover. For a while in 1966, Kanigher, Andru and Esposito tried to recapture the Golden Age vibe by offering tales taking place during World War II, but the audience didn't really respond and, in 1968, a brand new creative team took over the title. Mike Sekowsky, an artist familiar with the Amazon princess (he drew her in the Justice League—the team replacing the Justice Society) and Denny O'Neil, a young writer who came from Charlton Comics, would completely revamp the series. During their run, Diana lost her powers, her costume and her link with the mysterious Amazon Island. The hero became a private investigator and a fashion store owner, living adventures in the vein of the television characters of that era. This enchanted interlude came to an end in 1973 with the return of Kanigher as editor, followed quickly by Julius Schwartz.

Schwartz was a man with revolutionary ideas. He had already set the Silver Age in motion decades earlier with relaunches of Flash, Green Lantern and Hawkman. Under his watch, Wonder Woman was returned to her former role in the DC Universe. From summer 1974 to early 1976, the Amazon had to execute twelve labors, challenges created by her teammates to prove herself worthy of reinstatement in the Justice League. These issues benefited from unprecedented media exposure, thanks to the new *Wonder Woman* television series starring Lynda Carter. After two unsuccessful attempts to bring the Amazon Princess to the small screen (there had been an unaired pilot in 1967 and a TV movie with Cathy Lee Crosby in 1974), this version proved to be immensely popular, running for three seasons until 1979.

Meanwhile, the comic book returned to an older era, with many issues taking place during World War II. The creators explained that this Golden Age Wonder Woman was from another Earth… Earth-2, a place where the Justice Society still fought.

With the dawn of the 1980s, Wonder Woman came back to Earth-1 and modern times. Many writers contributed to her adventures: Jack C. Harris, Gerry Conway, Paul Levitz, Roy Thomas, Dan Mishkin and Mindy Newell, the first female writer ever on the series.

The final notes for this version of Wonder Woman came in the CRISIS ON INFINITE EARTHS saga, a cosmic crossover event that created a new universe and had repercussions on every DC Comics character and series. In the very last issue before the crossover, we saw Diana Prince and Steve Trevor marry, right before their world was erased from reality. As a farewell message, writer Kurt Busiek and artist Trina Robbins created a four-issue mini-series called THE LEGEND OF WONDER WOMAN.

Wonder Woman
By Charles Moulton
TAP!
TAP!
TAP!
WONDER WOMAN--BEAUTIFUL AS APHRODITE, WISE AS ATHENA, SWIFTER THAN MERCURY, AND STRONGER THAN HERCULES--IS ENTIRELY DIFFERENT IN THE OTHER GUISE OF HER DUAL IDENTITY KNOWN TO NO ONE! NOW, FOR THE FIRST TIME, THE BREATHLESS STORY BEHIND HER IMPERSONATION IS REVEALED IN THE STARTLING ADVENTURE STAMPED...
TOP SECRET!
1

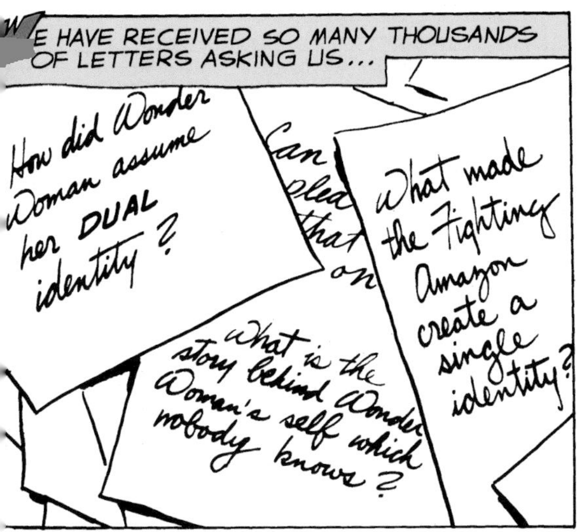
WE HAVE RECEIVED SO MANY THOUSANDS OF LETTERS ASKING US...
How did Wonder Woman assume her DUAL identity?
What made the Fighting Amazon create a single identity?
What is the story behind Wonder Woman's self which nobody knows?

IT ALL STARTED EARLY SATURDAY MORNING WHEN...

"...COL. STEVE TREVOR OF MILITARY INTELLIGENCE PERFORMED AN AMAZING STUNT..."
THUNDERBOLTS OF JOVE! STEVE REALLY PERFORMED THE STUNT OF PLUCKING MY SCARF OFF THAT POLE!
3
4

"AS THE INTREPID PILOT ZOOMED UP..."
SHADES OF PLUTO! A WING IS BREAKING OFF STEVE'S PLANE!
CRACK!

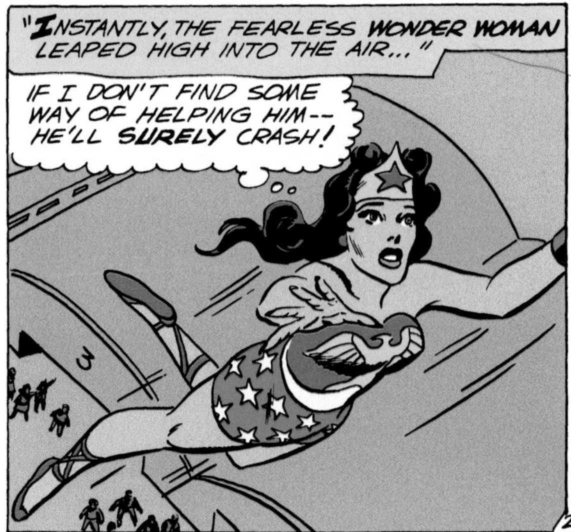
"INSTANTLY, THE FEARLESS WONDER WOMAN LEAPED HIGH INTO THE AIR..."
IF I DON'T FIND SOME WAY OF HELPING HIM-- HE'LL SURELY CRASH!
3
2

"THE STARTLED SPECTATORS ON THE FIELD WITNESSED AN AMAZING SIGHT..."
LOOK! WONDER WOMAN'S CAUGHT THE RIPPED-OFF WING!
WHAT CAN SHE HOPE TO DO WITH IT?

"A GASP AROSE AS THE MIGHTY AMAZON, WITH PERFECT TIMING..."
ANGEL--I CAN'T BELIEVE WHAT I SEE--YOU'VE STUCK THE WING BACK INTO PLACE!
I DON'T KNOW HOW LONG I CAN HOLD IT--HURRY AND LAND--HURRY--!
NC-30
THUD!

"BREATHLESSLY THE PILOT HEADED DOWN FOR A LANDING..."
LET GO, ANGEL! BEFORE YOU'RE CRUSHED AGAINST THE GROUND!

NO--YOU'LL CRASH IF I LET THE WING DROP! COMPLETE YOUR LANDING--I'LL TAKE CARE OF MYSELF!
3

"WITH HAIRBREADTH TIMING, WONDER WOMAN LET GO OF THE WRECKED WING THE PRECISE MOMENT STEVE SAFELY LANDED..."
SHE DID IT-- SHE DID IT-- I CAN'T BELIEVE MY EYES!
YOU'LL BELIEVE THE PICTURES CAMERAS ARE TAKING OF THIS IMPOSSIBLE STUNT!
NC 306
THUD!

"A MOMENT LATER..."
YOU MUST LOVE ME TO RISK YOUR LIFE FOR ME LIKE THAT, ANGEL! WHEN ARE YOU GOING TO MARRY ME? YOU KNOW HOW I FEEL ABOUT YOU!
I DO, STEVE, BUT I CAN'T MARRY YOU-- UNTIL MY SERVICES ARE NO LONGER NEEDED TO BATTLE CRIME AND INJUSTICE! ONLY THEN CAN I THINK ABOUT MYSELF!

IT'S NOT FAIR! I CAN'T LIVE WITHOUT YOU, ANGEL! WHY--EVEN WHEN I'M SURROUNDED BY AN ARMY OF PEOPLE-- ALL I SEE IS YOU! WHY--I COULD PICK YOU OUT IF YOU WERE JUST A SINGLE GRAIN OF SAND ON A BEACH--OR ONE STAR IN THE SKY!

THAT WAS A VERY PRETTY SPEECH, STEVE! BUT YOU KNOW YOU REALLY COULDN'T PICK ME OUT IF I WERE IN A HUGE CROWD--OR DISGUISED!
PROMISE TO MARRY ME IF I CAN PROVE IT?

ALL RIGHT, STEVE! I'LL TELL YOU WHERE I'LL BE--AND IF YOU CAN PICK ME OUT THREE TIMES IN TWENTY FOUR HOURS--I'LL MARRY YOU!

WONDER WOMAN DOESN'T KNOW IT-- BUT I CAN'T LOSE--!
4

"THE NEXT DAY..."
SINCE WE'RE PRACTICALLY MARRIED, ANGEL--YOU MIGHT AS WELL SLIP ON THIS ENGAGEMENT RING!

YOU HAVEN'T WON YET, STEVE! SO PLEASE TAKE BACK YOUR RING UNTIL YOU DO!

"AN HOUR LATER... ENGULFED AMONG THE MILLIONS OF SUNDAY BATHERS ON THE BEACH..."
STEVE SAID HE'D FIND ME IF I WERE BUT A SINGLE GRAIN OF SAND ON A BEACH! WELL--THAT'S JUST WHY I AM HERE--HE'LL NEVER FIND ME

HE'S LOST IN THE JUNGLE OF PEOPLE--!

HE CAN'T POSSIBLY--!
LIFE GU

HE CAN'T--!
LIFE

"TO WONDER WOMAN'S AMAZEMENT..."
IT'S A TRICK--A TRICK--THERE'S NO OTHER WAY YOU COULD HAVE DONE IT--YOU WENT STRAIGHT TOWARD ME--AS IF BY A COMPASS!
I TOLD YOU I'D FIND YOU IN A CROWD, ANGEL! READY TO GIVE UP? READY TO WEAR MY ENGAGEMENT RING?

"IN ANSWER--WONDER WOMAN SUDDENLY LEAPED INTO THE WATER AS HIGH ABOVE HER..."
CRASH!

"WITH INCREDIBLE SKILL THE INGENIOUS AMAZON STARTED WEAVING TRACKS WITH HER UNIQUE LASSO, AT FLASHING SPEED..."
HERA HELP ME!
RROAR!

"AND THEN, A SENSATIONAL SPECTACLE, AS THE MIGHTY WONDER WOMAN SKILLFULLY GUIDED THE RUNAWAY ROLLERCOASTER DOWN THE TRACKS OF UNBREAKABLE LINKS..."
THE AMAZON SAVED OUR LIVES!
THANK GOODNESS FOR WONDER WOMAN!
RRUMBLE!
6

"LATER..."
DON'T YOU SEE NOW WHY I MUST THINK ONLY OF OTHERS--TO PERFORM MY TASKS TO THE BEST OF MY ABILITY, STEVE?
A BET'S A BET, ANGEL! READY TO PUT ON MY ENGAGEMENT RING?

I HAVEN'T LOST! YOU HAVE TO PICK ME OUT TWICE MORE WITHIN TWENTY FOUR HOURS!
YOU HAVEN'T A CHANCE, ANGEL! YOU MIGHT AS WELL GIVE UP! I CAN PICK YOU OUT EVEN IF YOU ARE DISGUISED!

"A FEW HOURS LATER..."
STEVE WILL NEVER FIND ME IN THIS DISGUISE!
JUDGES

EVEN IF HE IS A JUDGE AT THIS VERY CONTEST FOR THE BEST COSTUME!

"BUT TO THE DISGUISED AMAZON'S UTTER AMAZEMENT..."
READY TO WEAR MY ENGAGEMENT RING NOW, ANGEL?
NO--BUT I DON'T KNOW HOW YOU DO IT?
7

"AT THAT MOMENT, AN OMINOUS CRACKLING SOUNDED AS..."
MERCIFUL MINERVA--LIGHTNING HEADING STRAIGHT FOR THOSE BATHERS IN THE WATER!
CRAAACK!

"AGAIN, WONDER WOMAN'S BREATHLESS PROWESS WITH HER AMAZON LASSO IS DISPLAYED AS..."
SHE'S SAVING THE PEOPLE--BY ATTRACTING THE LIGHTNING TO HERSELF!
CRANNGG!

"BUT AT THE LAST MOMENT, THE FEARLESS AMAZON WHIPPED THE LIGHTNING INTO THE SEA..."
THANK HERA--THE LIGHTNING IS GROUNDING ITSELF AWAY FROM ANYBODY!

"AGAINST WONDER WOMAN'S PLEAS..."
HOW CAN I HELP PEOPLE IN TROUBLE IF I'M WITH YOU, STEVE?
IF I PICK YOU OUT ONCE MORE--YOU'LL MARRY ME? OR ARE YOU READY TO GIVE UP NOW, ANGEL--AND WEAR MY ENGAGEMENT RING?
8

"LATER... AS FIREWORKS SHOWERED THE SKIES IN ALL THEIR COLORFUL BRILLIANCE..."
WHOOOOSH!
YOU'VE GOT UNTIL TO-MORROW NOON TO OUTWIT ME, ANGEL--OR BE MY BRIDE!
WHAT MAKES HIM ABLE TO PICK ME OUT ANYWHERE AS IF I'M MARKED?

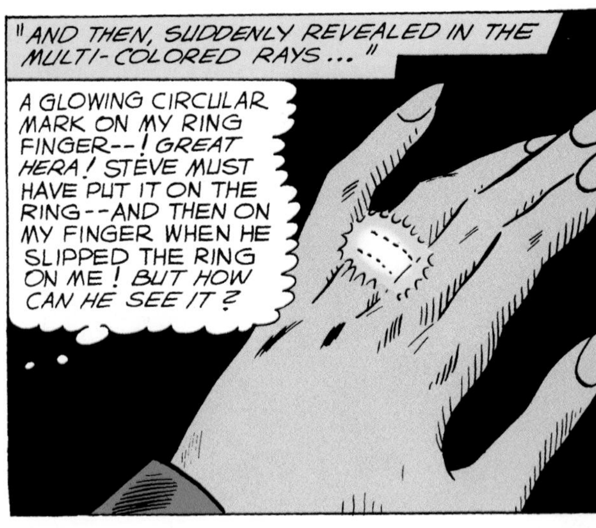
"AND THEN, SUDDENLY REVEALED IN THE MULTI-COLORED RAYS..."
A GLOWING CIRCULAR MARK ON MY RING FINGER--! GREAT HERA! STEVE MUST HAVE PUT IT ON THE RING--AND THEN ON MY FINGER WHEN HE SLIPPED THE RING ON ME! BUT HOW CAN HE SEE IT?

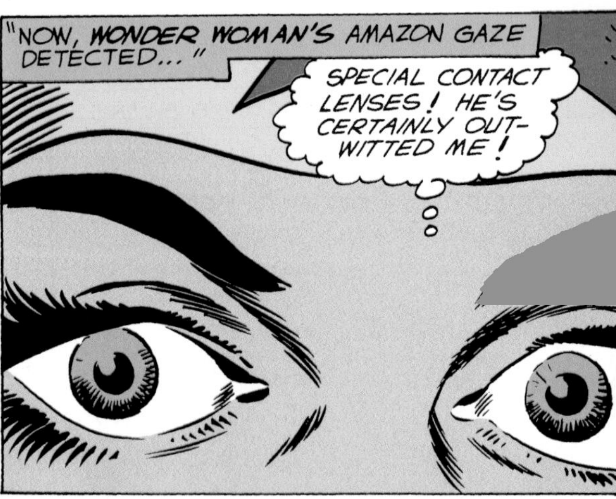
"NOW, WONDER WOMAN'S AMAZON GAZE DETECTED..."
SPECIAL CONTACT LENSES! HE'S CERTAINLY OUT-WITTED ME!

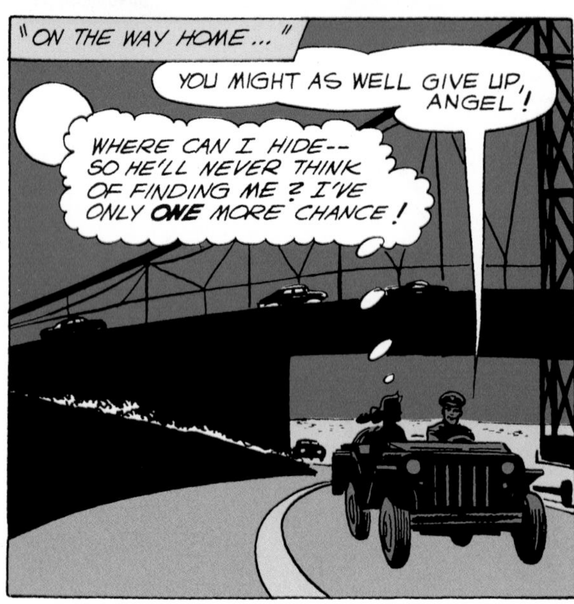
"ON THE WAY HOME..."
YOU MIGHT AS WELL GIVE UP, ANGEL!
WHERE CAN I HIDE--SO HE'LL NEVER THINK OF FINDING ME? I'VE ONLY ONE MORE CHANCE!

"THE NEXT MORNING AS THE PERPLEXED AMAZON IDLY GLANCED AT THE PAPER..."
HMMM--! THIS AD GIVES ME AN IDEA! IT MIGHT--JUST--WORK!

SHORTLY, AT MILITARY INTELLIGENCE..."
LADIES--ONLY ONE AMONG YOU WILL BE ABLE TO PASS THE DIFFICULT MENTAL AND PHYSICAL COMPETITIONS AHEAD OF YOU FOR THE POSITION! GOOD LUCK!

"AFTER THE WRITTEN EXAMINATION..."
ONLY YOU FIVE STILL QUALIFY FOR THE POSITION, LADIES! NOW FOR THE ORAL EXAMINATION!

"EXHAUSTIVE QUESTIONING REDUCED THE NUMBER OF CANDIDATES STILL FURTHER.."
NOW, FOR THE LAST SERIES OF TESTS--WHICH ONLY ONE OF YOU CAN FINALLY COMPLETE! WHICH ONE SHALL IT BE?

" ONE GRUELING TEST FOLLOWED ANOTHER UNTIL..."
HERE IS YOUR COMMISSION, LIEUTENANT! THE OTHER APPLICANT DROPPED OUT OF THE RACE! CONGRATULATIONS!

"LATER, BACK AT MILITARY INTELLIGENCE.."
YOUR NEW ASSISTANT, LT. DIANA PRINCE, STEVE!
EXCUSE ME! I HAVE UNTIL NOON TO LOOK FOR SOMEONE!

"AND THAT'S THE STORY OF WONDER WOMAN'S DUAL IDENTITY!"
WHAT BETTER PLACE TO CONCEAL MYSELF FROM STEVE--AFTER THE STAIN WORE OFF--THAN RIGHT UNDER HIS NOSE?
The End
10

SUPERMAN DC NATIONAL COMICS
Wonder Woman
JULY NO. 107
10¢
APPROVED BY THE COMICS CODE AUTHORITY
HERE'S THE SURPRISE STORY OF THE YEAR!...
WONDER WOMAN'S ADVENTURES AS AN... "AMAZON TEEN-AGER!"

Wonder Woman
By Charles Moulton
WONDER WOMAN PRESENTS A WONDER GIRL STORY!
DEAR READERS! WE'VE RECEIVED SO MANY REQUESTS FOR STORIES ABOUT MY ADVENTURES AS A TEEN-AGER--THAT WE'RE GOING TO TAKE YOU ALONG ON ASTOUNDING TRAILS TO EXCITEMENT AND SUSPENSE.. STARTING WITH HOW I WON MY COSTUME FOR ...
Wonder Woman
AMAZON TEEN-AGER!
HERA HELP ME TO HOLD ONTO THIS ROC! ONLY IT CAN LEAD ME TO WHERE MY COSTUME IS HIDDEN!
1

AS WONDER GIRL SURFACES AFTER A DIVE IN THE SEA OFF PARADISE ISLAND...
SHADES OF PLUTO! WH-WHERE DID YOU COME FROM? WE'RE THOUSANDS OF MILES FROM LAND! EXCEPT FOR PARADISE ISLAND! AND YOU CAN'T GO ASHORE! ATHENA'S LAW FORBIDS ALL MALES!

LAND? I NEVER GO ASHORE! HAHAHA!
GREAT HERA! H-H-H-HE'S A MERBOY!
SPLASH!

PLAYFULLY AS A DOLPHIN, THE MERBOY LEAPS OVER WONDER GIRL'S HEAD...
YOU ARE THE PRETTIEST FISH I HAVE EVER SEEN!
I'M AN AMAZON! NOT A FISH!

MY NAME IS RONNO, WONDER GIRL! FAREWELL! IF EVER YOU SHOULD NEED ME--I WILL BE NEARBY!

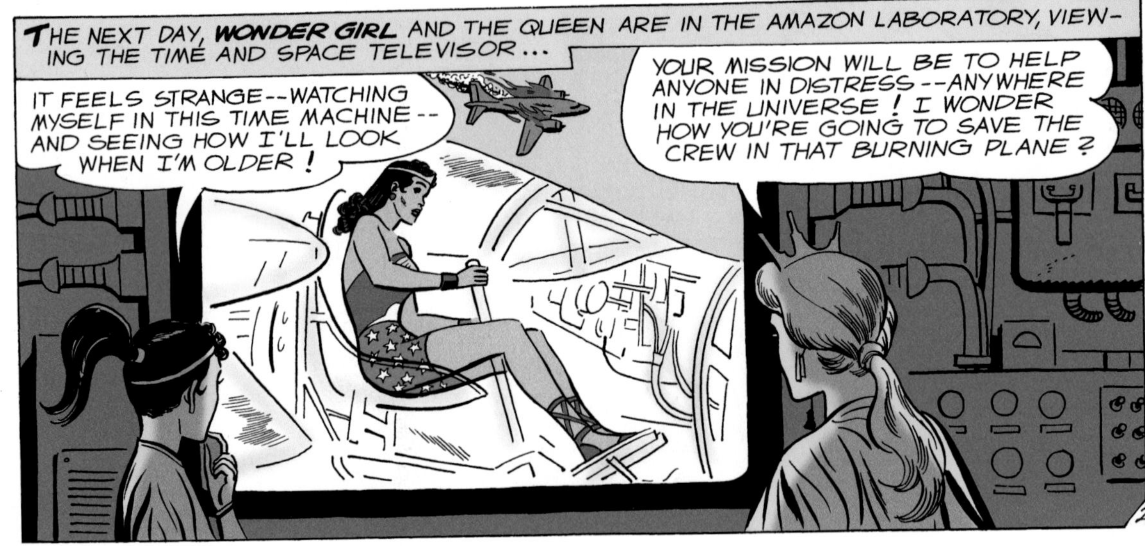
THE NEXT DAY, WONDER GIRL AND THE QUEEN ARE IN THE AMAZON LABORATORY, VIEWING THE TIME AND SPACE TELEVISOR...
IT FEELS STRANGE--WATCHING MYSELF IN THIS TIME MACHINE--AND SEEING HOW I'LL LOOK WHEN I'M OLDER!
YOUR MISSION WILL BE TO HELP ANYONE IN DISTRESS--ANYWHERE IN THE UNIVERSE! I WONDER HOW YOU'RE GOING TO SAVE THE CREW IN THAT BURNING PLANE?
2

THE RAPT AUDIENCE WATCHES WONDER WOMAN DIVE HER ROBOT PLANE AT SUCH FLASHING SPEED--THAT SHE WHIPS THE FLAMES AWAY FROM THE PLANE IN DISTRESS...
WHOOSH!

AT THE END OF THE PREVIEW INTO **WONDER GIRL'S** FUTURE CAREER AS **WONDER WOMAN**...

MOTHER! I WAS THINKING ABOUT THE COSTUME I'M GOING TO WEAR WHEN I'M OLDER! IT'S BEAUTIFUL! CAN'T I START WEARING IT NOW?

WONDER WOMAN HAD TO **WIN** THE RIGHT TO **WEAR** THAT COSTUME--BY PERFORMING INCREDIBLE FEATS! ARE YOU PREPARED TO DO THE SAME?

WHEN WONDER GIRL EAGERLY AGREES TO THE TRIALS... ALL THE AMAZONS ON THE ISLAND ARE TOLD TO SEND IN SUGGESTIONS ABOUT WHAT WONDER GIRL'S COSTUME SHOULD LOOK LIKE...
Golden Clasps
TOGA Green with Gold Athena Emblem
TOGA
WHITE STARS ON BLUE
Costume Wonder Girl
HIGH TOP SANDALS
Red Leather
RED CAPE
WHITE TOGA

AND THEN, WHEN ONE IS FINALLY SELECTED...
OH, MOTHER! AREN'T YOU GOING TO LET ME SEE THE WINNING SKETCH?
IT'S A SECRET, DIANA! YOU'LL HAVE TO WIN IT FIRST--BEFORE YOU CAN SEE IT! BUT I CAN TELL YOU IT'S COMPOSED OF THREE PARTS! AND NOW, WE MUST SELECT THE FEATS YOU WILL PERFORM!

TO REMOVE ANY POSSIBILITY OF FAVORITISM, ALL THE AMAZONS SUBMIT THEIR IDEAS OF DIFFICULT TASKS... WITHOUT THEIR SIGNATURES...
SUGGESTION BOX
3

FINALLY, AN IMPARTIAL BOARD OF AMAZONS MAKES THE SELECTIONS FROM ALL THE ENTRIES...
WE CHOSE THESE THREE FEATS AS THE MOST DIFFICULT SUBMITTED! THEY WERE UNSIGNED SO WE DON'T KNOW WHO THOUGHT THEM UP, NOBLE QUEEN!

THE MOMENT THE QUEEN GLANCES AT THEM...
GREAT HERA! IT'S DIANA'S HAND-WRITING! YOU SELECTED THE MOST DIFFICULT TASKS ANYONE THOUGHT OF!
I WANTED TO BE WORTHY OF THE COSTUME, MOTHER! JUST AS WONDER WOMAN IS WORTHY OF HERS!

A HUSH FALLS UPON THE ASSEMBLED AMAZONS AS THE QUEEN ANNOUNCES...
AS YOU ALL KNOW-- WONDER GIRL'S COSTUME CONSISTS OF THREE SEPARATE PARTS! SHE WILL FIND OUT WHAT THESE PARTS ARE--ONLY IF SHE SUCCEEDS IN WINNING THEM! IT WILL TAKE DAYS FOR US TO PLACE THEM WHERE SHE WILL HAVE TO BE A REAL WONDER GIRL-- TO RECOVER THEM!

DAYS LATER WONDER GIRL EAGERLY READS THE FIRST COMMAND...
YOU MAY PERFORM THESE IN ANY ORDER! ONE OF THE THREE PARTS ON YOUR COSTUME IS INSIDE THE CANNIBAL CLAM!

INSTANTLY, THE TEEN-AGE AMAZON BEGINS THE FIRST OF HER STARTLING MISSIONS WITH THE BENDING OF A TREE OVERLOOK-ING THE SEA...
THIS WILL HELP ME GET TO MY DESTINATION QUICKER!
TWAAANG!

AS WONDER GIRL DIVES INTO THE SEA, SHE IS UNAWARE THAT BELOW HER...
Ahh! 'TIS MY WONDER GIRL! I SHALL KEEP MY EYE ON HER IN CASE SHE NEEDS MY HELP!

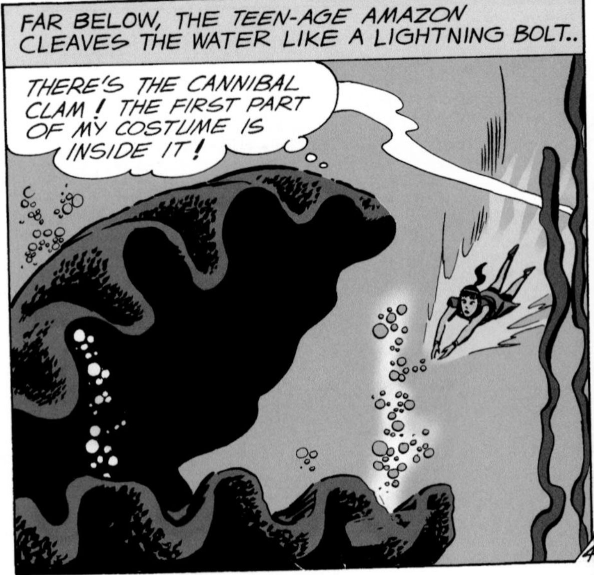
FAR BELOW, THE TEEN-AGE AMAZON CLEAVES THE WATER LIKE A LIGHTNING BOLT..
THERE'S THE CANNIBAL CLAM! THE FIRST PART OF MY COSTUME IS INSIDE IT!
4

AS WONDER GIRL NEARS THE GIANT CLAM...
HOW BEAUTIFUL! STARS FOR MY COSTUME--JUST LIKE WONDER WOMAN'S! AMAZONS MUST HAVE PLACED THEM INSIDE!

BUT THE PRESENCE OF THE DARING GIRL CAUSES THE SINISTER CLAM TO OPEN AND CLOSE ITS MASSIVE JAWS...
IF I GO INSIDE THE CLAM FOR THE STARS--I'LL BECOME A PRISONER--HOW CAN I GET THEM OUT?
CLUMP!

SEEING A CORAL FORMATION NEARBY, WONDER GIRL GETS AN INGENIOUS IDEA...
I'LL FASHION A PIECE IN THE SHAPE OF A SWORD!

A MOMENT LATER, THRUSTING THE SWORD OF CORAL BETWEEN THE CLASHING JAWS OF THE GIANT CLAM...
THANK HERA! THIS WILL KEEP THE CLAM OPEN LONG ENOUGH FOR ME TO TAKE OUT THE STARS FOR MY COSTUME!

EAGERLY, THE TEEN-AGE AMAZON FULFILLS HER FIRST TASK...
I'VE WON THE FIRST PART OF MY COSTUME!

WITH GIRLISH ENTHUSIASM SHE PLACES THEM ON HER TOGA...
THERE'S A SPECIAL ADHESIVE ON THEM--SO I CAN PUT THEM ON WITHOUT SEWING THEM ON!

5

BUT, AS SHE STEPS OUTSIDE, WONDER GIRL IS CONFRONTED BY AN OMINOUS SIGHT...
IT'S THE MERBOY! COME TO WARN ME ABOUT THIS GIANT SWORDFISH! ONLY TO FALL INTO DEADLY PERIL HIMSELF!

THE ONLY WEAPON I HAVE AGAINST THIS MONSTER-- IS THIS SWORD!

BUT NO SOONER HAS SHE SNATCHED THE SWORD FROM BETWEEN THE GIANT CLAM'S JAWS THAN...
SHADES OF PLUTO! MY FOOT IS CAUGHT!
PART TWO OF THIS EXCITING STORY CONTINUES..
6

Wonder Woman

WONDER GIRL -- TEEN-AGE AMAZON... PART TWO

SUCCESSFULLY COMPLETING THE FIRST OF HER THREE TASKS TO WIN THE RIGHT TO A UNIQUE COSTUME ALL HER OWN -- WONDER GIRL IS MENACED BY A GIANT SWORDFISH...

EVEN THOUGH SHE IS A PRISONER OF THE GIANT CLAM, **WONDER GIRL** BEGINS THE MOST AMAZING DUEL IN HISTORY... BATTLING A HUGE SWORDFISH WITH A SWORD OF CORAL...

HERA HELP ME WIN THIS BATTLE!

KLUNK!

KLUNK

THANK HERA! HE'S HAD ENOUGH!

THEN, WITH A MIGHTY BLOW OF HER SWORD...
HOW GOOD IT IS TO BE FREE AGAIN!
CRAACK!

NEXT, THE AMAZON TEEN-AGER TENDS TO THE PROSTRATE MERBOY...
A LITTLE FRESH AIR WILL DO US BOTH GOOD!
7

ON THE SURFACE, THE MERBOY RECOVERS AND...
WHEN I SAW YOU IN DEADLY PERIL FROM THE SWORDFISH-- ALL I COULD THINK OF-- WAS TO SAVE YOU--NO MATTER WHAT THE COST!
THANK YOU! IT WAS VERY BRAVE OF YOU!

AS SOON AS WONDER GIRL IS SURE THAT THE MERBOY IS RECOVERED...
I MUST BE OFF ON MY NEXT QUEST! FAREWELL!
FAREWELL! BUT IF YOU SHOULD NEED ANY HELP--I SHALL BE AROUND!

THE SECOND FEAT WONDER GIRL MUST PERFORM DIRECTS HER TO...
ANOTHER PART OF MY COSTUME IS ON THE GIANT ROC'S NEST--ON TOP OF THAT CLIFF!

BUT AS THE TEEN-AGE AMAZON ATTEMPTS TO CLIMB UP...
THE ROCK IS COATED WITH A SLIPPERY SUBSTANCE--I CAN'T GET A HOLD--ANYWHERE!

WONDER GIRL NEXT TRIES TO RIDE THE UP AND DOWN DRAFTS... BUT AGAIN...
AIR CURRENTS--

NOT STRONG ENOUGH--

--TO CARRY ME U--
8

THE YOUNG AMAZON TURNS TO THE THIRD AND LAST DIRECTIVE ...
I CAN TAKE THESE FEATS IN ANY ORDER! I'LL COME BACK TO THE ROC'S NEST LAST! I'LL TRY THIS ONE INSTEAD! ANOTHER PART OF YOUR COSTUME IS IN THE CRATER OF VOLCANO ISLAND!

AT FLASHING SPEED, THE TIRELESS TEEN-AGER SWIMS TOWARDS THE MYSTERIOUS ISLAND ...
VOLCANO ISLAND! NOW TO FIND A PART OF MY COSTUME IN THE CRATER!

UP TO THE EDGE OF THE BOILING CRATER WONDER GIRL RUNS ...
THERE'S THE SECOND PART OF MY COSTUME! A LASSO--JUST LIKE THE ONE I'LL USE WHEN I'M OLDER!

DARINGLY, THE AMAZON TEEN-AGER LEAPS DOWN...
IT'S A GOOD THING WE AMAZONS WERE TRAINED TO WITHSTAND TREMENDOUS HEAT AND COLD! NO ORDINARY PERSON WOULD BE SAFE TRYING THIS!

AS SHE FLASHES BY...
I'VE GOT THE LASSO!

AND THEN, WITHIN SIGHT OF THE YAWNING LAVA, WONDER GIRL'S PLUNGE IS HALTED WHEN...
JUST AS I HOPED! THE TREMENDOUS UPDRAFTS CREATED BY THE HOT AIR--ARE STOPPING ME!
9

WITH HER UNCANNY SKILL, THE AMAZON TEEN-AGER "RIDES" THE UPDRAFTS TO SAFETY...

I'M OUT AT LAST! NOW--TO GET BACK TO THE ROC'S NEST ON TOP OF THE CLIFF!

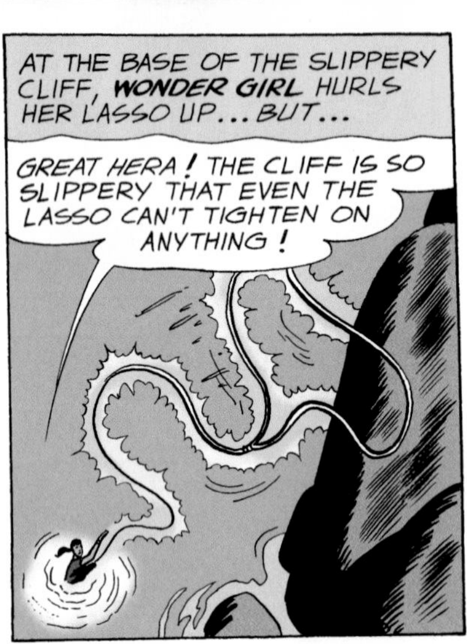

AT THE BASE OF THE SLIPPERY CLIFF, WONDER GIRL HURLS HER LASSO UP... BUT...
GREAT HERA! THE CLIFF IS SO SLIPPERY THAT EVEN THE LASSO CAN'T TIGHTEN ON ANYTHING!

AND THEN... AN OUTCRY...
LOOK OUT! WONDER GIRL!
THE MERBOY HAS FALLEN INTO THE CLUTCHES OF THE GIANT ROC HIMSELF!

INSTANTLY, THE YOUNG AMAZON HURLS HER GLEAMING LASSO UPWARDS...
DON'T WORRY--I'LL SAVE YOU!
THANK HERA! THE LASSO WILL HELP ME TO SAVE THE MERBOY!

AGILELY WONDER GIRL CLIMBS UP THE LASSO..
WHEN I SAW THE ROC FLY TOWARDS YOU--I TRIED TO FRIGHTEN HIM OFF!
THAT WAS VERY COURAGEOUS OF YOU!
10

ABOVE ITS NEST, THE HUGE WINGED-MONSTER RELEASES THE MERBOY...
THUNDERBOLTS OF JOVE! THERE'S THE LAST PART OF MY NEW COSTUME IN THE ROC'S NEST--THE EAGLE EMBLEM I WEAR AS WONDER WOMAN!

DANGLING FROM THE LASSO, WONDER GIRL SEIZES THE EAGLE EMBLEM IN ONE HAND...
THE LAST PART OF MY COSTUME!

INSTANTLY, THE SPECIAL ADHESIVE QUALITY OF THE EMBLEM ENABLES THE TEEN-AGER TO FASTEN IT ON...
YOU LOOK-- BEAUTIFUL!

BUT--THEN--AN UNEXPECTED DEVELOPMENT...
SUFFERING SAPPHO! THE ROC! HE'S FLYING AWAY WITH MY LASSO! IF I DON'T RECOVER IT--ALL MY EFFORTS WILL BE FOR NOTHING!

SEIZING THE MERBOY, WONDER GIRL HURLS HERSELF DESPERATELY AFTER THE GREAT BIRD...
IF I DON'T RECOVER THE LASSO--MY COSTUME WILL BE INCOMPLETE--AND I SHALL HAVE FAILED!
11

HER PRODIGIOUS LEAP PLACES THE AMAZON TEEN-AGER WITHIN REACH OF THE LASSO...
BY PLUTO! YOU'VE YANKED YOUR LASSO FREE!

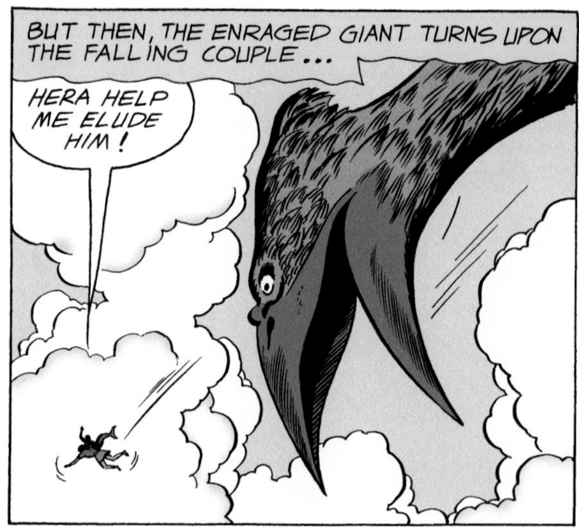
BUT THEN, THE ENRAGED GIANT TURNS UPON THE FALLING COUPLE...
HERA HELP ME ELUDE HIM!

FINDING AIR CURRENTS...
SNAP!

WONDER GIRL TWISTS AND TURNS ON THEM...
SNAP!

GRIMLY ELUDING THE WINGED PURSUER'S CLUTCHES...

UNTIL SHE COMES WITHIN REACH OF THE HOLE IN THE ROCK SHE USES TO ESCAPE INTO...
THANK HERA--THE ROC CAN NO LONGER FOLLOW US!

WHEN THE AMAZON GIRL AND THE MERBOY FINALLY SURFACE, THE WINGED FURY IS GONE...
I TOLD YOU I WOULD BE AROUND IN CASE YOU EVER NEEDED ME!
I CAN'T THANK YOU ENOUGH!
12

THEN, THE TWO PART...

I'LL KEEP YOUR HAIR RIBBON AS A SOUVENIR OF THE GIRL I LOST MY HEART TO! BUT YOU HAVEN'T SEEN THE LAST OF ME!

LATER, ALL THE AMAZONS HAIL **WONDER GIRL** IN HER NEW COSTUME...

YOU HAVE EARNED THE RIGHT TO WEAR THIS COSTUME! CONGRATULATIONS!

I'LL TRY TO BE WORTHY OF IT, MOTHER!

MANY ARE THE THRILLING ADVENTURES WHICH BEFALL **WONDER GIRL** IN HER NEW COSTUME! PLEASE WRITE AND TELL US IF YOU WOULD LIKE TO READ MORE OF THEM!

The End

13

SUPERMAN DC NATIONAL COMICS
IT'S GOODBYE TO THE PAST FOR...
APPROVED BY THE COMICS CODE AUTHORITY
DEC. NO. 179
THE NEW WONDER WOMAN
12¢

THIS IS THE BEGINNING OF THE MOST BIZARRE ADVENTURE YOU HAVE EVER WITNESSED! IT BEGINS QUIETLY... WITH A MUTED CONVERSATION BETWEEN TWO MEN AT THE OFFICE OF A GOVERNMENT AGENCY SO SECRET IT MUST REMAIN NAMELESS...
YOU'RE CERTAIN YOU WANT TO UNDERTAKE OUR MISSION, COLONEL TREVOR? IT *IS* VOLUNTARY, YOU KNOW!
I'M CERTAIN, GENERAL!
I'M COMMITTED TO THE WELFARE OF THE UNITED STATES... AND I'M READY TO GO WHEREVER THAT COMMITMENT TAKES ME!
IN THE PRESENT CASE, IT WILL TAKE YOU INTO GRAVE DANGER-- AND *DISGRACE!*
BECAUSE... TO BE EFFECTIVE, YOU MUST ESTABLISH YOURSELF AS A *TRAITOR!*
UM-HUM! WHEN DO I START?
AT ONCE! BUT ONE WORD OF CAUTION... AS SOON AS THE CRIMINAL ORGANIZATION CONTACTS YOU, LET ME KNOW WITHOUT DELAY!
YES SIR!... NOW, IF YOU'LL PARDON ME, GENERAL...
I'LL LAUNCH MY CAREER AS... AN ENEMY OF THE PEOPLE!
WAP

IN--AGH!--
INDEED...
GENERAL!
A-ANY ORDERS?!
WHAM!
MP
MP
ONE MORE PUNCH SHOULD BRING THE GUARDS!

SEIZE HIM! THIS MAN IS A SPY!
IT'LL TAKE MORE THAN A PAIR OF TIN SOLDIERS...
MP

...TO STOP STEVE TREVOR!
SOK
THIS HURTS ME MORE THAN IT DOES YOU, SOLDIER...

IT'S AGAINST ALL MY TRAINING... EVERYTHING I BELIEVE IN...
YET I MUST MAKE IT BELIEVABLE! I MUST BECOME AN OUTCAST--HATED, HUNTED, DESPERATE!
MP
2

UH... GET HIM! USE YOUR GUNS!
THAT DOES IT-- I'M STRICTLY ON MY OWN! THE GENERAL WARNED ME THAT IF I'M CAUGHT--NEITHER HE --NOR HIS AGENCY-- WILL HELP!
SO...GOT TO CONCENTRATE ON GETTING OUT WITH MY WHOLE SKIN!
HUH-OH! MAIN EXIT'S BLOCKED!
MY MISSION IS TOO VITAL TO BE STOPPED BEFORE IT GETS STARTED!
BUT IT LOOKS LIKE THAT'S WHAT'S HAPPENING--! THE BACK DOOR'S CUT OFF, TOO!
FIRE EXIT
MAYBE I CAN HIDE IN HERE 'TIL THE GUARDS LEAVE!
THERE HE GOES...
...INTO THE CONFERENCE ROOM!
GET THOSE HANDS UP, CHUM... AND I MEAN QUICK!
THE LIGHT FROM THE WINDOW IS HITTING THEM SMACK IN THE EYES! THAT GIVES ME MY ONE CHANCE--!
3

SUDDENLY-- AS STEVE TREVOR LUNGES FORWARD, GLASS EXPLODES IN A RAINBOW OF TINY, JAGGED PIECES...
CCRRASSHH!
BLAM
BLAM
BLAM
HE'S HEADING FOR THE PARKING LOT!
4

BULLETS WHINE ACROSS THE PAVEMENT AS STEVE FORCES HIMSELF TO ALMOST INHUMAN SPEED...
SOUND THE ALARM!
ONLY ONE WAY TO GET TO THE ENEMY-- AND THIS IS IT!
PARKING
F-WHIIING
F-WHIIING
HOLD IT--
HE'S OUT OF RANGE!
I NEVER SAW A MAN MOVE THAT FAST!
MP
MP
MP
3N7D
DON'T WORRY, GENERAL! HE WON'T GET FAR!
MP
WE'LL HAVE EVERY MILITARY AND CIVILIAN UNIT ON THE LOOKOUT FOR HIM!
GOOD LUCK, STEVE--AND GODSPEED!
5

RETURN TO YOUR POSTS, MEN!
SO FAR, SO GOOD! COLONEL TREVOR, THE MOST LOYAL OFFICER I'VE EVER KNOWN, IS BRANDED A TRAITOR!
MP
6

...THE WORLD HAS GOTTEN PRETTY ROTTEN TO FORCE ME INTO A LIE LIKE THAT! BUT THE WORLD WILL GET A GREAT DEAL MORE ROTTEN...
...UNLESS WE CAN BRING DOCTOR CYBER AND HIS HIGH-POWERED CUT-THROATS TO JUSTICE!
LEAVE THE GENERAL TO HIS THOUGHTS, HIS TORMENT...AND PREPARE YOURSELF FOR AN EXCURSION INTO THE STRANGE, THE SPECTACULAR, THE TERRIFYING--PREPARE YOURSELF FOR A WHOLLY UNIQUE KIND OF IMAGINATIVE EXPERIENCE!
EDITOR: JACK MILLER
WRITER: DENNIS O'NEIL
CONTINUITY & PENCILS MIKE SEKOWSKY
INKS: DICK GIORDANO

Wonder Woman

WONDER WOMAN'S LAST BATTLE!
PART II
A BRIGHT, SUNNY DAY IN LOWER MANHATTAN SUDDENLY TURNS CHILL FOR DIANA PRINCE AS SHE HEARS...
POLICE AGENCIES ARE SEEKING STEVEN TREVOR, A COLONEL IN THE U.S. ARMY...
YA CAN'T TRUST ANYBODY OVER 30--
GREAT HERA! IT'S TRUE!
DAILY HERALD
HUNT COL. TREVOR
ARMY OFFICER LABELED SPY BY SUPERIORS!
MEDAL-OF-HONOR WINNER TREVOR IS CHARGED WITH STEALING TOP-SECRET DOCUMENTS! AN ARMY SPOKESMAN HAS CALLED HIM A GRAVE THREAT TO NATIONAL SECURITY...
HAVE YOU SEEN THIS MAN?
IT CAN'T BE TRUE--! STEVE MAY HAVE HIS FAULTS...
...BUT DISLOYALTY CERTAINLY ISN'T ONE OF THEM! THERE'S BEEN A HORRIBLE MISTAKE-- A MISTAKE WONDER WOMAN MAY BE ABLE TO CORRECT! I'LL CHANGE TO MY COSTUME AND...
DIANA! THIS IS YOUR MOTHER...
...QUEEN HIPPOLYTA! REPORT TO PARADISE ISLAND AT ONCE!
I MUST HEED MOTHER'S TELEPATHIC SUMMONS!
7

AN HOUR LATER, AS WONDER WOMAN'S INVISIBLE PLANE WINGS SILENTLY THROUGH A BLUE PACIFIC SKY...
MOTHER'S MESSAGE SEEMED... URGENT! I CAN'T IMAGINE WHAT KIND OF TROUBLE SHE COULD BE IN--!
I'VE ALWAYS BEEN AFRAID THAT SOME DAY HIS STUBBORNNESS WOULD GET HIM INTO DIFFICULTY!
THE AMAZONS COMMAND MY FIRST LOYALTY! BUT I WANT SO MUCH TO FIND STEVE... TO HELP HIM!

LATER, AS WONDER WOMAN SETS FOOT ON FABLED PARADISE ISLAND...
I BID YOU WELCOME, DAUGHTER! MAY THE BRIGHT BEINGS BEHOLD YOU!
THANK YOU, MOST GRACIOUS MOTHER!
THE FORMAL GREETING--! THE ADDRESS USED ONLY ON THE MOST SOLEMN AND GRAVE OCCASIONS!

IT IS MY DUTY TO DEMAND A DECISION OF YOU, DIANA!
OUR TIME ON EARTH GROWS SHORT! FOR TEN THOUSAND YEARS, WE HAVE LIVED HERE, PERFORMING THE MISSION ASSIGNED TO US...
... HELPING MANKIND FIND MATURITY! BUT NOW, OUR MAGIC IS EXHAUSTED!

WE MUST JOURNEY TO ANOTHER DIMENSION, TO REST AND RENEW OUR POWERS! WE ARE TIRED, DIANA... THE AGES WEIGH HEAVILY UPON US!
WILL YOU COME--?

BUT YOU HESITATE, DAUGHTER...?
I LOVE YOU, MOTHER...

...YOU AND MY SISTER AMAZONS! BUT STEVE TREVOR DESPERATELY NEEDS ME...

I MUST STAY!
SO BE IT!
8

GAZE NOW UPON A CEREMONY NEVER BEFORE SEEN ON THIS PLANET... THE AWESOME AMAZON RITE OF RENUNCIATION!
I HEREBY RELINQUISH ALL MYSTIC SKILLS! I LAY UPON THE SACRED ALTAR THE GLORIES OF THE AMAZONS AND WILLINGLY CONDEMN MYSELF TO THE TRAVAILS OF MORTALS!
MAY THE GODS BE MERCIFUL TO ME!
THUS IT SHALL BE DONE!
OH, MOTHER... MOTHER... I'LL MISS YOU!
AND I YOU! PERHAPS WE WILL AGAIN COME TOGETHER SOME DAY...
THROUGH A BLUR OF TEARS, DIANA PRINCE WATCHES PARADISE ISLAND SHIMMER, DISSOLVE, VANISH... LEAVING ONLY THE AZURE OCEAN...
GOODBYE... MY HOME...
GONE... EVERYTHING THAT SUSTAINED ME... MY CHILDHOOD... MY FAMILY... ALL GONE!
WHEN I REACH THE MAINLAND, THE PLANE WILL FOLLOW THE ISLAND INTO OBLIVION...
THEN I SHALL BE TRULY ALONE... AN ORPHAN... WITHOUT FRIENDS, WITHOUT A HOME... A STRANGER AND ALONE...
9

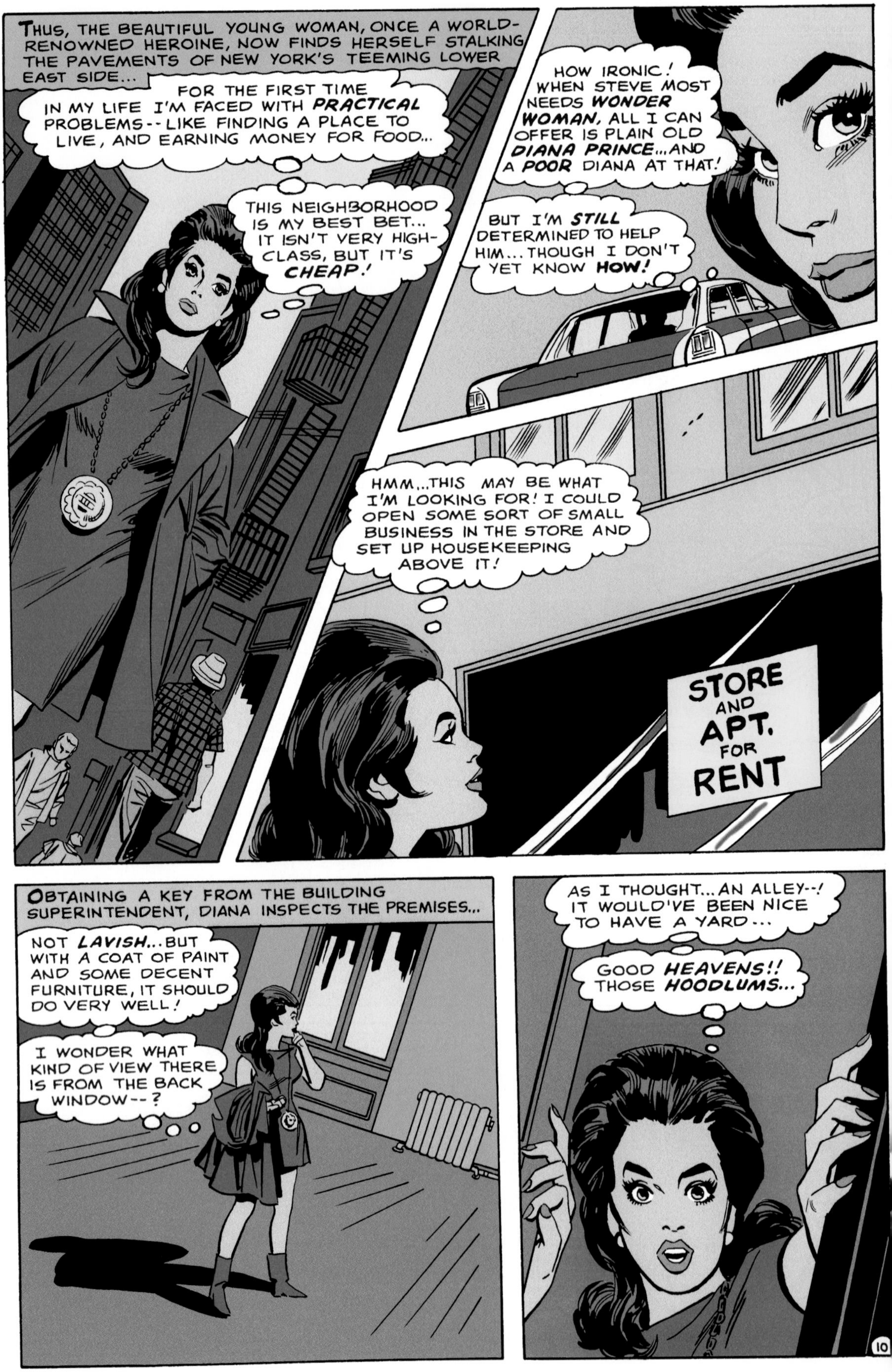

THUS, THE BEAUTIFUL YOUNG WOMAN, ONCE A WORLD-RENOWNED HEROINE, NOW FINDS HERSELF STALKING THE PAVEMENTS OF NEW YORK'S TEEMING LOWER EAST SIDE...
FOR THE FIRST TIME IN MY LIFE I'M FACED WITH **PRACTICAL** PROBLEMS--LIKE FINDING A PLACE TO LIVE, AND EARNING MONEY FOR FOOD...
THIS NEIGHBORHOOD IS MY BEST BET... IT ISN'T VERY HIGH-CLASS, BUT IT'S **CHEAP!**

HOW IRONIC! WHEN STEVE MOST NEEDS **WONDER WOMAN**, ALL I CAN OFFER IS PLAIN OLD **DIANA PRINCE**...AND A **POOR** DIANA AT THAT!
BUT I'M **STILL** DETERMINED TO HELP HIM... THOUGH I DON'T YET KNOW **HOW!**

HMM...THIS MAY BE WHAT I'M LOOKING FOR! I COULD OPEN SOME SORT OF SMALL BUSINESS IN THE STORE AND SET UP HOUSEKEEPING ABOVE IT!
STORE AND APT. FOR RENT

OBTAINING A KEY FROM THE BUILDING SUPERINTENDENT, DIANA INSPECTS THE PREMISES...
NOT **LAVISH**...BUT WITH A COAT OF PAINT AND SOME DECENT FURNITURE, IT SHOULD DO VERY WELL!
I WONDER WHAT KIND OF VIEW THERE IS FROM THE BACK WINDOW--?

AS I THOUGHT...AN ALLEY--! IT WOULD'VE BEEN NICE TO HAVE A YARD...
GOOD **HEAVENS!!** THOSE **HOODLUMS**...
10

...THEY'RE ATTACKING THAT POOR BLIND MAN!
GOT ANY MONEY, POPS?!
LET'S HAVE US SOME FUN! IT'S A CINCH THE OLD GEEZER WON'T IDENTIFY US.
PLEASE LET ME PASS, YOUNG GENTLEMEN!
HAW! HAW!
NO TIME TO CALL THE POLICE! MAYBE I CAN FRIGHTEN THEM OFF!
BUT, AS DIANA REACHES THE ALLEY...
PLEASE TO RECALL THIS PAIN, YOUNG GENTLEMEN, WHEN NEXT TEMPTED TO HARM FELLOW BEING!
IT...IT'S UNBELIEVABLE! THE OLD MAN HAS KNOCKED ALL THREE OF THEM UNCONSCIOUS!
DIANA PRINCE? PERMIT ME TO INTRODUCE SELF! I CHING!
HOW DID YOU KNOW I'M HERE? AREN'T YOU... BLIND?
11

WERE YOU LOOKING...UH, SEEKING ME, MR. CHING?
EYES ARE ONLY ONE PORTAL TO THE SOUL! THE MIND IS WHAT TRULY SEES!

INDEED! I REQUIRE YOUR ASSISTANCE, DIANA PRINCE! CERTAIN POWERS GIVEN TO MY CARE REVEAL THAT YOU ARE WONDER WOMAN!
I WAS WONDER WOMAN, MR. CHING! NOW...

NOW YOU HAVE LOST STRENGTH, SWIFTNESS AND MAGIC! YOU WISH TO AID STEVE TREVOR, BUT DO NOT KNOW HOW! THESE THINGS I UNDERSTAND!
THE LINES OF OUR FATES CONVERGE! FOR THE ENEMIES OF STEVEN TREVOR ARE ALSO MY ENEMIES--AND THE ENEMIES OF MANKIND!
12

LISTEN, PLEASE! HEAR MY STORY! HEAR THE EVIL OF HIM WHO IS CALLED DOCTOR CYBER!
THEN YOU WILL COMPREHEND WHY HE MUST BE DESTROYED!
CHING'S AMAZING TALE FOLLOWS ON THE PAGE FOLLOWING...

Wonder Woman

I AM LAST SURVIVING MEMBER OF ANCIENT SECT! OUR MONASTERY WAS HIDDEN HIGH IN MOUNTAIN! IT WAS OUR TASK TO MAINTAIN AGELESS KNOWLEDGE LOST CENTURIES PAST-- WHEN MEN FOOLISHLY CONCLUDED THAT MAGIC AND SCIENCE ARE DIFFERENT! ONLY WE KNEW THEY ARE TWO SIDES OF SAME COIN!
WONDER WOMAN'S LAST BATTLE PART III
IN OUR TEMPLE RESTED TREASURES OF PRECIOUS METAL AND GEMS! THE AGENTS OF DOCTOR CYBER WISHED TO POSSESS THEM! SO THEY STRUCK AT US...
WE RESISTED BRAVELY! BUT WE WERE HELPLESS BEFORE THEIR WEAPONS! WITH GUN AND BOMB, THEY SPREAD DEATH!
AT LAST, THE BREATH OF MY BROTHERS WAS STILLED! ALTHOUGH I, TOO, WAS WOUNDED, I WAS ABLE TO ESCAPE! I HID UNTIL THE MURDERERS HAD FLED WITH THEIR BOOTY!
I DON'T BLAME YOU FOR HATING THEM!
CHING DOES NOT HATE! RATHER, I PURSUE DOCTOR CYBER FOR REASONS OF LOVE! I LOVE HUMANITY-- AND IF DOCTOR CYBER'S PLANS OF CONQUEST ARE REALIZED...
...MEN AND WOMEN WILL BE REDUCED TO LIVING AUTOMATONS-- SLAVES TO DO HIS BIDDING!
WHO IS THIS DOCTOR CYBER?
13

A MONSTROSITY! A CREATURE--HALF MAN, HALF MACHINE... BUT MORE OF HIM LATER! FOR THE PRESENT, YOU MUST LEARN SKILLS!
SKILLS?
ABILITIES TO REPLACE YOUR LOST AMAZON TRAITS! YOUR AMAZON TRAINING MAKES YOU UNIQUELY SUITED TO MY TEACHING!
IF YOU SAY SO--! WHEN DO WE BEGIN?
IMMEDIATELY! I AM AT YOUR SERVICE! LET US START WITH A COURSE IN SIMPLE FIGHTING--KARATE!
WEEKS PASS... WEEKS FILLED WITH STRENUOUS PHYSICAL AND MENTAL LABOR! DIANA'S BODY STRETCHES, STRAINS, ACQUIRES UNCANNY REFLEXES--HER MIND IS FORCED TO UNBELIEVABLE DISCIPLINE!
RUBBING YOUR HANDS IN RICE GRAINS WILL GIVE THEM TOUGHNESS!
DO NOT BE STIFF! YOUR LIMBS MUST BE LIMBER AS STRINGS!
CONCENTRATE! PUT YOUR WHOLE WILL INTO YOUR FINGERS WHEN YOU STRIKE!
THE HUMAN FORM CAN SMASH STEEL WALLS! BUT YOU MUST BELIEVE IT CAN!
14

DIANA MASTERS IN A FEW SHORT MONTHS THE KNOWLEDGE AN ORDINARY GIRL WOULD SPEND YEARS ACQUIRING! BY DAY, SHE PRACTICES THE DEADLY BATTLE ARTS OF THE ORIENT... AND BY NIGHT, SHE QUESTIONS UNDERWORLD INFORMERS, STUDIES THE NEWS COLUMNS, SEEKING SOME TRACE OF STEVE TREVOR...
DAILY PRESS
STILL HUNT
STEVE TREVOR
NEWS
...UNTIL, AT A GYM WHERE SHE IS HONING TO FINE SHARPNESS THE THINGS CHING HAS BEEN TEACHING, STEVE FINDS HER...
STEVE!! HE'S SHOT!
15

I SHALL SUMMON MEDICAL AID!
MUST... MUST TALK... CYBER'S THUGS... DIDN'T BELIEVE ME... TRAITOR! GUNNED ME... LEFT ME FOR DEAD... I CRAWLED AWAY...
REST, STEVE... DON'T TRY TO TALK!
PLEASE, STEVE! YOUR STORY CAN WAIT!
NO!... THEY'RE HIDING AT ABANDONED FACTORY... EDGE OF CITY... PUTTING BOMBS IN TOYS... PLAN TO SEND THEM TO CONGRESS-MEN'S KIDS... CAUSE CHAOS IN GOVERNMENT... EASY FOR CYBER TO TAKE OVER...

AAAGH! HURTS, DIANA... HURTS SO MUCH--!
AMBULANCE COMES!
YOU'LL BE ALL RIGHT, STEVE! I KNOW YOU WILL!
NEVER MIND... ME! GET WONDER WOMAN... TO STOP CYBER...

ARRRRRR
AM I TO LOSE EVERYONE--? EVERYONE WHO MEANS... LOVE... TO ME?
OH, STEVE... PLEASE DON'T DIE!
16

DIANA! YOU HAVE PITY IN YOUR HEART-- PITY FOR STEVEN TREVOR AND FOR YOURSELF!
THIS MUST STOP! WE HAVE JOB TO DO!
SOFT EMOTIONS CLOUD INTELLECT! GRIEVE WHEN WE ARE FINISHED, IF YOU MUST!
WHAT I'M FEELING ISN'T SOFT, CHING... I HATE CYBER--!
HATE, TOO, WILL INTERFERE WITH TASK! PUT IT ASIDE! COME! CAR IS WAITING!
AT MIDNIGHT, A RENTED AUTOMOBILE GLIDES TOWARD AN OMINOUS BLACK BUILDING...
HOW DO YOU FEEL, DIANA?
FRANKLY... I'M FRIGHTENED! I'VE NEVER FACED CRIMINALS WITHOUT MY AMAZON POWERS BEFORE!
PUT FRIGHT AWAY! HAVE FAITH IN YOUR INSTINCTS--AND IN YOURSELF! BE ALERT NOW! DESTINATION LIES AHEAD!
WE GOT COMPANY, BOSS!
FOOL! TREVOR ESCAPED--AND NOW, WE HAVE FURTHER DIFFICULTIES!
IF YOU WOULD ESCAPE PUNISHMENT FOR YOUR STUPIDITY, YOU WILL ELIMINATE THE INTRUDERS!
I CAN NOT PERSONALLY SUPERVISE! THERE ARE IMPORTANT MATTERS ELSEWHERE AWAITING MY ATTENTION!
REPORT TO ME AT MAIN HEADQUARTERS WHEN IT IS DONE!
SURE, BOSS! YOU GOT NOTHIN' TO WORRY ABOUT!
17

HERE THEY COME, GUYS! GET READY--

NOW!

AS I SENSED! HOSTILE GENTLEMEN! PREPARE, DIANA! STANCE ONE!

THEY'RE ATTACKING US WITH *TOYS!*

--*DEADLY* TOYS!

MORE DEADLY THAN YOU SUSPECT! MY NOSE DETECTS *POISON* ON SMALL SWORDS! A NICK MEANS INSTANT DOOM!

MY FIRST REAL TEST OF CHING'S TRAINING... SO FAR, SO GOOD!

BEFORE I CAN *THINK* ABOUT DANGER, MY REFLEXES ACT TO STOP IT!

HARK, DIANA! I PERCEIVE *ANOTHER* PERIL!

A HUGE *FRANKENSTEIN* DOLL!

PLEASE DISABLE SAME!

18

YEOW! THE THING WANTS TO SCALP ME! BUT WE'VE PRACTICED A COUNTERATTACK...
I PULL ITS HAND FORWARD TO RELIEVE THE PRESSURE...
...AND STAB AN ELBOW INTO ITS MIDSECTION!
KWOP!
AND FINALLY, DISABLE IT WITH A HAITO CHOP!
GREAT HERA! IT'S STILL COMING!
FIGURE HAS HEAT-SEEKING DEVICE HIDDEN IN BODY--LIKE MISSILES!
YOU MUST SMASH ENGINE IN SOLAR PLEXUS! SUGGEST MAE GERI KICK!
KLAT!
THAT DID IT!
THEY AIN'T HUMAN! BUT HUMAN OR NOT, THE FLYIN' CIRCUS'LL GIT 'EM!
19

WHAT'S THAT? DO YOU HEAR--?
BRRRR
SMALL PROPELLERS! REMEMBER STEVEN TREVOR'S WORDS... TOY PLANES WITH BOMBS!
BRATATATAT
THEY'RE MODEL FOKKER TRIPLANES!
FIRING MINIATURE MACHINE GUNS!
WHILE THE CHINAMAN AND THE DAME ARE BUSY DODGING SLUGS, YOU GUYS GIT BEHIND 'EM WITH YOUR CHOPPERS!
CHECK!
AS MY FAVORITE COMIC STRIP CHARACTER WOULD SAY-- TAKE THAT, RED BARON!
SWAT!
OBVIOUSLY STEVE TREVOR LEARNED ONLY PART OF CYBER'S PLANS FOR TOYS! MANY EVILS BUILT INTO INNOCENT PLAY-THINGS--!
I NEVER GUESSED I'D BEGIN MY POST-AMAZON CAREER PLAYING KING KONG!
20

HE'S **INCREDIBLE!** HE ACCOMPLISHES MORE **BLIND** THAN ANYONE I EVER MET WITH PERFECT VISION!

I'D BETTER STOP ADMIRING CHING-- AND PAY ATTENTION TO THESE **HOODS!**

SOON I SHALL QUALIFY AS WORLD WAR ONE **ACE!**

DID SOMETHING MAKE YOU THINK I'M TIRED, UGLY?

ZOK

UNNGK!

HOLD STILL, BLAST YOU... **OOMPH!**

THIS IS CALLED THE **NAKADATE IPPON KIN ZUKI PUNCH!**--A LONG NAME TO MAKE **SHOPT** WORK OF YOU!

WHOOFF

THAT TAKES CARE OF THEM ALL!
NOT SO, DIANA! I HEAR FOOTSTEPS APPROACHING FROM OTHER ROOM!

YOU PUT ON A REAL FINE SHOW, CHUMPS! TAKE A BOW-- YOUR LAST BOW!
21

FOR THIS, DOC CYBER'LL GIVE ME A FAT, JUICY BONUS!
ZRRRRRR

BRATATAT
TATATAT

BRAT-A-TAT-A-TAT
V-ROOOOOM

DIANA-- DOWN!
KRUNCH
BRAT-A-TAT
NOW, I AM ACE!
SOMEHOW, CHING, I HADN'T REALIZED YOU HAVE A SENSE OF HUMOR!
LAUGHTER IS MEDICINE OF GODS-- AND MAN!

EARLY THE NEXT MORNING, AT A CITY HOSPITAL...
STEVE...
HE CAN'T HEAR YOU, MISS PRINCE!

HE'S IN A DEEP STATE OF SHOCK FROM THE BEATING AND GUN WOUNDS! IT'S A MIRACLE HE'S ALIVE AT ALL!
WE CAN'T TELL HOW EXTENSIVE THE DAMAGE IS! THERE COULD BE BRAIN INJURY!

HE MAY SPEND THE REST OF HIS LIFE AS HE IS NOW!
GET WELL, STEVE! PLEASE... GET WELL!
22

THEN, OUTSIDE, IN THE COOL DAWN AIR...
I'M EXHAUSTED... AND A BIT NUMB! MY LIFE HAS CHANGED SO MUCH...
NO! WE HAVE BARELY STARTED! DOCTOR CYBER IS STILL FREE! HE IS LIKE AN INFECTION IN HUMAN STRAIN! OUR TASK IS TO CURE DISEASE--BY CRUSHING HIM!
23

AS FOR CHANGES-- THEY HAVE JUST BEGUN!
A GOOD-LOOKING DAME AND A BLIND CHINESE... THOSE THE PEOPLE I'M AFTER, ALL RIGHT!

THUS, THE FIRST CHAPTER IN THE SAGA OF THE ***NEW WONDER WOMAN*** ENDS... WITH DIANA AND HER AGED MENTOR BEING OBSERVED BY A SINISTER FIGURE HIDDEN IN THE SHADOWS! MORE DANGER--MORE HIGH-VOLTAGE EXCITEMENT--MORE HEARTBREAK--AWAIT DIANA PRINCE AS SHE AND CHING CONTINUE THEIR PURSUIT OF THE SUPREMELY DEPRAVED ***DOCTOR CYBER!***

NEW ADVENTURES OF THE ORIGINAL
DC
WONDER WOMAN
20¢
WONDER WOMAN
APPROVED BY THE COMICS CODE AUTHORITY
NO. 204
FEB.
UNLESS I REVEAL THERE ARE TWO WONDER WOMEN--
MY DAUGHTER DIANA WILL DIE!
"The SECOND LIFE OF WONDER WOMAN!"
INTRODUCING NUBIA!

THE SECOND LIFE OF THE ORIGINAL WONDER WOMAN
IT IS A DAY LIKE ANY OTHER DAY IN FUN CITY...
ONE OF ITS UNSUNG, UNKNOWN, FACELESS MILLIONS IS STARTING WORK EARLY...
KAPOWW
AT 12:01 THE SNIPER'S FIRST BULLET FELLS DOTTIE COTTONMAN, WOMAN'S MAGAZINE, EDITOR...
1

K-POWWW
AT 12:03 DELIVERY BOY JIMMY GREENE FALLS...
TZIINNNG
DELIVERY
IT SOUNDS AS IF WE ARE BEING SERVED VIOLENCE WITH OUR FIRST COURSE, DIANA?
A RUNAWAY CAR-- I CHING!
2

AT 12:06-- ONE HOUR AFTER THEY ARE MARRIED-- MARY AND JOHN MASON'S HONEY-MOON ABRUPTLY ENDS...
TZING!
BEEOOH
THE DRIVERLESS CAR SWERVES AND HURTLES TOWARD DINERS IN A RESTAURANT...
PRIOR'S LUCK RESTAURANT
JUST MARRIED
SCREEEEE!
CRAS-SH
3

ANY UNFORTUNATES IN THE CAR, DIANA?
A YOUNG COUPLE, I CHING-- **DEAD!**
POOR SOULS!
JUST MARRIED

AGAIN FLAME SPURTS FROM THE SNIPER'S RIFLE...
K-POWW

OHH NO-- NO! NOT YOU-- I CHING--
NOT YOU--!
T-ZIIING!

FATE HAS A... **LONG ARM**... DIANA--**NONE** CAN... **ESCAPE** ITS REACH--
FAREWELL-- **DAUGHTER** I **NEVER** HAD--
WEEP NO... M—

FAREWELL...
...**FATHER**...
I **NEVER** HAD...
4

ARE YOU GOING AFTER THE SNIPER BY HELICOPTER?
THERE'S NO OTHER WAY TO REACH HIM, DIANA!
HE'S ON THE ROOF OF 480--A SKYSCRAPER! JAMMED ALL ELEVATORS! LOCKED ALL DOORS!
HE'S A FORTRESS!
WHUPP-WHUPP-WHUPP

STAND CLEAR!
YOU'VE GOT ANOTHER PASSENGER!

POLICE HELICOPTER COMIN' UP!
THEY'LL TRY TO SMOKE ME OUT WITH GAS-- BUT I'LL BE READY FOR THEM WITH THIS TNT "BOUQUET"!

AS DIANA DANGLES BELOW THE SOARING HELICOPTER...
KRAAAKH--
THE SNIPER WAS READY FOR US!..
WITH A RIFLE GRENADE!
5

THE HELICOPTER PLUNGES DOWN LIKE A FLAMING CARTWHEEL...
W-A-A-R-O-O-M-M

BUT NOT BEFORE DIANA PRINCE HAS HURLED HERSELF DOWN THROUGH GIDDY SPACE AT THE KILLER...
I DON'T NEED MY SNIPER-SCOPE TO GET YOU, CHICK!

THE HOSPITAL THOUGHT I'D LOST MY TASTE FOR KILLIN' AFTER THEY SHOT ME FULL OF BUG JUICE-- BUT THE SHRINKS WERE WRONG!
KRAAACK

LET ME TAKE YOU IN-- YOU DON'T KNOW WHAT YOU'RE DOING!
I'M DOIN' JUST WHAT COMES NATURALLY TO ME-- CHICK!
PLEASE LISTEN-!
THUDD-
SMASHIN' IN THE FACE OF THIS WHOLE STINKIN' WORLD!
YOU INCLUDED!

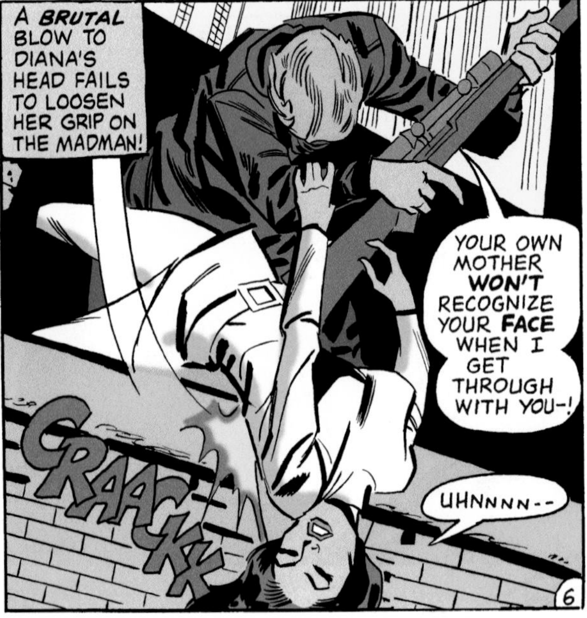
A BRUTAL BLOW TO DIANA'S HEAD FAILS TO LOOSEN HER GRIP ON THE MADMAN!
YOUR OWN MOTHER WON'T RECOGNIZE YOUR FACE WHEN I GET THROUGH WITH YOU-!
CRAACKK
UHNNNN--
6

HURLED OFF BALANCE BY HIS OWN SAVAGE BLOW AT DIANA—KILLER AND HIS UNCONSCIOUS VICTIM TOPPLE OVER...
MAMA-- MAMA-- HELP MEEEEEEE..

DIANA HURTLES ONTO A METAL DECORATION...THE SNIPER PLUNGES TO HIS DOOM ...
EEEEEEEE

DIANA PRINCE! UNCONSCIOUS! IT'S A WONDER SHE'S STILL ALIVE!
CALL FOR AN AMBULANCE! HURRY!--HURRY!

SHORTLY... THROUGH A SWIRLING HAZE...
DIANA?... DIANA PRINCE?... CAN YOU HEAR ME?
DIANA... ANSWER ME!
7

WHO IS... DIANA PRINCE--?
WHY--YOU--OF COURSE! NATURALLY--YOU'RE DAZED, DIANA!
YOU REMEMBER BATTLING A SNIPER?
FALLING FROM THE ROOF WITH HIM!
YOU LANDED ON A PROJECTION!
IT SAVED YOUR LIFE!

I--I'M AFRAID--THE MADMAN KILLED YOUR FRIEND I CHING!
I CHING?... I DON'T KNOW ANY-ONE BY THAT NAME?

LET'S START AT THE BEGINNING! IT WILL ALL COME BACK TO YOU! NO HURRY... TAKE YOUR TIME, DIANA!
NOW... WHAT DO YOU REMEMBER?
NOTHING... NOTHING--IT'S ALL A BLANK!

ALL I KNOW IS--I'VE GOT TO GET BACK!
GET BACK--WHERE--DEAR?
I--I DON'T KNOW! BUT--LET ME UP!
8

I'VE GOT TO GET BACK--!
OF COURSE--DEAR ...OF COURSE...
I'M GIVING YOU SOMETHING TO SLEEP, DIANA! NOW RELAX--WE'RE HERE TO HELP YOU--

THE POOR GIRL! NO WONDER SHE HAS AMNESIA--AFTER ALL SHE'S BEEN THROUGH TODAY!
I NEVER SAW ANYONE STRUGGLE LIKE THAT--TO GET BACK! BUT--WHERE, DOCTOR?
WHERE?
WHO KNOWS? THE MIND'S A TRICKY MAZE!
I HOPE WE'LL FIND OUT WHEN SHE WAKES UP--ABOUT EIGHT HOURS FROM NOW!

SHORTLY...
DOCTOR!-- DOCTOR!-- DIANA PRINCE IS GONE!
HER CLOTHES TOO!
SHE COULDN'T HAVE LEFT THROUGH THE DOOR-- I HAD MY EYE ON IT ALL THE TIME-- FROM THE HALL DESK!
THE WINDOW-- IT'S OPEN!

WHAT DROVE HER TO SHAKE OFF THE EFFECTS OF THE SEDATIVE? NO ORDINARY PERSON COULD!
SHE WAS DRIVEN BY A POWERFUL SUBCONSCIOUS DRIVE! THE SAME IRRESISTIBLE FORCE THAT PROPELS FISH AND BIRDS HALF-WAY ACROSS THE WORLD TO THEIR DESTINATION!
BUT--WHAT IS DIANA'S?

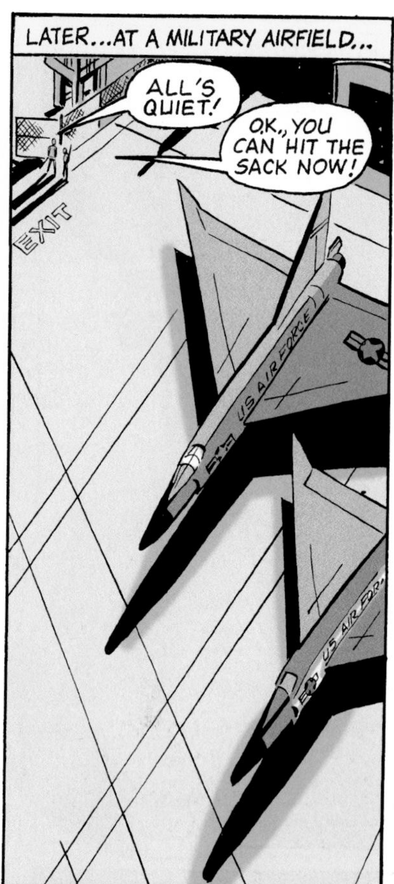

LATER...AT A MILITARY AIRFIELD...
ALL'S QUIET!
O.K., YOU CAN HIT THE SACK NOW!
EXIT
U.S. AIR FORCE

LOOK-! NO SHIP'S DUE TO TAKE OFF NOW! MUST BE A SABOTEUR! SOUND THE ALARM!
OFFICER OF THE GUARD!

AND IN THAT SUPERSONIC PLANE, DRIVEN BY AN OVERWHELMING FORCE, DIANA PRINCE ROCKETS THROUGH THE NIGHT SKIES TOWARDS A STARTLING RENDEZVOUS WITH FATE!
I'VE GOT TO GET BACK! -- I'VE GOT TO GET BACK!
9

THROUGH THE CLOUDY NIGHT... OVER DARK SEAS... DIANA HURTLES...
I--I DON'T KNOW WHERE I'M GOING--
BUT--I FEEL--AS IF A HAND ON MINE--IS GUIDING ME--
BACK--BACK--BACK!
OUT OF SIGHT IN THE SKIES BEHIND HER...
ROVER LEADER TO ROVER BASE! TARGET DOES NOT ANSWER CHALLENGE! HAVE TARGET ON RADAR GRID! -- OVER!

ROVER BASE TO ROVER LEADER! TARGET MUST NOT FALL INTO HOSTILE HANDS! ATTACK! OVER!
FIRE!

VRUUM
VRUUUMM..
VRUUUM
LETHAL MISSILES SLASH THROUGH THE SKIES AT DIANA'S PLANE...

ROVER LEADER TO ROVER BASE! DIRECT HIT ON TARGET! OVER!
ROVER BASE TO ROVER LEADER! RETURN TO BASE!-- OVER!

AT THAT MOMENT--OUT OF SIGHT MILES AWAY--DIANA PRINCE HURTLES SEAWARDS IN THE FLAMING PLANE--
WHREEEEEE-
10

GOT TO BRING THE NOSE UP-- OR THE SHIP WILL DIVE TO THE BOTTOM OF THE SEA!
CRAAAASH

THANK HERA-- I WAS THROWN CLEAR!
THANK HERA? WHERE IN THE WORLD DID THAT COME FROM--?

SHARK--!

GOT TO PRETEND I'M DEAD-- MAYBE THE SHARK WILL PASS BY ME?

HE'S COMING AT ME FOR THE KILL!

IF I CAN ONLY HOLD ON--

--KEEP AWAY FROM ITS JAWS!
11

LUNGS BURSTING FOR AIR--
I'VE GOT TO LET GO--
HEAD FOR THE SURFACE--
EVEN IF IT'S FOR MY LAST BREATH!
BEFORE THE SHARK TURNS ON ME!

DESPERATELY HURLING HERSELF FREE OF THE UNDERSEA CANNIBAL, DIANA'S HAND SUDDENLY--IT IS GRIPPED BY...

IT'S A GOOD THING WE WERE PATROLLING PARADISE ISLAND-- OR WE WOULDN'T BE ABLE TO HELP THIS POOR GIRL!
GREAT HERA-- DO YOU REALIZE WHO SHE IS?
WE MUST BRING HER TO QUEEN HIPPOLYTA'S PALACE!

BACK TO PARADISE ISLAND AT ONCE!

IN THE QUEEN'S PALACE... AFTER DIANA'S TATTERED ATTIRE IS CHANGED...

THANK HERA-- FOR BRINGING YOU BACK TO ME!
WHO... ARE... YOU--?
12

DIANA-- WHAT'S HAPPENED?
DON'T YOU KNOW ME?
I'M YOUR MOTHER!

MOTHER? ...YOU?
I NEVER SAW YOU BEFORE-- IN MY LIFE?
DON'T-- DON'T LOOK AT ME-- YOUR OWN MOTHER-- AS IF I WERE A STRANGER!

DIANA'S SUFFERED A TOTAL LOSS OF MEMORY! OUR ONLY CHANCE OF RESTORING IT IS AT THE AMAZON MEMORY BANK, O QUEEN!
SO BE IT, DOCTOR! TAKE HER THERE AT ONCE!

DON'T BE FRIGHTENED, DIANA! EVERY-THING WILL BE ALL RIGHT!
YOU MUST STAND CLEAR OF THE MEMORY ELECTRODES, O QUEEN! WE ARE READY TO START TOTAL REPLAY!

NOT TOTAL REPLAY, DOCTOR!
OMIT CHANNELS 3-5!
WHY SHOULD DIANA KNOW MY SECRET?
EDIT OUT THAT SINGLE EPISODE!
I UNDERSTAND, O' QUEEN!

START MEMORY REPLAY ON ALL CHANNELS EXCEPT 3-5-
FROM THE BEGINNING OF TIME...
13

THE MEMORY CHANNELS REPLAY THE ORIGIN OF THE AMAZONS... SHOWING-

AND WOMEN HAVE WEPT...

UNTIL APHRODITE, GODDESS OF LOVE AND BEAUTY, SHAPED WITH HER OWN HANDS A RACE OF SUPER WOMEN-- STRONGER THAN MEN!
I SHALL BREATHE LIFE INTO THESE WOMEN-- AND ALSO THE POWER OF LOVE!
THEY SHALL BE CALLED AMAZONS! AND YOU SHALL BE THEIR QUEEN, HIPPOLYTA!

SO LONG AS YOU WEAR MY MAGIC GIRDLE, YOU AMAZONS SHALL BE UNCONQUERABLE, QUEEN HIPPOLYTA!

BUT, APHRODITE'S RIVAL, THE SCHEMING MARS, GOD OF WAR, PLOTTED TO DESTROY THE AMAZONS WITH THE MIGHTY HERCULES, STRONGEST MAN IN THE ANCIENT WORLD!
THE AMAZONS ARE A SUPER RACE, HERCULES! BUT, THEIR WEAKNESS IS THAT THEY ARE STILL ONLY WOMEN--
--LED BY THEIR HEARTS!
THIS IS WHAT YOU MUST DO! SEE QUEEN HIPPOLYTA AND...
14

ACCORDING TO PLAN, HERCULES COURTED QUEEN HIPPOLYTA...
YOU ARE AS BEAUTIFUL AS APHRODITE HERSELF! YOU FILL MY VEINS WITH FIRE! I DREAM OF YOU NIGHT AND DAY-- MY QUEEN!
NO MAN-- HAS EVER SPOKEN TO ME LIKE THIS-- HERCULES...

SUDDENLY...
HERCULES! WHA-?

MARS WAS RIGHT! WOMEN ARE BLIND-- WHEN THEY ARE BEING WOOED!
WITHOUT APHRODITE'S MAGIC GIRDLE-- YOU AMAZONS ARE POWERLESS!

NEVER TRUST A WOMAN! CHAIN THEM!

APHRODITE, FORGIVE MY SIN! GIVE US STRENGTH TO BREAK OUR CHAINS AND RECOVER YOUR MAGIC GIRDLE!
15

LATER THAT NIGHT--THE GODDESS APHRODITE ANSWERED THE CAPTIVE QUEEN'S PRAYER...
I WILL BREAK YOUR CHAINS, HIPPOLYTA!
BUT YOU MUST WEAR THESE HEAVY WRIST BANDS ALWAYS TO TEACH YOU THE FOLLY OF EVER SUBMITTING TO MEN!
I WILL NEVER FORGET!

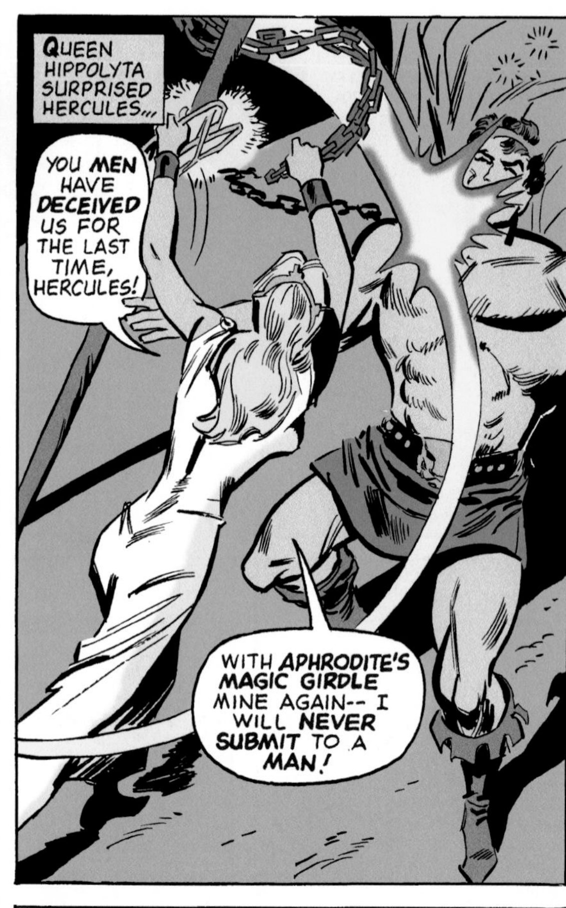
QUEEN HIPPOLYTA SURPRISED HERCULES...
YOU MEN HAVE DECEIVED US FOR THE LAST TIME, HERCULES!
WITH APHRODITE'S MAGIC GIRDLE MINE AGAIN-- I WILL NEVER SUBMIT TO A MAN!

THE AMAZONS SEIZED HERCULES' SHIPS AND GUIDED BY APHRODITE SAILED THE DISTANT SEAS...
YOU WILL BUILD A SPLENDID CITY ON THIS ISLAND WHICH NO MAN MAY ENTER! IT WILL BE A PARADISE-- FOR WOMEN ONLY!
16

THE CITY ROSE... THE AMAZONS THRIVED WITHOUT MEN... BUT THE AMAZON QUEEN STILL HAD THE YEARNINGS OF A WOMAN-- AND UNDER THE DIRECTION OF ATHENA, GODDESS OF WISDOM, LEARNED THE SECRET OF MOULDING HUMAN FORMS:
THEY'RE BEAUTIFUL, ATHENA! IF ONLY THEY WERE ALIVE!
MEMORY CHANNELS 3-4-5
WHAT SECRET WAS NOT SHOWN TO DIANA? AS HER ORIGIN CONTINUES WITH MEMORY CHANNEL 6...

APHRODITE GRANTED THE QUEEN'S PRAYER--
I NAME THEE DIANA--AFTER THE MOON GODDESS--MISTRESS OF THE HUNT!
AND I ENDOW THEE...

WITH THE BEAUTY OF APHRODITE--THE STRENGTH OF HERCULES--THE WISDOM OF ATHENA--AND THE SPEED OF MERCURY!

MAMA--
O' DIANA--!

MY LITTLE WONDER CHILD!

AS DIANA GREW UP--SHE PROVED HERSELF AS UNIQUELY ENDOWED AS HER LEGENDARY NAMESAKES!

YOU HAVE MADE ME VERY HAPPY, DIANA! YOU ARE INDEED A WONDER WOMAN!
I LOVE YOU, MOTHER!
17

THE YOUNG AMAZON RECEIVED HER BRACELETS OF SUBMISSION AT APHRODITE'S ALTAR...
I PLEDGE MYSELF TO YOUR SERVICE, APHRODITE! TO GIVE LOVE AND KINDNESS FOREVER!

MY OWN SPECIAL OUTFIT!
AND THE GOLDEN MAGIC LASSO TO AID YOU IN YOUR BATTLES AGAINST EVIL!

AS THE MULTI-DIMENSIONAL MEMORY CHANNELS FADE THE MEMORY ELECTRODES REPLAYING THE PAST--END! ALL AT THE AMAZON MEMORY BANK ARE BREATHLESS, NOT DARING TO BREAK THE TENSE SILENCE--
APHRODITE-- PLEASE BRING BACK MY DAUGHTER TO ME!... PLEASE GRANT A MOTHER'S PRAYER!

MOTHER--!
THANK APHRODITE-- YOU'VE COME BACK TO ME!
SUMMON ALL THE AMAZONS FOR A CELEBRATION!

HOLA-- PRINCESS DIANA!
HOLA, WONDER WOMAN!
YOU ARE THE MIGHTIEST AMAZON IN THE WORLD!
18

SUDDENLY... AN ASTOUNDING INTRUDER-!
I CHALLENGE THIS USURPER!
THERE IS ONLY ONE WONDER WOMAN!
I AM WONDER WOMAN!

W-WHY DOES THIS STRANGER MAKE MY HEART POUND?
BY AMAZON LAW-- I CLAIM THE RIGHT TO PROVE IN HAND-TO-HAND COMBAT-- WHICH OF US IS WONDER WOMAN!
YOU DO HAVE THAT RIGHT! AND YOU SHALL BE GIVEN YOUR CHANCE!

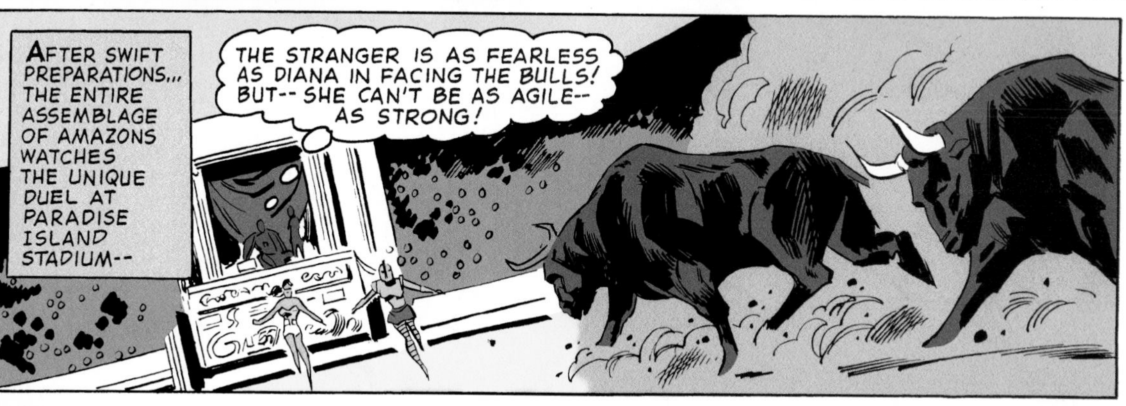
AFTER SWIFT PREPARATIONS... THE ENTIRE ASSEMBLAGE OF AMAZONS WATCHES THE UNIQUE DUEL AT PARADISE ISLAND STADIUM--
THE STRANGER IS AS FEARLESS AS DIANA IN FACING THE BULLS! BUT-- SHE CAN'T BE AS AGILE-- AS STRONG!

BOTH DIANA AND THE MASKED CHALLENGER DARINGLY LEAP OVER THE LUNGING HORNS OF THE BULLS!
19

BY HERA-- STRANGER! NO ONE BUT I HAS EVER CONQUERED THE BULLS BEFORE!
A TRIFLE FOR ME! I AM WONDER WOMAN!

THE STRANGER REMINDS ME OF--? NO--IT'S IMPOSSIBLE!
THEN--WHY AM I TORN--LEST THE STRANGER FALLS BEFORE DIANA IN THE DUEL OF THE SWORD AND THE SCARF?
CLANG!
CLANG
CLANG
CLANG!

CLANG
CLANG!

20

DIANA'S HAND LUNGES AT THE SWORD-
YOU HESITATED TOO LONG TO KILL ME, STRANGER!

WHY?-WHY?-WHY?
I-- I DON'T KNOW!

BY AMAZON LAW-- THE DUEL ENDS IN A DRAW!
STRANGER--RISE! REMOVE YOUR HELMET AND IDENTIFY YOURSELF-- THAT ALL OF US MAY HONOR YOU!
CLAP!
CLAP!
CLAP!
CLAP

I AM NUBIA!
WONDER WOMAN OF THE FLOATING ISLAND!
HOLA! NUBIA!

IS IT POSSIBLE?-- AFTER ALL THESE YEARS-
THAT NUBIA IS- IS-?
21

WE MUST CELEBRATE OUR MEETING, NUBIA!
NO-- I MUST GO BACK TO MY BOATS-MEN!
MY PEOPLE ARE WAITING ON OUR FLOATING ISLAND-- CONCEALED IN THE MIST OFFSHORE!

WILL WE SEE EACH OTHER AGAIN, NUBIA?
WE WILL, DIANA!
UNTIL ONE OF US PROVES SHE IS THE ONLY WONDER WOMAN!
FAREWELL! UNTIL WE MEET AGAIN!

LATER... BACK AT THE PALACE...
B-BUT, MOTHER? I WANT TO FIND OUT MORE ABOUT NUBIA?
AND-- AND ISN'T MY PLACE HERE AT PARADISE ISLAND WITH YOU?!
NO, DIANA! YOU BELONG TO TWO WORLDS! BUT-- YOU MAY COME HERE AS OFTEN AS YOU WISH!
IT IS YOUR DESTINY TO RETURN--AND TRY TO STOP MAN FROM DESTROYING HIMSELF AND HIS WHOLE WORLD!

AN AMAZON SUB IS WAITING TO TAKE YOU BACK-- I-- I WISH IT WEREN'T--
SO DO I--

FAREWELL-- DIANA-- MY DAUGHTER...!
NOW I MUST GO TO THE MEMORY BANK--AND CHECK THE CHANNEL 3 THAT DIANA WASN'T SHOWN! AND SEE IF IT'S POSSIBLE THAT NUBIA IS REALLY-?

LATER...
DIANA-- WE'VE REACHED OUR DESTINATION! WE'RE LETTING YOU OFF HERE! HAVE YOU CHANGED INTO YOUR OTHER ATTIRE?
YES, CAPTAIN!
22

FATE LEFT ME OFF AT THE U.N. BUILDING! I WONDER WHY?

WE'RE GREATLY IN NEED OF GUIDES WHO SPEAK AS MANY LANGUAGES AS POSSIBLE!
NOW-- HOLD YOUR HANDS UP TO INDICATE THAT YOU SPEAK ENGLISH? SPANISH? FRENCH? GERMAN? RUSSIAN? CHINESE? JAPANESE? HEBREW? AFRICAN DIALECTS...

THAT PLAIN JANE WOULD BE A UNIVERSAL LINGUIST!
WELL-- I SUPPOSE I COULD LOSE HER AMONG ALL THE BEAUTIFUL GIRLS I'M GOING TO HIRE WHO CAN ONLY SPEAK A FEW LANGUAGES!
WHAT'S YOUR NAME?
WH-WHO-- ME? ER... DIANA PRINCE!

WE HAVE BEEN HIRED TOO! -- WE WOULD BE HONORED IF YOU WOULD SHARE AN APARTMENT WITH US NEAR THE U.N.?
WHAT SHE MEANS IS THAT WE COULD ONLY AFFORD IT IF YOU WOULD SHARE THE RENT WITH US!
WHY-- I'D LOVE TO--!
23

I FEEL AS IF I'VE BEEN REBORN!
I WONDER WHAT'S GOING TO HAPPEN TO ME-- THE SECOND TIME AROUND?
END

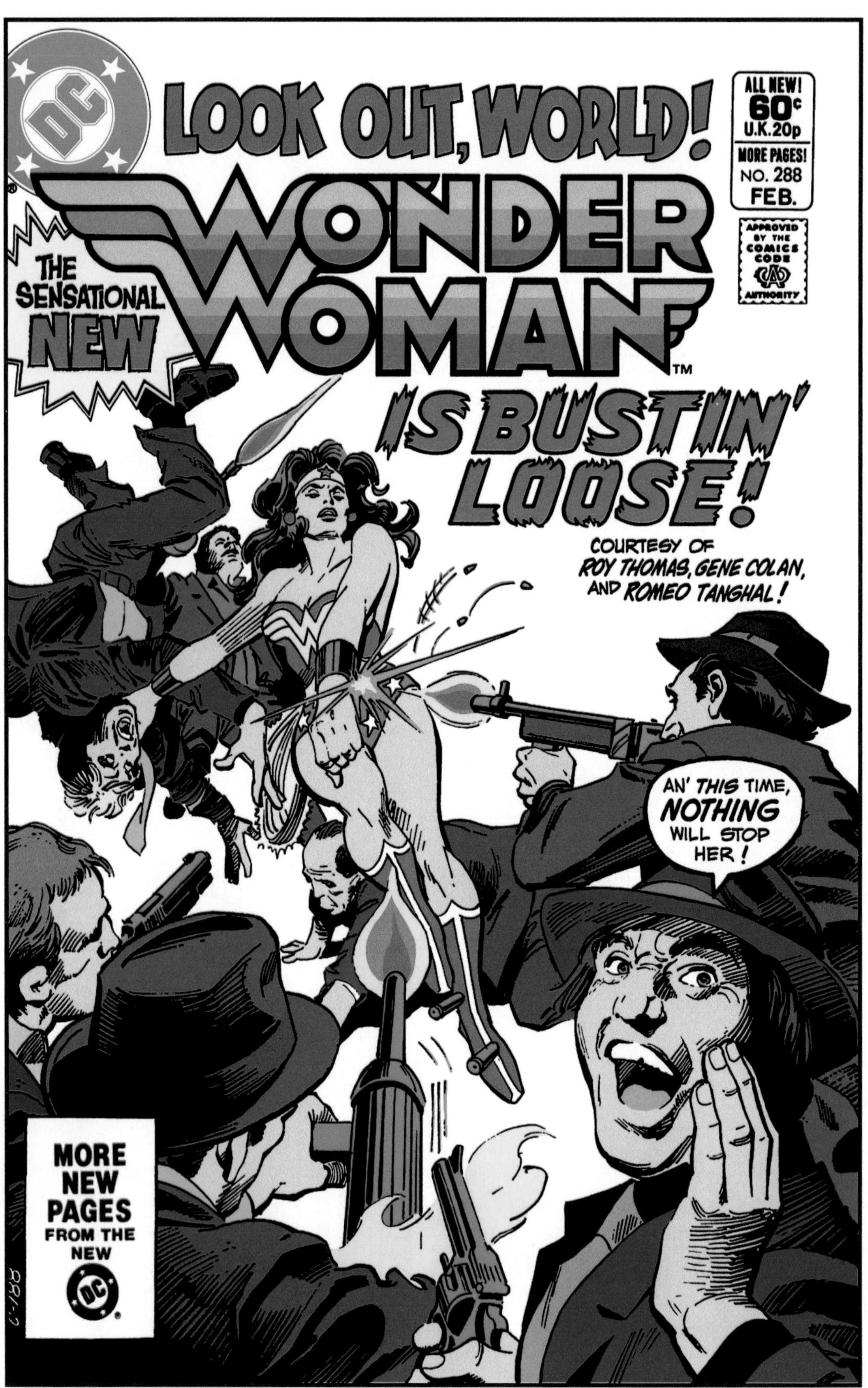
LOOK OUT, WORLD!
ALL NEW! 60¢ U.K. 20p
MORE PAGES! NO. 288 FEB.
APPROVED BY THE COMICS CODE AUTHORITY
THE SENSATIONAL NEW
WONDER WOMAN
IS BUSTIN' LOOSE!
COURTESY OF ROY THOMAS, GENE COLAN, AND ROMEO TANGHAL!
AN' THIS TIME, NOTHING WILL STOP HER!
MORE NEW PAGES FROM THE NEW DC

SHE WAS BORN A FANTASTICALLY-POWERED PRINCESS --DAUGHTER OF HIPPOLYTA, QUEEN OF THE AMAZONS-- BUT SHE LEFT THE TRANQUIL GROVES OF PARADISE ISLAND, TO BATTLE EVIL IN A WORLD SHE NEVER MADE! SHE IS BEAUTIFUL AS APHRODITE... WISE AS ATHENA... STRONGER THAN HERCULES... SWIFTER THAN MERCURY! SHE IS DIANA PRINCE, KNOWN TO OUR WORLD AS...
WONDER WOMAN™
LEARN WHY WE CALL HER FIRST ADVENTURE IN A NEW AND EXCITING ERA--
SWAN SONG!
HINT: THERE ARE MORE REASONS THAN ONE!
AM I TOO LATE? I DON'T DARE STOP NOW--FOR ANYONE OR ANYTHING!
I--I CAN'T BELIEVE IT!
WONDER WOMAN-- HERE, IN METRO GENERAL HOSPITAL!?
UH--HOLD UP, PLEASE! YOU CAN'T GO PAST THIS POINT WITHOUT A PASS!
NEVER MIND THAT, NURSE! JUST GET ME AN AUTOGRAPH!
QUIET, SON! SHE'S OBVIOUSLY HERE ON URGENT BUSINESS!
WONDER IF SHE'S BOOKED UP FOR THE WEEKEND...!?
Beginning the fifth fabulous decade of the Amazing Amazon's exploits, courtesy of the new kids on the block:
ROY THOMAS WRITER
GENE COLAN PENCILLER
aided and abetted by:
ROMEO TANGHAL INKER
CARL GAFFORD - COLORIST
BEN ODA - LETTERER
LEN WEIN EDITOR
With special thanks to GERRY CONWAY TECHNICAL ADVISOR

ER, PARDON ME, NURSE...
...BUT THIS IS THE WAY TO COLONEL STEVE TREVOR'S ROOM, ISN'T IT?
I'M...SORT OF A FRIEND OF HIS...!
IT'S DOWN THAT WAY --BUT WOULD YOU MIND SIGNING THIS FIRST?
THEN MINE, OKAY?
AND COULD YOU MAKE IT OUT "TO RALPH, WITH--"?
I'M SORRY.
MAYBE LATER.
WELL! ISN'T SHE THE STUCK-UP CELEBRITY!
WHO DOES SHE THINK SHE IS-- BO DEREK?
ACTUALLY, WONDER WOMAN'S THINKING NOTHING OF THE SORT JUST NOW...
SHE'S MERELY... REMEMBERING:
REMEMBERING HOW, AS CAPT. DIANA PRINCE, SHE AND STEVE WERE ATTACKED BY ENEMY AGENTS EARLIER TODAY...
...AND HOW STEVE, FALLING IN BATTLE, LATERALED HER THE BRIEFCASE-FULL OF SECRET DOCUMENTS THEY WERE AFTER.
AS WONDER WOMAN, SHE DEALT WITH THE FLEEING SPIES EASILY ENOUGH...
...EVEN SPARED A FEW MOMENTS FOR A WOMEN'S ORGANIZATION WHICH WANTED HER TO WEAR A NEW EMBLEM THEY HAD DESIGNED:
IF YOU DO, OUR NEW "WONDER WOMAN FOUNDATION" WILL BE ABLE TO GET FINANCIAL BACKING TO PROMOTE EQUALITY FOR WOMEN EVERYWHERE!
I'LL... THINK ABOUT IT.
AND, WHEN THE AMBULANCE HAD TAKEN STEVE AWAY, THAT'S JUST WHAT SHE DID...
I'M TEMPTED TO GO ALONG WITH THEM.
AFTER ALL, THEY SAID THE "W" STANDS FOR "WOMEN"-- NOT JUST FOR MY NAME.
SINCE STEVE'S HEAD-WOUND WAS SO MILD, MAYBE IT'LL DO ME GOOD TO TALK IT OVER WITH MY--
2

-- MOTHER!?

YET, ARRIVING ON *PARADISE ISLAND*, SHE FOUND THE AMAZONS ALL IN *MALE-FORGED* CHAINS--

--AND QUEEN HIPPOLYTA HERSELF DIVESTED OF HER *MAGIC BELT*, THE SOURCE OF MUCH OF HER IMMORTAL *STRENGTH*.

SHE OUTRACED *MERCURY*, ONE OF THE CULPRITS, TO RECOVER THE HARD-HURLED *BELT*--

--AND EVEN THE STEEL SINEWS OF THE MAIN SCHEMER, *HERCULES*, COULD NOT BEST THOSE OF *WONDER WOMAN*.*

*ALL FLASHBACK SCENES FROM OUR SPECIAL *PREVIEW* IN *DC PRESENTS #41*. -- *Len*.

THEN, THE AMAZONS FREED AND THE MAN-GODS BANISHED BACK TO OLYMPUS, SHE TOLD HER MOTHER OF THE PLEA OF THE WOMEN'S GROUP, AND...
MY ADVICE IS-- WEAR THE NEW HALTER FOR A TIME, AT LEAST... FOR THE GOOD THAT IT MAY DO.
SHE DECIDED TO TAKE HER MOTHER'S ADVICE...

...AND DEPARTED AGAIN FOR WHAT THE AMAZONS HAVE LONG CALLED "MAN'S WORLD"...
GOOD-BYE, BERMUDA TRIANGLE! HIDE YOUR SECRETS WELL!
BY NOW, HOPEFULLY, STEVE WILL BE FULLY RECOVERED.
BUT INSTEAD, UPON RETURNING TO WASHINGTON, SHE LEARNED AT THE HOSPITAL'S FRONT DESK THAT STEVE TREVOR --THE MAN SHE LOVES--MAY WELL BE DYING!

IS IT ANY WONDER SHE HAS LITTLE PATIENCE FOR AUTOGRAPH HOUNDS?
IF HE DIES-- I'LL NEVER FORGIVE MYSELF FOR--
THERE'S STEVE'S ROOM!
6
NO! DON'T EVEN THINK ABOUT IT, DIANA! HE'S GOING TO BE ALL RIGHT!...
3

JUST KEEP CALM, SO NO ONE MAKES TOO MUCH OUT OF YOUR BEING CONCERNED ABOUT--
STEVE!
WHO--? OH, ER, I MEAN--
IT'S READILY APPARENT WHO SHE IS, NURSE...

IT'S WHAT SHE'S DOING HERE THAT I WANT TO KNOW!
I TAKE IT YOU KNOW COLONEL TREVOR, WONDER WOMAN?
MORE OR LESS! WE MET A FEW MONTHS AGO...
...WHEN I SAVED HIM FROM A PLANE CRASH.*
*IN THE ALREADY-IMMORTAL TRILOGY, ISSUES #269-271. --Len.

OH? WELL, I JUST WISH WHAT HE'S FACING NOW HAD THE CLASSIC SIMPLICITY OF AN AIRPLANE ACCIDENT.
IS IT THE HEAD WOUND HE--?
DEFINITELY NOT...

OR AT MOST, THAT ONLY TRIGGERED WHATEVER'S HAPPENING TO HIM NOW.
IT'S ALMOST AS IF HE--I DON'T EVEN KNOW HOW TO PUT THIS IN MEDICAL TERMINOLOGY--
--AS IF HIS BODY AND HIS SOUL ARE STRUGGLING TO GET OUT OF THIS WORLD--INTO ANOTHER ONE!
MAY I... BE ALONE WITH HIM A MOMENT... PLEASE?
MERCIFUL MINERVA!
YOU SEE? I TOLD YOU I DIDN'T KNOW HOW TO SAY IT.
4

IF IT WERE ANYONE ELSE, I'D SAY NO, BUT--WELL, I SUPPOSE JUST FOR A MINUTE.
BUT DON'T EXPECT ANY RESPONSE FROM HIM. HE HASN'T OPENED HIS EYES SINCE HE WAS BROUGHT IN.
AN HOUR AGO, I THOUGHT HE WAS DYING-- BUT NOW, I DON'T KNOW.
I JUST DON'T KNOW.

THANK YOU FOR YOUR HONESTY, DOCTOR...
PRESCOTT. REMEMBER... JUST A MINUTE, NOW.
I... UNDERSTAND.
EVEN THOUGH WE'VE BEEN OUT TOGETHER IN PUBLIC ONCE OR TWICE, I'VE TRIED TO KEEP PEOPLE FROM SUSPECTING THERE WAS ANY-THING BETWEEN STEVE AND ME.
BUT DR. PRESCOTT KNEW. I SAW IT IN HER EYES.

STEVE...YOU CAN'T HEAR ME, I KNOW... AND I PROBABLY WOULDN'T BE SAYING THIS IF YOU COULD.
BUT SOMEHOW, I FEEL I'VE KNOWN YOU... SO MUCH LONGER THAN A FEW SHORT MONTHS.*
I CAN'T EVEN BEGIN TO SAY WHY... BUT I HAD THAT FEELING ALMOST FROM THE MOMENT I SAW YOU.
I'LL FIND OUT WHAT'S HAPPENING TO YOU... I SWEAR IT.
I'LL PULL YOU BACK, IF I CAN, FROM THAT OTHER WORLD YOU'RE WITHDRAWING INTO.
*DIANA IS UNAWARE THAT THIS STEVE TREVOR IS FROM A PARALLEL EARTH... OR THAT SHE HAS EVER KNOWN ANY OTHER! --Len.

OH, AND ONE OTHER LITTLE ITEM, STEVE TREVOR...

I LOVE YOU.

...A-ANGEL? IS TH-THAT...YOU...?
STEVE! YOU'RE--
5

S-SURE! BUT, I FEEL... LIKE I'VE BEEN... FAR AWAY SOMEWHERE...
...LIKE I WAS... SOMEBODY ELSE...!
P-PLEASE, STEVE... DON'T TRY TO TALK ANY MORE. JUST REST.

WHATEVER... YOU SAY, ANGEL. BUT TELL ME... THAT BRIEFCASE... I WAS DELIVERING...
IT'S SAFE. DON'T WORRY.
AND... CAPTAIN PRINCE... IS SHE...?

SHE'S SAFE, TOO. NOW GO BACK TO SLEEP, OKAY?
EVERYTHING'S GOING TO BE ...ALL RIGHT.
AND STEVE TREVOR DOES RETURN TO A STATE OF SLEEP... OR ELSE TO SOMETHING DESPERATELY LIKE IT.
MOMENTS LATER, OUTSIDE THE ROOM...
HE SPOKE TO ME, DR. PRESCOTT.
WHAT? WHAT DID HE--?
THAT'S NOT IMPORTANT, IS IT? HE'S ASLEEP NOW.
I'D BETTER EXAMINE HIM. WILL YOU BE HERE WHEN I--?
I'M NOT SURE

I PROMISED... TO PICK UP SOMETHING FOR HIM.
BUT IF I'M NOT, I'LL BE BACK, DOCTOR... YOU CAN RELY ON IT!
WELL! SHE WALKED RIGHT PAST US, LIKE WE WEREN'T EVEN HERE!
NEXT TIME, LET'S STAKE OUT THE SUPREME COURT BUILDING.
I REALLY WANTED JUSTICE O'CONNOR'S AUTO-GRAPH, ANYWAY!

NEXT INSTANT, IGNORING THE SNIVELINGS OF THE SELF-ABSORBED, WONDER WOMAN IS RACING THROUGH THE BUSTLING STREETS OF HER ADOPTED NATION'S CAPITAL...

AND THOUGH SHE DOES NOT FLY, HER HEART, AT LEAST, HAS WINGS.

HE'S ALIVE! THE MAN I LOVE-- IS ALIVE!

HE EVEN HAD ENOUGH PRESENCE OF MIND TO REMEMBER BOTH THE BRIEFCASE... AND DIANA PRINCE...

...EVEN IF HE DID REMEMBER THEM IN THAT ORDER.

THAT'S PROGRESS OF A SORT! HE'S ALWAYS SEEMED TO BE TERMINALLY SMITTEN WITH WONDER WOMAN... YET HE WOULDN'T NOTICE DIANA UNLESS SHE CAUGHT ON FIRE.

OF COURSE, I DO TRY TO SPEAK AND CARRY MYSELF A BIT DIFFERENTLY WHEN I'M DIANA, BUT STILL--SUFFERING SAPPHO!

WHAT CAN THAT MATTER TODAY? HE'S ALIVE--AND NOTHING'S GOING TO RUIN MY MOOD... NOTHING!

NOTHING, AMAZON?

NOT EVEN... THIS?
UH-OH, SAMMY! WE GOT US A PROBLEM OVER HERE!
TWO CARLOADS OF COPS COME SCREECHING UP, THE MINUTE WE TRY TO ROB A NICE QUIET BANK--AND YOU THINK WE GOT PROBLEMS OVER THERE?
JUST THE SAME, THESE SOUPED-UP GUNS OF OURS OUGHTTA--
BANK

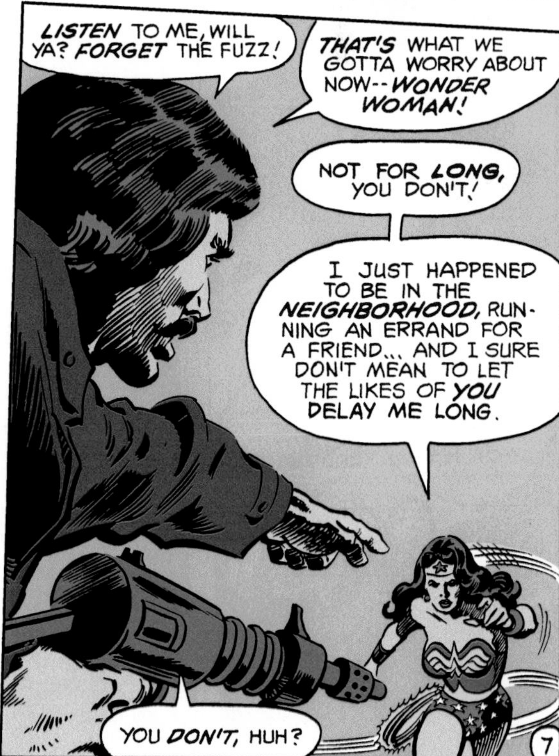

LISTEN TO ME, WILL YA? FORGET THE FUZZ!
THAT'S WHAT WE GOTTA WORRY ABOUT NOW--WONDER WOMAN!
NOT FOR LONG, YOU DON'T!
I JUST HAPPENED TO BE IN THE NEIGHBORHOOD, RUNNING AN ERRAND FOR A FRIEND... AND I SURE DON'T MEAN TO LET THE LIKES OF YOU DELAY ME LONG.
YOU DON'T, HUH?
7

HOW ABOUT LIKE... FOREVER?
BRAKKA BRAKKA
"FOREVER" IS HOW LONG I COULD PLAY BULLETS-AND-BRACELETS WITH YOU, PUNK, IF I FELT LIKE IT--
PTINK
--WHICH, AS IT HAPPENS, I DON'T!
THANKS FOR THE WRAPPING PRACTICE, THOUGH! AFTER ALL, CHRISTMAS IS COMING UP.
NOW, WHERE'S YOUR FUTURE PRISON ROOMIE?...
FOR PETE'S SAKE UP THERE--GET HER OFF MY BACK!
AH, THERE HE IS!
CLIMBING THE ROPE-LADDER OF SUCCESS, OBVIOUSLY.
YOU BETTER BELIEVE IT, WONDER BROAD!
NOW STAY WHERE YOU ARE-- AND DON'T SO MUCH AS BREATHE TILL WE'RE LONG GONE--
--OR I'M GONNA GIVE THAT CROWD SOMETHING TO REMEMBER YOU BY!
KEEP BACK, EVERYBODY! HE'S STILL GOT HIS GUN!
HER IMPULSES AND FEELING RAGING A VERITABLE WAR WITHIN HER, THE DAUGHTER OF HIPPOLYTA IS INDEED JUST TAKING A STEP BACKWARD--THEN SUDDENLY, FROM OUT OF THE VERY SKY--
HOLY COW! LOOK AT THAT--A WOMAN--!
SHE'S FLYING--STRAIGHT FOR THE 'COPTER! NOT ONLY THAT--BUT SHE'S A KNOCKOUT!
IF THE BEMUSED BYSTANDER MEANS SHE'S A FEMME FATALE...
8

--HE MAY BE RIGHT IN MORE WAYS THAN ONE, AS--
N-NOOOO! DON'T!
STOP WHINING, FRIEND! I'VE GOT YOU.
WHOEVER THAT WOMAN IS, I HOPE SHE KNOWS HOW TO FLY A HELICOPTER, TOO!
THAT, HOWEVER DOES NOT APPEAR TO BE ONE OF THE SILVERY-FEATHERED NEWCOMER'S PRIORITIES...
...AS, INSTEAD, SHE MERELY KICKS HERSELF UPWARD INTO THE AIR...
...THEREBY SENDING THE CHOPPER, PILOT AND ALL, SPINNING DOWNWARD...
...WHILE SHE SWOOPS SLOWLY, GRACEFULLY AFTER IT, AS IF CHARTING ITS SICKENING FALL.
WHOEVER SHE IS-- SHE'S APPARENTLY WILLING TO LET THE PILOT DIE!
WITH MY MAGIC LASSO, I CAN GUIDE THE 'COPTER DOWN--
--BUT I'VE GOT TO FIND SOMEPLACE WHERE IT CAN DO THE LEAST HARM!
WOW! LOOK AT THAT BABY LOOP THE LOOP!
AND THAT MAKES THE PERFECT LANDING-SPOT NOT LAND AT ALL--
9

...BUT A GOOD OLD-FASHIONED 1960'S-TYPE SPLASHDOWN!
THE PILOT'S ALIVE, I SEE-- BUT HE'S OUT LIKE A LIGHT!
GOOD! NO USE GETTING SUED FOR WHIPLASH.
WHUMP!
NOW TO FIND OUT WHO THAT BIRD-LADY IS, 'CAUSE SHE SURE ISN'T SACAJAWEA... OR THE BLACK CANARY!
HELLO, EVERYONE! MAY I HAVE YOUR ATTENTION PLEASE?
I'M CALLED THE SILVER SWAN--
--AND I'D LIKE TO THANK WONDER WOMAN, FOR GIVING ME AN ASSIST ON THAT CAPTURE!
WHY, SHE --SHE'S BEAUTIFUL!
HARRY--!
"ASSIST"? NOW LOOK, MISS... I DON'T CARE WHO GETS CREDIT FOR STOPPING THOSE THUGS...
BUT, AT LEAST YOU COULD HAVE--
THE LOVELY STRANGER, HOWEVER, SEEMS HARDLY TO NOTICE THE PRINCESS... AS SHE SPEAKS WITH A VOICE LIKE A MELODIOUS WATERFALL...
I MUST LEAVE YOU NOW... BUT REMEMBER MY NAME, WON'T YOU?
YEAH-- THE SILVER SWAN!
HAR-RY...!
10

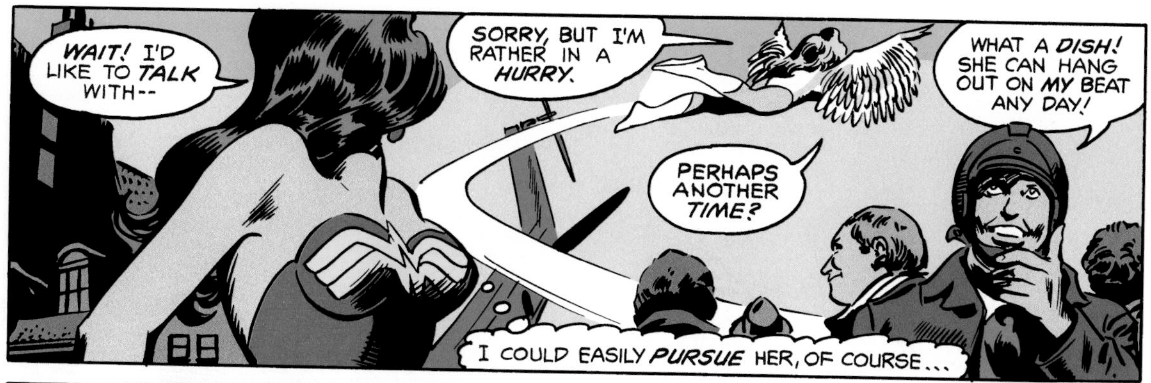
WAIT! I'D LIKE TO TALK WITH--
SORRY, BUT I'M RATHER IN A HURRY.
WHAT A DISH! SHE CAN HANG OUT ON MY BEAT ANY DAY!
PERHAPS ANOTHER TIME?
I COULD EASILY PURSUE HER, OF COURSE...

...BUT SHE DOES HAVE A RIGHT TO HER PRIVACY.
FUNNY, THOUGH, HOW HER BEAUTY SEEMED TO AFFECT THOSE MEN SO STRONGLY.
ARE MEN REALLY THAT SHALLOW-- OR AM I JUST GIVING VENT TO A KIND OF ENVY I'VE ALWAYS THOUGHT BENEATH ME?
WELL, I'LL WORRY ABOUT THAT LATER.

RIGHT NOW, IT'S NOT A NEW SUPER-HEROINE THAT INTERESTS ME... BUT A CERTAIN BRIEFCASE.
LET'S SEE, I LEFT IT RIGHT IN--
--HERE!?
SUFFERING SAPPHO!

I CAN STILL SEE THE IMPRINT OF WHERE IT LAY--
--BUT IT'S NOT THERE!

IT COULD HAVE BEEN CARRIED OFF BY ANYONE, OF COURSE... A CHILD, A DERELICT.
OR IT COULD EVEN NOW BE IN THE HANDS OF AGENTS OF A FOREIGN POWER!
DON'T PUSH THE PANIC BUTTON YET, THOUGH, DIANA--

--TILL YOU'VE TALKED TO GENERAL DARNELL, AND AT LEAST LEARNED WHAT WAS IN THAT BRIEFCASE.
CALLING ROBOT PLANE... HOVER FOR BOARDING...!
AND THAT MEANS AN AFTERNOON EXCURSION OUT TO--
11

--THE PENTAGON!
NOW THERE'S A PLACE THAT'S REALLY GONE THROUGH SOME CHANGES IN THE PAST FOUR DECADES--AT LEAST, IN PEOPLE'S MINDS.
WHEN IT WAS FINISHED IN '43, IT WAS A SYMBOL OF DEMOCRACY... THEN, DURING THE COLD WAR, A SYMBOL OF STRENGTH.
SINCE THEN--WELL, IT'S HAD A LOT OF BAD PRESS, AND ZEUS KNOWS IT'S PROBABLY DESERVED A LOT OF IT--
--THOUGH THE FINAL VERDICT'S DEFINITELY NOT IN YET.

ANYWAY, NOW THAT I THINK OF IT, IT'S HIGH TIME I PUT IN AN APPEARANCE HERE...

...NOT AS WONDER WOMAN, OF COURSE...
...BUT AS DIANA PRINCE, WHO ACTUALLY WORKS IN THE PLACE...
...AS COL. STEVE TREVOR'S EVER-HELPFUL ADJUTANT.

IT'S BEEN HOURS SINCE WE LEFT WITH THAT BRIEFCASE.
FOR ALL I KNOW, BY NOW I MAY BE LISTED AS AWOL...OR WORSE.

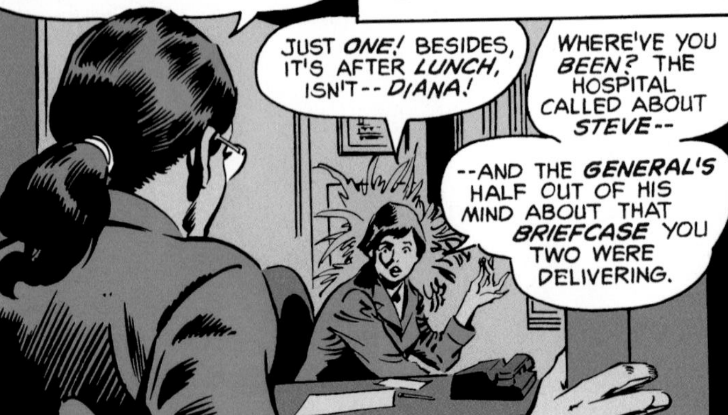
HELLO, ETTA! HAVING YOURSELF A CHOCOLATE, I SEE?
JUST ONE! BESIDES, IT'S AFTER LUNCH, ISN'T--DIANA!
WHERE'VE YOU BEEN? THE HOSPITAL CALLED ABOUT STEVE--
--AND THE GENERAL'S HALF OUT OF HIS MIND ABOUT THAT BRIEFCASE YOU TWO WERE DELIVERING.

UH--I HOPE YOU'VE GOT IT UNDER YOUR HAIRDO SOMEWHERE...!
I DON'T.
IS THE GENERAL IN?
TO YOU, ROOMIE, HE'S ALWAYS IN.
12

ER, GENERAL DARNELL...
WHAT IS IT, LT. CANDY? I TOLD YOU I WASN'T TO BE--
CAPTAIN PRINCE IS HERE, SIR.
THEN SEND HER IN, BLAST IT!
SEE?

WELL, CAPTAIN? WHAT HAPPENED OUT THERE TODAY?
FOREIGN AGENTS, SIR. DIDN'T THE POLICE--?
YES, AND THANK GOD TREVOR'S NOT DEAD...BUT WHAT ABOUT THAT BRIEFCASE?

THINKING FAST, DIANA SPINS A TALE WHICH IS TECHNICALLY TRUE...
...AND BY THE TIME I CAME BACK FROM GOING FOR HELP, IT WASN'T IN THE TRASHCAN.
HOW COULD YOU HAVE LET IT OUT OF YOUR SIGHT--
--EVEN FOR AN INSTANT?

I'M AFRAID...I'VE SAID ALL I CAN SAY, SIR.
LOOK, PRINCE... DIANA... I'M NOT TRYING TO BROWBEAT YOU.
BUT THOSE PAPERS WERE IMPORTANT, AND YOUR STORY'S SO VAGUE...!

WELL, DON'T WORRY. NO MATTER WHAT HAPPENS, YOU KNOW I'LL PROTECT YOU FROM ANY INQUIRIES THAT--
I DON'T WANT ANY SPECIAL FAVORS, SIR.
MAY I GO NOW...GENERAL DARNELL?

VERY WELL, CAPTAIN. I'LL ACT ON WHAT YOU'VE TOLD ME...
...AND WE'LL TALK AGAIN TOMORROW.
YES, SIR.

ETTA CANDY! WERE YOU EAVESDROPPING ON US?
WHO, ME? I JUST DROPPED MY BON-BON, THAT'S ALL!
C'MON! IT'S TIME TO GO HOME.

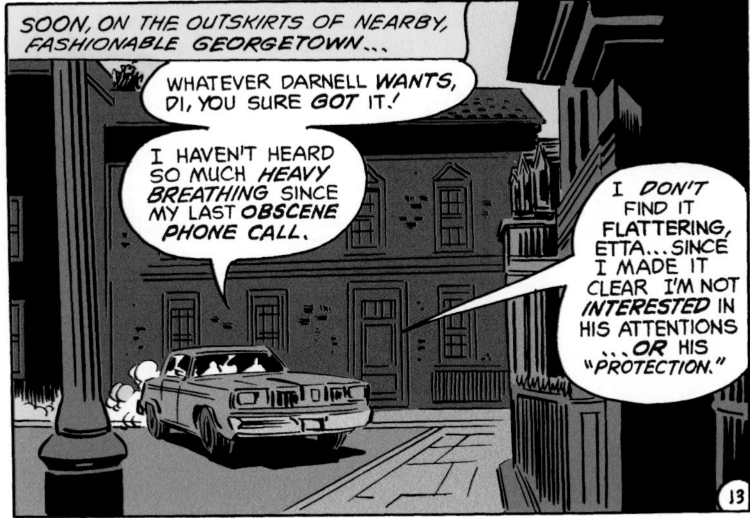
SOON, ON THE OUTSKIRTS OF NEARBY, FASHIONABLE GEORGETOWN...
WHATEVER DARNELL WANTS, DI, YOU SURE GOT IT.!
I HAVEN'T HEARD SO MUCH HEAVY BREATHING SINCE MY LAST OBSCENE PHONE CALL.
I DON'T FIND IT FLATTERING, ETTA...SINCE I MADE IT CLEAR I'M NOT INTERESTED IN HIS ATTENTIONS ...OR HIS "PROTECTION."
13

LORD, BUT IT'LL FEEL GREAT TO SLIP INTO A NICE HOT -- EH? WHAT'S THIS?
ROOMMATE WANTED INQUIRE WITHIN AFTER 5 P.M. OR CALL 555-3578
OH, ER, I FORGOT TO TELL YOU, DI.
YOU AND ME GOTTA LINE UP A THIRD ROOMIE-- PRONTO!

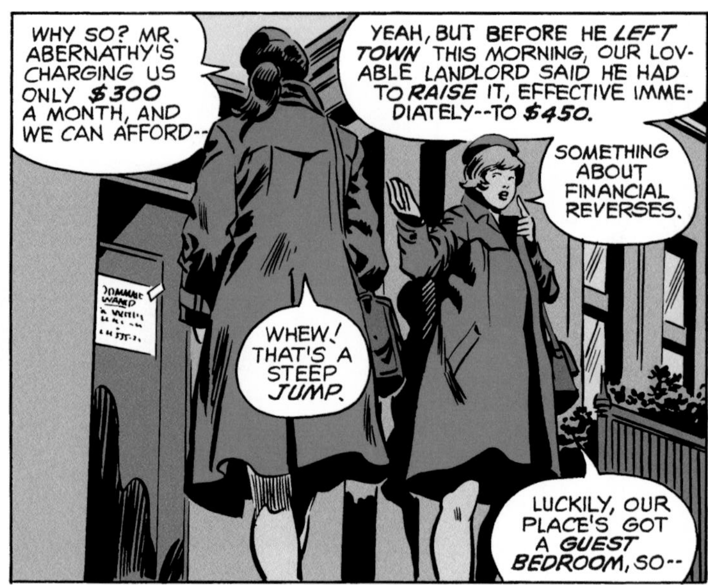
WHY SO? MR. ABERNATHY'S CHARGING US ONLY $300 A MONTH, AND WE CAN AFFORD--
YEAH, BUT BEFORE HE LEFT TOWN THIS MORNING, OUR LOVABLE LANDLORD SAID HE HAD TO RAISE IT, EFFECTIVE IMMEDIATELY--TO $450.
SOMETHING ABOUT FINANCIAL REVERSES.
WHEW! THAT'S A STEEP JUMP.
LUCKILY, OUR PLACE'S GOT A GUEST BEDROOM, SO--

WELL, I GUESS IF WE MUST... THEN WE MUST.
CAN'T LET ON THAT WHAT I REALLY FEAR IS THAT SOMEONE WILL FIND OUT I'M WONDER WOMAN.

BUT IT WOULD LOOK SUSPICIOUS IF I USED SOME OF THE AMAZONS' WEALTH TO--
BUZZZ
I'LL GET IT, ETTA.
Eggs
THANKS, DI.
Butter
I'D GO, BUT MY HANDS ARE FULL.

GOOD AFTERNOON. YOU WERE LOOKING FOR...?
UH... MY NAME'S HELEN... HELEN ALEXANDROS... AND I CAME ABOUT YOUR SPARE ROOM.
I'M DIANA PRINCE. WON'T YOU COME IN?
MAY I HELP YOU WITH ONE OF THOSE...?
WELL, ACTUALLY, MISS PRINCE...

...I THINK ONE OF THEM BELONGS TO YOU.
14

WHY, IT--IT'S THE BRIEFCASE I, ER, LOST TODAY!
HOW ON EARTH DID YOU KNOW THAT I--?
ANOTHER LITTLE THING I FORGOT TO MENTION, DI...

HELEN CALLED DARNELL'S OFFICE EARLIER, ASKING FOR YOU.
SHE DIDN'T THINK TO MENTION THE BRIEFCASE, I GUESS...
...BUT I DID LET IT SLIP WE WERE LOOKING FOR AN APARTMENT MATE, SO--
HI, HELEN... I'M ETTA.
I... I HOPE I'M NOT BEING PUSHY, COMING OVER LIKE THIS.
BUT ROOMS ARE SO SCARCE IN THE WASHINGTON-ARLINGTON AREA...!
NOT AT ALL... BUT HOW DID YOU KNOW I HAD ANY CONNECTION WITH THIS BRIEFCASE?

THE MEN WHO WERE EXPECTING IT... THEY CAME DOWN AFTER ALL THE EXCITEMENT ...AND I HEARD YOUR NAME MENTIONED, ALONG WITH THAT COLONEL'S.
THEY SAID YOU BOTH WORKED AT THE PENTAGON, SO I DECIDED TO TRY CALLING YOU THERE.

...BUT, WELL, I GUESS I MAY AS WELL ADMIT IT... MEN FRIGHTEN ME A LITTLE... THEY ALWAYS HAVE.
I SUPPOSE IT COMES FROM BEING SO PLAIN ALL MY LIFE... NOT TO MENTION THIS SKIN PROBLEM.
YEAH, THAT CAN BE TOUGH ON A GIRL, ALL RIGHT.
WANT A PIECE OF CAKE?

ANYWAY, THANKS, HELEN. YOU'LL MAKE A MIDDLE-AGED GENERAL VERY HAPPY, WHEN I GIVE THIS TO HIM IN THE MORNING.
DOES THAT MEAN... I CAN HAVE THE ROOM?
WHY NOT?
HEY, MAYBE WE CAN ALL GO OUT FOR PIZZA LATER!?

THERE'S SOMETHING ABOUT HELEN'S STORY THAT JUST DOESN'T ADD UP, SOMEHOW.
WELL, I CAN ALWAYS CHECK IT OUT, EASILY ENOUGH.
OH, YOU'RE JUST ON EDGE, DIANA.
MAYBE YOU SHOULD TAKE GENERAL DARNELL THAT MYSTERIOUS BRIEFCASE TONIGHT.
AT LEAST IT MIGHT TAKE YOUR MIND OFF STEVE FOR A WHILE.
15

YOU SURE I WON'T BE TOO MUCH TROUBLE, LT. CANDY?
ETTA. AND DON'T WORRY ABOUT THOSE ZITS, SWEETIE... I USED TO HAVE 'EM, TOO.
MY SKIN CLEARED UP; THERE'S JUST A LOT MORE OF IT NOW.
SEE YOU AFTER YOU UNPACK!
BUT, WHEN ETTA HAS CLOSED THE DOOR SOFTLY BEHIND HER, HELEN ALEXANDROS THROWS BACK HER UNPREPOSSESSING HEAD... AND LAUGHS.
IT IS NOT A NICE LAUGH, FOR THERE IS IN IT BOTH A MALIGNANT TRIUMPH... AND A LINGERING, HALF-STIFLED BITTERNESS.
THE BITTERNESS BEGAN WHEN SHE WAS JUST A LITTLE GIRL... AND ALAS, BY OUR CULTURAL STANDARDS, NOT A PARTICULARLY PRETTY ONE.
HAW! YOU COULD PLAY CONNECT-THE-DOTS ON HELEN'S FACE!
NOR DID HER MOTHER'S CONSTANT UPBRAIDINGS HELP MUCH...
I DON'T UNDERSTAND WHY YOU DIDN'T TURN OUT TO FAVOR MY SIDE OF THE FAMILY MORE.
YOU ALWAYS DID TAKE AFTER YOUR FATHER, THAT DIRTY--!
WHAT IS IT THE SONG IN THAT BROADWAY MUSICAL SAID?
"EVERYONE IS BEAUTIFUL AT THE BALLET."
SO, IN BETWEEN CRYING JAGS, SHE CONTINUED THE DANCING LESSONS WHICH NOW BECAME HER ONLY ESCAPE FROM AN UGLY REALITY: HERSELF!
SHE WAS NO PAVLOVA... BUT SHE GOT BY, AND EVEN BECAME PART OF A PROFESSIONAL BALLET TROUPE.
HER AMBITION?
WHY, TO DANCE THE LEAD IN "SWAN LAKE," OF COURSE.
FOR SUCH AS HELEN ALEXANDROS, WHAT ELSE IS THERE?
HER TROUPE TRAVELED ABROAD... EVENTUALLY EVEN GAVE A SPECIAL OUTDOOR PERFORMANCE AT AN ANCIENT GREEK THEATRE NEAR ATHENS.
HELEN WAS STILL JUST ONE OF THE DANCERS, BUT SHE GAVE IT HER ALL...
KLAP KLAP KLAP
KLAP
16
...AND HOPED FOR BETTER THINGS.

THAT'S WHY IT HURTS SO MUCH LATER THAT NIGHT, WHEN SHE ACCIDENTALLY OVERHEARD...
MARIA'S QUITTING, SO WE NEED A NEW PRIMA BALLERINA.
HOW ABOUT HELEN ALEXANDROS?
SHE DANCES WELL ENOUGH, BUT SHE'S SO... WELL...

THE WORD YOU'RE GROPING FOR, HAL, IS "UGLY."
YEAH, I GUESS YOU'RE RIGHT. IN REAL LIFE, THE UGLY DUCKLING NEVER REALLY GETS TO PLAY THE SWAN.
WE'LL GIVE KARINA A TRY, EH?

HELEN STAYED BEHIND THAT NIGHT, TO BE ALONE IN THE AMPHITHEATRE WHOSE BRILLIANT ACOUSTICS HAD ONCE DELIGHTED PERICLES AND SOPHOCLES...

WHY, YOU GODS IN YOUR FAR-OFF HEAVENS??

WHY DID YOU MAKE ME SO PLAIN--IN A WORLD THAT VALUES BEAUTY OVER EVERYTHING?

I--WHO WAS NAMED FOR HELEN OF TROY, MOST DESIRABLE WOMAN OF ALL TIME!

OH, HOW I HATE MEN--MEN, AND THIS CRUEL AND HORRIBLE WORLD THEY'VE MADE!!

DO YOU HEAR ME, YOU GODS? I HATE MEN!!

THAT'S WHEN HELEN SUDDENLY NOTICED THE STORM CLOUDS, WHICH HAD GATHERED AS IF OUT OF NOTHINGNESS.

THAT'S WHEN SHE HEARD THE OMINOUS, RUMBLING THUNDERCLAP.

AND THAT'S WHEN SHE HEARD THE VOICE:

YES, HELEN ALEXANDROS, I HAVE HEARD YOU --EVEN IN DISTANT, MIST-SHROUDED OLYMPUS!

I HAVE HEARD YOU--AND I HAVE COME!

CONVINCED FOR A MOMENT THAT SHE WAS LOSING HER MIND, HELEN THREW HERSELF THEN UPON THE TIME-WORN FLAGSTONES OF THE MOON-WASHED THEATRE...

17

...AND STARED UPWARD, EYES WIDE WITH FEAR:

WH-WHO ARE YOU??

WHAT ARE YOU??

I AM HE WHOM THE ANCIENT GREEKS DID CALL ARES-- THE ROMANS, MARS, GOD OF WAR!

BELIEVE, GIRL! YET, YOU HAVE AN EQUALLY LUSTROUS HERITAGE ON YOUR MOTHER'S SIDE.

DO YOU NOT RECOGNIZE, BY INSTINCT, YOUR OWN IMMORTAL ANCESTOR?

WHAT? I--I CAN'T--

MY--?

FOR, ZEUS IT WAS-- KING OF THE OLD GODS --WHO CAME IN THE FORM OF A SWAN TO THE BEAUTEOUS LEDA--

--AND FROM THIS UNION, HELEN OF SPARTA WAS BORN--

--SHE WHO BECAME FOREVER KNOWN TO LEGEND AS HELEN OF TROY, AFTER THE TROJAN PRINCE PARIS PERSUADED HER TO FORSAKE HER GREEK HUSBAND FOR HIM!

IF YOU'RE-- WHO YOU SAY YOU ARE--

--THEN YOU MUST KNOW I HEARD THESE STORIES AS A CHILD, FROM MY PARENTS.

WHAT DO THEY HAVE TO DO WITH ME?

YOU WERE NAMED, AS YOU SAID, FOR HER WHOSE MATCHLESS FACE DID LAUNCH A THOUSAND GRECIAN SHIPS AGAINST TROY--

--AND BRING DEATH AND DESTRUCTION TO ITS BRAVE WARRIORS--

--IN THE FORM OF A HOLLOW WOODEN HORSE, WHICH THE FOOLISH TROJANS THEMSELVES CARRIED PAST THEIR ELSE-UNBREACHABLE WALLS.

I--I LIKE THAT PART--
I KNOW!
--THE PART ABOUT BRING DEATH AND DESTRUCTION TO MEN!
FOR, IT WAS SENSING THIS PASSION WITHIN YOUR BREAST-- THIS HATRED FOR ALL HUMAN MALES--
--THAT BROUGHT ME HERE TO OFFER YOU THE CHANCE TO DWARF YOUR NAMESAKE'S GRIM ACHIEVEMENT!

ARE YOU WILLING, HELEN ALEXANDROS, TO ACCEPT YOUR DIVINE HERITAGE OF BLOOD?
YES! YES!
WHAT MUST I DO??
18

ONLY WATCH-- AND BE RECEPTIVE--
--AS WONDROUS WAVES OF MY OLYMPIAN POWER WASH OVER YOUR FACE AND FORM, LIKE UNTO THE FROTHING WHITECAPS OF OCEAN!
CAN YOU FEEL THEM-- TRANSFORMING YOU, WHO WERE DESPISED BY MEN FOR YOUR PLAINNESS--
--INTO ONE POSSESSED OF THE BEAUTY OF HELEN OF TROY, WHICH TURNED STRONG MALES INTO STAMMERING FOOLS, AND BROUGHT A WORLD CRASHING DOWN AROUND THEIR HEADS?
I--I CAN FEEL MYSELF CHANGING-- MY CLOTHES-- MY VERY SHAPE--EVEN THE COLOR OF MY HAIR!
I'M NO LONGER HELEN ALEXANDROS AT ALL!
NAY! YOU ARE NOW SHE WHOM I WOULD CALL-- THE SILVER SWAN!
A NAME I'LL WEAR PROUDLY AS LONG AS I CAN GO ON LOOKING LIKE THE WAY I CAN SENSE THAT I--
NO! PLEASE-- DON'T LIFT ME INTO THE SKY WITH YOU!
I'LL FALL--!
WILL YOU, LASS--EVEN WHEN I RELEASE YOU?
THROW WIDE YOUR ARMS-- AND SEE!
WAIT! I'M NOT FALLING AT ALL--I-- I'M FLYING!
I'M AS BEAUTIFUL AS A MORTAL GODDESS--AND NOW YOU'VE GIVEN ME GODLIKE POWERS AS WELL!
POWERS THE FULLER EXTENT OF WHICH YOU'LL REALIZE--WHEN YOU TRY YOUR STRENGTH.
THERE! I'VE LANDED EASILY-- JUST BY WILLING IT.
BUT, WHAT DID YOU MEAN--"TRY MY STRENGTH"?
THAT BROKEN PILLAR... PULL IT UP, MY SILVERY ONE!
19

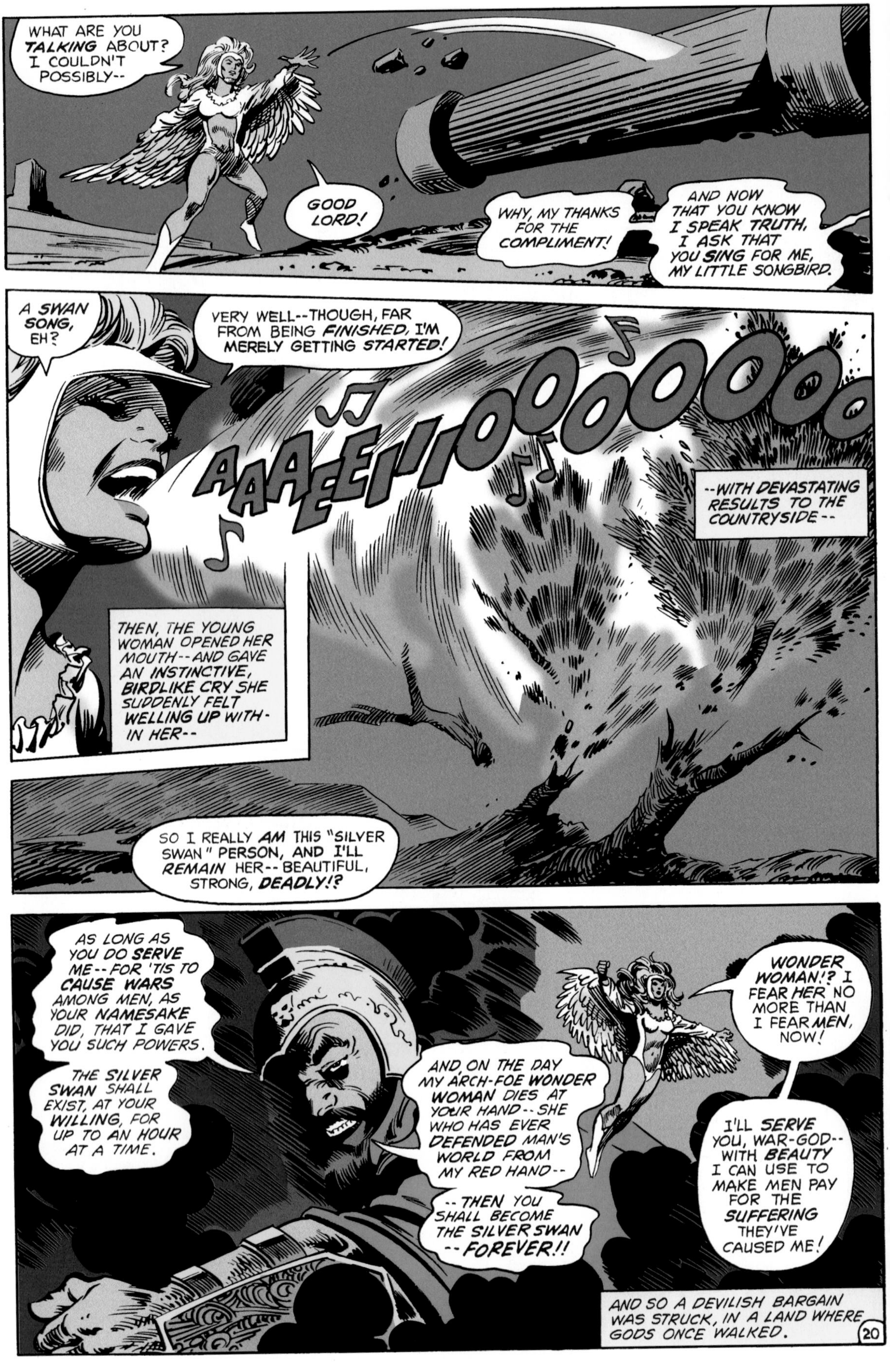

WHAT ARE YOU **TALKING** ABOUT? I COULDN'T POSSIBLY--

GOOD LORD!

WHY, MY THANKS FOR THE COMPLIMENT!

AND NOW THAT YOU KNOW I SPEAK **TRUTH**, I ASK THAT YOU **SING** FOR ME, MY LITTLE SONGBIRD.

A **SWAN SONG**, EH?

VERY WELL--THOUGH, FAR FROM BEING **FINISHED**, I'M MERELY GETTING **STARTED!**

AAAEEIIIOOOOOOOO

--WITH **DEVASTATING** RESULTS TO THE COUNTRYSIDE--

THEN, THE YOUNG WOMAN OPENED HER MOUTH--AND GAVE AN **INSTINCTIVE, BIRDLIKE CRY** SHE SUDDENLY FELT **WELLING UP** WITH-IN HER--

SO I REALLY **AM** THIS "SILVER SWAN" PERSON, AND **I'LL REMAIN** HER--BEAUTIFUL, STRONG, **DEADLY!?**

AS LONG AS YOU DO **SERVE** ME--FOR 'TIS TO **CAUSE WARS** AMONG MEN, AS YOUR **NAMESAKE** DID, THAT I GAVE YOU SUCH POWERS.
THE **SILVER SWAN** SHALL EXIST, AT YOUR **WILLING**, FOR UP TO AN HOUR AT A TIME.
AND, ON THE DAY MY ARCH-FOE **WONDER WOMAN** DIES AT YOUR HAND--SHE WHO HAS EVER **DEFENDED** MAN'S **WORLD** FROM MY RED HAND--
--**THEN** YOU SHALL BECOME THE **SILVER SWAN** --**FOREVER!!**
WONDER WOMAN!? I FEAR **HER** NO MORE THAN I FEAR **MEN**, NOW!
I'LL **SERVE** YOU, WAR-GOD--WITH **BEAUTY** I CAN USE TO MAKE MEN PAY FOR THE **SUFFERING** THEY'VE CAUSED ME!
AND SO A DEVILISH BARGAIN WAS STRUCK, IN A LAND WHERE GODS ONCE WALKED.
20

SOON AFTERWARD, IT WAS **HELEN ALEXANDROS** WHO BEGAN TO STUDY CAREFULLY THE ITINERARY OF **WONDER WOMAN**... AND LEARNED SHE HAD BEEN SEEN RECENTLY IN THE COMPANY OF **COL. STEVE TREVOR** OF U.S. MILITARY INTELLIGENCE.

FROM THERE, IT WAS A SIMPLE MATTER, WITH THE HELP OF MARS, TO CONTACT FOREIGN AGENTS CONCERNING A CERTAIN DELIVERY TREVOR WAS TO MAKE...

AND, THOUGH IT WAS CAPT. DIANA PRINCE SHE SAW HIDING A VALUED BRIEF-CASE IN A WASHINGTON GARBAGE CAN...

...IT WAS SOMEONE ELSE THAT DIANA TURNED INTO:
WONDER WOMAN!
SO SHE'S GOT A PLAIN-JANE ALTER EGO, TOO!

THAT WAS THE **TURNING POINT!**

FOR NOW, I NOT ONLY KNOW WONDER WOMAN'S **SECRET IDENTITY**--

BUT, WITH THE UNWITTING HELP OF **ETTA CANDY**--

--I EVEN SHARE AN **APARTMENT** WITH HER.

PERHAPS, HOWEVER--**NOT FOR LONG!**

THEN, HELEN **CONCENTRATES**, AS SHE HAS DONE MORE THAN ONCE OF LATE, AND--

HOW **WONDERFUL** IT IS TO SHED THE DOUGHTY FEATHERS OF **HELEN ALEXANDROS**--

--FOR THE PEERLESS PLUMAGE OF THE **SILVER SWAN!**

PERHAPS I SHOULD HAVE **ATTACKED** WONDER WOMAN OUTRIGHT THIS AFTERNOON--SOUGHT TO **DESTROY** HER.

BUT, I NEED **PRACTICE** WITH MY POWERS--SO I COULD BE CERTAIN THAT, WHEN I **DO** STRIKE AT HER, I SHALL **PREVAIL**.

BESIDES, IT BROUGHT A RUSH OF **PLEASURE** TO SENSE THE LUSTFUL **DESIRES** OF MEN, WHEN THEY **SEE** ME IN THIS GUISE.

IF ONLY THEY KNEW THAT THE **WAR-GOD** PLANS TO **USE** THOSE DESIRES--TO BRING THEIR WORLD TO A **FIERY END**--

--THEY WOULD **REVILE** THE SILVER SWAN, AS MUCH AS THEY NOW **ADMIRE** HER!

21

MEANWHILE, NOT FAR AWAY, DIANA PRINCE HAS STEPPED FROM THE SHOWER... TO GRAB A GLEAMING LASSO IN-STEAD OF A TOWEL...
...AND, WHILE WE MUST LEAVE IT TO PROPHETS AND PUNDITS TO PONDER JUST HOW HOW HER SPINNING LARIAT WEAVES THE GARMENTS OF WONDER WOMAN ABOUT HER WATER-SPLASHED FORM...
...THE FACT REMAINS:
IT WORKS.
A FEW MOMENTS MORE, AND THE AMAZING AMAZON LEAPS HEAD-LONG FROM HER UPPER-STORY WINDOW...
...TOWARD A DANGLING ROPE-LADDER WHICH IS WHOLLY INVISIBLE TO MORTAL EYES.
THE NARROWED EYES WHICH FURTIVELY WATCH HER NOW, HOWEVER, ARE SOMEHOW MORE THAN MERELY MORTAL...
AND THE SHINING SILVER FORM WHICH STREAKS SKYWARD AFTER HER NEXT INSTANT, IS SOMEHOW BOTH MORE AND LESS THAN HUMAN...
I DON'T EVEN NEED TO KEEP UP WITH HER... SINCE I CAN GUESS WHERE SHE'S GOING.
I KNEW SHE'D BE UNABLE TO RESIST, ONCE SHE HAD THE BRIEFCASE IN HER POSSESSION.
IT'S IN MY OWN INTEREST THAT I LET HER REACH THE PENTAGON BEFORE I ATTACK.
22

THAT WAY, THE WHOLE WORLD WILL SOON LEARN WHICH OF US IS THE STRONGER, AS WELL AS THE MOST BEAUTIFUL.
I WANT ACKNOWLEDGMENT FROM A WORLD RULED BY MEN--BEFORE I HELP MY IMMORTAL ANCESTOR DESTROY IT.
TO GET THAT, I MUST GAIN PERMANENT POSSESSION OF THIS EXQUISITE FORM--BY KILLING WONDER WOMAN!
AH! WE'RE NEARLY ABOVE THE PENTAGON ALREADY...
...SO IT'S TIME TO MAKE MY MOVE!
SILVER SWAN! WHAT DO YOU WANT?
--WHEN I'M IN MY INVISIBLE ROBOT PLANE?
NO ANSWER! BUT HOW COULD SHE EVEN HAVE FOUND ME--

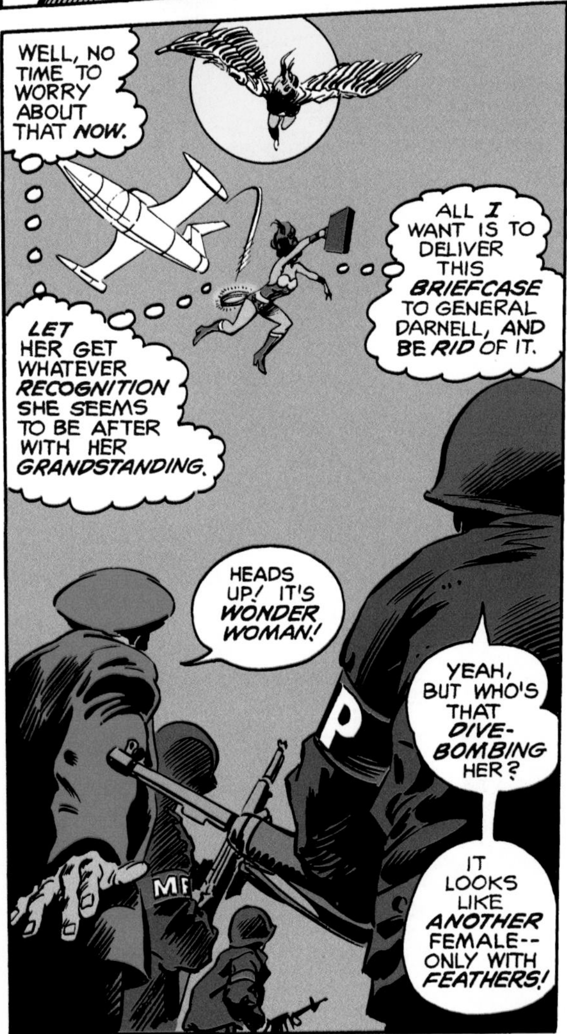
WELL, NO TIME TO WORRY ABOUT THAT NOW.
ALL I WANT IS TO DELIVER THIS BRIEFCASE TO GENERAL DARNELL, AND BE RID OF IT.
LET HER GET WHATEVER RECOGNITION SHE SEEMS TO BE AFTER WITH HER GRANDSTANDING.
HEADS UP! IT'S WONDER WOMAN!
YEAH, BUT WHO'S THAT DIVE-BOMBING HER?
IT LOOKS LIKE ANOTHER FEMALE--ONLY WITH FEATHERS!
MP
P

I'LL JUST TAKE THIS OFF YOUR HANDS, AMAZON.
WHAT IN PLUTO'S NAME--?
I WAS CARELESS--BECAUSE SHE HELPED CAPTURE THOSE SPIES BEFORE!
IF SHE'D WANTED THE BRIEFCASE, I THOUGHT IT WOULD'VE BEEN SHE WHO FOUND IT... RATHER THAN TIMID LITTLE HELEN ALEXANDROS.
WHATEVER HER SCHEME, THOUGH, IT WON'T WORK--
23

--NOT WITH ME!
YOUR GRIP--IT'S AS STRONG AS MINE!
RRIP
IS THAT WHAT THIS IS ALL ABOUT, SWAN?
IN ORDER TO BE ACCEPTED, DO YOU FEEL A NEED TO PROVE YOU'RE QUEEN OF THE HILL?
WELL, I DON'T HAVE TIME TO PLAY EGO GAMES WITH YOU.
I'VE GOT A BRIEFCASE TO DELIVER--BY AIR EXPRESS.
THANK HERA THAT ALBATROSS IS OFF MY NECK!
GENERAL DARNELL--DO YOU SEE--?
LIKE MANNA FROM HEAVEN, MAJOR!
THUMP
YOU STAR-SPANGLED FOOL!
THAT BRIEFCASE MEANS NOTHING TO ME.
IT'S YOUR DEATH I WANT! YOUR DEATH!
SHE SEIZED HER CHANCE TO HURL ME DOWNWARD--WHILE I WAS BUSY WITH THE 'CASE.
I CAN'T FLY AS SHE APPARENTLY CAN--
--BUT, ANYTIME THERE'S A HALFWAY DECENT WIND CURRENT AROUND, I CAN AT LEAST RIDE IT AS I'D RIDE AN OCEAN WAVE.
I CAN'T KEEP THIS UP FOREVER, OF COURSE.
STILL, IT WILL BE EASY TO GLIDE SAFELY TO EARTH, WHEN I'VE DEALT WITH THE SILVER SWAN.
IF ONLY I KNEW WHY SHE ATTACKED ME THIS TIME... BUT NOT WHEN WE FIRST MET.
I DON'T KNOW--MAYBE I'M CARRYING NON-VIOLENCE TOO FAR, BY NOT ATTACKING HER OUTRIGHT IN RETURN.
PERHAPS I SHOULD QUESTION LESS... AND FIGHT MORE.
BUT IT'S JUST NOT MY WAY... NOT WITH-OUT AT LEAST TRYING TO FIND OUT WHY--
24

ARRRH!
NOW WE'LL SEE WHO'S THE STRONGEST ONE OF ALL, DAUGHTER OF HIPPOLYTA!
THRAM!
STRUCK AT NEAR LIGHTNING SPEED BY THE HURTLING HARPIE, WONDER WOMAN SPIRALS GROUNDWARD AGAIN--INSTINCTIVELY USING THE WIND CURRENTS TO SLOW HER FALL SOMEWHAT--
--THOUGH NOT ENOUGH:
HOLY MOSES!
THAT WINGED WOMAN UP THERE SURE CAN SCRAP!
BY WHY IS SHE FIGHTING THE AMAZON?
MAYBE WONDER-LADY CAN TELL YOU THAT HERSELF, GENERAL.
LOOK! SHE'S RECOVERED ALREADY --HARDLY EVEN SCRATCHED!
ALL I KNOW AT THIS MOMENT, SOLDIER, IS THAT THE GLOVES ARE OFF.
I'M TANGLING WITH THAT KILLER PARAKEET--RIGHT NOW!
HMMM...THAT DOESN'T SOUND LIKE THE WONDER WOMAN I'VE MET.
I COULDN'T SEE WHO REALLY STARTED THAT BATTLE UP THERE.
I WONDER IF SHE--!?
GIVING YOUR ALL FOR ONE LAST TRY, ARE YOU?
IT'LL BE THE LAST--WHEN I'VE COLLARED YOU, SWAN, AND NOT BEFORE!
25

THIS IS *MY* GAME, WONDER WOMAN--AND WE PLAY BY ***MY RULES.***
OH, AND I JUST WANTED TO DEMONSTRATE ONE ***LAST*** POWER OF MINE...!
ONCE MORE, THE SOUL-PIERCING ***CRY OF THE SWAN*** *IS HEARD IN THE LAND OF THE FREE, THE HOME OF THE BRAVE--*
AAAEEEIIOOOOO
--AND THE ***AMAZON PRINCESS,*** *UNPREPARED FOR THE SUDDEN VOCAL ONSLAUGHT, IS ABRUPTLY* ***BUFFETED ABOUT,*** *LIKE A STRAW CAUGHT IN A WHIRLWIND--*
WHILE, BELOW--
AGGGK! TH-THAT ***SOUND--!***
IT'S--***BEAUTIFUL!*** AND YET--SO ***PAINFUL***--INSIDE MY ***HEAD--!***

RIGHT THIS MOMENT, HOWEVER, WONDER WOMAN WOULD PROBABLY NOT EVEN GIVE THE SWAN'S SONG MARKS FOR BEAUTY--
FRAAKK!
--AS SHE FALLS TO EARTH A SECOND TIME--AGAINST A STONE WALL!

GOOD! NOW TO LAND AND SLAY HER BEFORE SHE CAN--
Y-YOU MUST BE THE SILVER SWAN WE HEARD ABOUT!
THAT'S RIGHT! THE ONE WHO CAUGHT THOSE SPIES!
MP
LOOK AT HER, GUYS! SHE'S GORGEOUS!
26

MOMENTS LATER...
WHY DON'T YOU... ASK HER... WHY SHE TRIED... TO KILL ME?
OH, SHE'S ALREADY EXPLAINED ALL ABOUT THAT, WONDER WOMAN.
GLAD TO SEE YOU'RE NOT HURT TOO BADLY, THOUGH.

SHE SAYS IT WAS ALL AN UNFORTUNATE MISUNDERSTANDING ...BECAUSE SHE THOUGHT YOU WERE STEALING IT.
AND...YOU BELIEVE THAT!?
WHY WOULD I LIE?
WELL PUT, SILVER SWAN... AND THANKS AGAIN.
YOU'RE AS PATRIOTIC AS YOU ARE LOVELY... AND THAT'S SAYING A LOT!

WHY, THANK YOU, GENERAL DARNELL-- AND NOW, AU REVOIR!
W-WAIT--!
SHE'S FLYING OFF-- YET I'M SURE SHE LANDED IN ORDER TO FINISH ME!
WHY DID SHE CHANGE HER MIND? WHY??

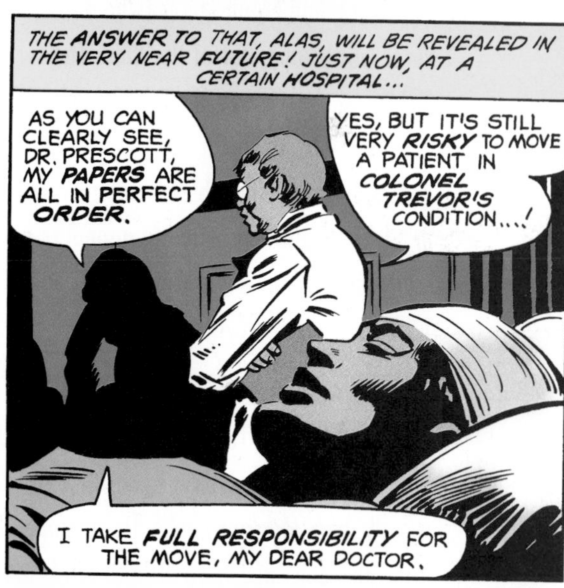
THE ANSWER TO THAT, ALAS, WILL BE REVEALED IN THE VERY NEAR FUTURE! JUST NOW, AT A CERTAIN HOSPITAL...
AS YOU CAN CLEARLY SEE, DR. PRESCOTT, MY PAPERS ARE ALL IN PERFECT ORDER.
YES, BUT IT'S STILL VERY RISKY TO MOVE A PATIENT IN COLONEL TREVOR'S CONDITION...!
I TAKE FULL RESPONSIBILITY FOR THE MOVE, MY DEAR DOCTOR.

AFTER ALL, ONE MUST BE DOUBLY TRUST-WORTHY, DOESN'T ONE -- WHEN ONE HAS A NAME LIKE--
--DOCTOR PSYCHO!
NEXT ISSUE: PSYCHO! THE SILVER SWAN! -PLUS- THE COMING OF CAPTAIN WONDER!

PART III: 1986-2010
THE AMBASSADOR

After CRISIS ON INFINITE EARTHS ended in 1985, a new modern unified DC Universe was created in lieu of the old multiverse. The Crisis epilogue had shown two different possible ends for the Wonder Women of Earth-1 and Earth-2. The latter ended up with her husband on Mount Olympus with the Gods, while the former sacrificed herself fighting the Anti-Monitor.

The new universe simplified the situation: now there was only one Wonder Woman. The new series was written and drawn by George Pérez (with help on script from Greg Potter, then Len Wein). Just like John Byrne (who took over Superman in MAN OF STEEL), and Frank Miller (who wrote Batman in BATMAN: YEAR ONE), George Pérez was a superstar of the time. The series didn't shy away from any major topic, tackling such issues as feminism, nuclear threats, drug abuse and teenage suicides, but remaining a spectacular superhero action book. Completely in sync with the decade's fears and problems, the creators delivered a character who was both close to her roots and renovated to appeal to a much wider audience. George Pérez's stint on the series is also marked by the addition of female creators such as Mindy Newell, Jill Thompson and Cynthia Martin.

With the Amazon's fiftieth anniversary in 1991, Pérez bowed out with the final crossover WAR OF THE GODS. Afterwards, every writer who stepped in to chronicle Wonder Woman's adventures threw a chunk of his or her own personality in the mix. William Messner-Loebs, for example, juxtaposed the balance between the Amazon's epic superhero life (he sends her to space, for instance) and very real everyday problems (Diana works as a fast-food waitress to pay her rent!). After Messner-Loebs, John Byrne took over, reintroducing concepts and characters that existed before Crisis. Then the next batch of writers, Eric Luke, Phil Jimenez and Greg Rucka (with fill-in writers Christopher Priest, Brian K. Vaughan and Walter Simonson) reinstated Diana in her role as ambassador of Themyscira, the Amazon Island.

The WONDER WOMAN series showed as many faces as Diana herself: warrior, upholder of the law, philosopher, friend, lover... Confronted constantly with the high expectations of what she represents, she quite often suffers when she's not able to meet that ideal. Her biggest failure came during the INFINITE CRISIS crossover in 2006. To free a mentally controlled Superman, she breaks villain Maxwell Lord's neck. To make amends for her action, she decides to take a secret identity again and becomes Diana Prince once more.

Allan Heinberg, then Jodi Picoult, wrote Wonder Woman's tales before Gail Simone ultimately became a more permanent writer on the series. Under her watch, Wonder Woman fights for justice once again, whether it's on Earth, or in space, or in a mystical dimension.

Finally, to close the chapter of the post-Crisis Wonder Woman, DC called in J. Michael Straczynski, creator of the television series *Babylon V* and writer of many comics, who imagined an amnesic Wonder Woman trying to follow the trail of the Amazons. With the unexpected help of one of her greatest enemies, Doctor Psycho, Diana recovered her memories, just in time for a new incarnation of the DC Universe.

GEORGE PEREZ

DC
FANTASTIC
1ST ISSUE!
75¢
1
WONDER WOMAN
APPROVED BY THE COMICS CODE AUTHORITY
POTTER, PEREZ AND PATTERSON

" THE GODS ARE DEAD, KILLED BY THE ONE GOD. BETWEEN THE MEN OF THE NEW AND THOSE OF ANCIENT TIMES THERE WILL NO LONGER BE A THOUGHT IN COMMON."
-- FERDINAND LOT

30,000 B.C.--TODAY, YOUR TRIBE CAST YOU OUT! THEY MOCKED YOU-- CALLED YOU USELESS...

...CALLED YOU AN ANIMAL!

ONLY YESTERDAY YOU WERE CALLED A MAN! YOU HUNTED WITH MEN AND FOUGHT WITH MEN.
THAT WAS BEFORE YOU MET THE SABERTOOTH...
...THE ONE WHO BESTED YOU...
NOW, YOU ARE A MAN NO MORE. FOR MEN ARE HUNTERS -- AND HUNTERS NEED HANDS!
THAT MAKES YOU AFRAID. BUT YOU MUST NOT SHOW YOUR FEAR.
REMEMBER WHAT THE TRIBE TEACHES:...
...FEAR IS FOR WOMEN!
SO YOU HIDE YOUR FACE--QUELL YOUR TREMBLING.
STILL, SOMEHOW, SHE KNOWS!

...THE ONE WHO TOOK YOUR HAND!

AND WHEN SHE TOUCHES YOU...
...WHEN YOU HEAR HER SYMPATHETIC WHINING...

...YOU CURSE HER!

SO YOU PULL AWAY--
BUT SHE INSISTS!
YOU TRY TO IGNORE HER--BUT HER WHIMPERING TAUNTS YOU...
...TEASES YOU...
...EMASCULATES YOU...
...MAKES YOU...SNAP!
AND WHEN YOUR TEMPER COOLS...
...WHEN THE ECHO OF HER SCREAM HAS BEEN SWALLOWED BY THE AIR...
...YOU HEAR IT!
A MUFFLED STIRRING WITHIN HER.
AND A VOICE--
--AS IF FROM THE EARTH ITSELF--
--WHISPERING--
--CALLING--
--BECKONING--
--MAKING SOMETHING HAPPEN...
...THAT YOU CANNOT UNDERSTAND!
AND IT MAKES YOU WANT TO...
...SCREAM!
2

DC Comics Proudly Presents
WONDER WOMAN
created by William Moulton Marston
the Princess and the POWER!
MOUNT OLYMPUS: 1,200 B.C.
LORD ZEUS, KING OF GODS! LISTEN NOT TO THESE BABBLING FOOLS! IT IS TRUE THAT MAN MUST NOW BE DEALT WITH--
GREG POTTER script - GEORGE PÉREZ co-plotters - pencils . BRUCE PATTERSON inks . JOHN COSTANZA letters . TATJANA WOOD colors . KAREN BERGER Editor

-- BUT IF THE GODS WISH TO SECURE THEIR POWER ON EARTH, HEED THE WORDS OF YOUR SON-- ARES-- GOD OF WAR!
MY HALF-SISTER ARTEMIS HAS PROPOSED TO CREATE A NEW RACE OF MORTALS ON EARTH-- A RACE WHICH, SHE CLAIMS, SHALL MAKE MEN WORSHIP US AS NEVER BEFORE! MY LORD, THIS PLAN IS LUNACY!
IF OLYMPUS TRULY DESIRES TO OWN MEN'S HEARTS-- IF POWER IS OUR ULTIMATE AIM-- THEN LET ARES DESCEND UPON THESE WEAK-KNEED MORTALS...
...AND WITH THE DOGS OF WAR, I SHALL CRUSH THEM INTO ETERNAL SUBMISSION!
NO, ARES. VIOLENCE WILL MAKE MAN FEAR US, NOT FOLLOW US. OUR INTENT WITH THIS NEW RACE IS TO SET AN EXAMPLE -- TO SHOW MAN AND WOMAN'S TRUE PLACE WITH EACH OTHER--
--AS GAEA HAD MEANT IT TO BE!
FORCE IS ALL MEN UNDERSTAND! FORCE IS ALL THEY WORSHIP!
AND I AM FORCE INCARNATE!
LORD ZEUS--ARES' WAY SHALL DESTROY US ALL. IF MAN DIES...
...SHALL WE NOT ALSO PERISH?
THERE IS TRUTH IN MY SISTER'S WORDS, FATHER ZEUS. MEN WORSHIP THE GODS-- AND THROUGH THEIR WORSHIP, WE GROW STRONG.
WITHOUT THEIR GOOD WILL, WE SHALL BECOME AS NOTHING IN MAN'S WORLD!
SO, APOLLO-- YOU AGREE WITH ARTEMIS!
DO YOU, TOO, SEE THIS NEW RACE AS FEMALE?
4

DOES THEIR GENDER TRULY MATTER, LORD ZEUS? THEY SHALL BE AS NO OTHER WOMEN EVER BEFORE SEEN BY MAN! STRONG...BRAVE... COMPASSIONATE!
THEY SHALL BE OLYMPUS' GLORY--
NAY, LORD! THEY SHALL BE OLYMPUS' SHAME!
WHAT ARE YOU AFRAID OF, ARES? THAT OLYMPUS SHALL BE REPRESENTED ON EARTH BY WOMEN?
OR THAT THESE NEW MORTALS SHALL BE ABLE TO RESIST EVEN YOUR BASE INFLUENCE?
NO MORTAL RESISTS ARES, ATHENA! MY ULTIMATE DOMINATION OF MAN IS INEVITABLE!
EVEN IN PROPHECY NOTHING IS INEVITABLE, AR MANKIND IS EV BLESSED --AN CURSED--WITH THE POWER OF CHOICE!
ENOUGH!

YOU SPEAK AS IF MAN WILL SOMEDAY FORGET THE GODS! I SAY IT SHALL NEVER COME TO PASS!
IT MATTERS LITTLE, THEREFORE, WHETHER YOUR NEW RACE IS BORN OR NOT!

SETTLE THIS TRIFLING MATTER AMONG YOURSELVES--AND BOTHER ZEUS WITH IT NO MORE!

HERA--WILL YOU NOT SPEAK WITH LORD ZEUS WE WOULD HAVE HIS BLESSING IN THIS VENTURE...AND HE WOULD LISTEN TO YOU.

MY HUSBAND IS PROUD--AND YOUR WORDS HAVE STIRRED A STORM WITHIN HIM.
MY ADVICE TO YOU IS THIS: WALK NOT LIGHTLY INTO SUCH A MAELSTROM!

AND DO NOT ASK YOUR QUEEN TO TAKE SIDES AGAINST HER LORD WHILE HE STILL RAGES!

SEE THERE? SHE TURNS HER BACK ON YOU! AS DOES ZEUS!
IN THE END, ARTEMIS, YOUR NEW RACE SHALL MATTER NOT!
MAN BUILDS HIS WORLD THROUGH EMPIRE--AND EMPIRES ARE BORN OF MURDER AND DESTRUCTION--BORN OF WAR!
THUS WILL MAN'S HEART ULTIMATELY BELONG TO ARES!
AND EVEN ZEUS HIMSELF SHALL SOMEDAY BOW BEFORE MY POWER!
HA HA HA HA HA
ARES' WORDS--THEY ARE BLASPHEMOUS, ATHENA!
AYE, ARTEMIS. ARES' THREATS MAKE THE SITUATION EVEN MORE GRAVE!
HERMES, THOUGH ZEUS TURNS HIS BACK ON US, WE CANNOT TURN OUR BACKS ON HIM!
THEN WE PROCEED WITHOUT OUR LORD'S BLESSING?
"AYE, HERMES. NOW, AS AGREED, TRANSPORT US TO THE EARTH'S DARKEST QUARTER!
"FOR THERE--IN HADES--BY A SHORE SO OMINOUS THAT NO IMMORTALS HAVE DARED GO BEFORE, OUR COMPANIONS WAIT!"
ARTEMIS! ATHENA! HAVE YOU NEWS?
6

AYE, DEMETER--BUT NOT THAT FOR WHICH WE'D HOPED. YOUR BROTHER ZEUS OPPOSES US NOT--YET HE DEFENDS US NOT, EITHER.
AND MY NEPHEW ARES?
WHY EVEN ASK, DEMETER? MY FORMER HUSBAND IS AGAINST US. APHRODITE KNOWS HIM ONLY TOO WELL!
I AM PLEASED THAT YOU, TOO, DID COME, HESTIA. I KNOW YOU USUALLY AVOID THAT WHICH DIVIDES THE GODS.
AS ALWAYS, I BOW TO YOUR WISDOM, ATHENA.
MY COMPANIONS! DO YOU NOT FEEL THE AIR GROW CHILL?
CHARON, THE FERRYMAN COMES!
ONLY HE WHO FERRIES SOULS ACROSS THIS RIVER TO ETERNAL REST--
--OR TO ETERNAL DAMNATION--CAN GUIDE US TO OUR DESTINATION!
YET, FOR HIS SERVICES, HE ASKS A PRICE!
GIVE TO HIM A LOCK OF YOUR HAIR, APHRODITE.
FOR EVEN IN THE COLD DEPTHS OF HADES THE SPELL OF YOUR INCOMPARABLE BEAUTY WORKS ITS MAGIC!
WHERE DOES THE FERRYMAN TAKE US, ATHENA?
TO A PART OF HADES SO SACRED--
--EVEN CHARON, OLDER THAN THE STYX ITSELF, HAS NEVER MADE THIS JOURNEY. YET, HIS INSTINCTS GUIDE HIM AS IF IT WERE HIS HOME!
I--I KNOW THIS PLACE.
I HAVE NEVER BEEN HERE--YET, SOMEHOW, I KNOW IT!

AYE, APHRODITE. IT IS THE WELL OF REBIRTH--
--THE CAVERN OF SOULS!

IT IS, IN TRUTH, THE SOURCE FROM WHICH ALL LIFE ONCE SPRUNG!
IT IS THE WOMB OF GAEA-- MOTHER OF US ALL!
THOSE LIGHTS ARE SOULS OF WOMEN--
--THEIR LIVES CUT SHORT BY MAN'S FEAR AND IGNORANCE.

GAEA TOOK THEM UNDER HER CARE BEFORE SHE LEFT THIS PLANE.
NOW, THEY AWAIT REBIRTH!
THEIR NEW DESTINY BEGINS HERE! THEY HAVE WAILED IN LIMBO FOR CENTURIES-- SOON, THEY SHALL WAIL NO MORE!

SOON, THEY SHALL SING THE SONG OF LIFE!

ARTEMIS OPENS HER MOUTH...
8

...AND THE SKIES ABOVE FAIR GREECE YAWN WIDE...
...POURING THOUSANDS OF SOULS FROM GAEA'S WOMB!
IT IS DONE, GODDESSES. WE ARE ALL OF US MIDWIVES TO GAEA'S NEW OFFSPRING!
NOW LET US PRAY THAT THESE CHILDREN DO NOT FAIL US--FOR THE FATE OF MEN AND GODS RESTS IN THEIR HANDS!
ATHENA... DO NOT GO YET. LOOK!
ONE SOUL YET REMAINS IN DARK LIMBO. BUT IT WAILS NOT LIKE THE OTHERS!
AYE, APHRODI THAT ONE HA A SPECIAL DESTINY. BU HER TIME IS YET COME!
FOLLOW ME MIDWIVES. W HAVE MUCH STILL TO DO
EARTH... A ONCE TRANQUIL LAKE BUBBLES WITH THE SOFT BREATH OF CREATION...
...UNTIL ITS SURFACE BURSTS...
...AND SHE WHO IS CALLED HIPPOLYTE BECOMES THE FIRST TO RISE AND KISS APOLLO'S SUN DRENCHED SKIES
BESIDE HER, HER SISTER ANTIOPE IS REBORN.
AND AROUND HER THOUSANDS MORE RE-EMBODIE SOULS EMERGE-- EACH DRINKING JO FULLY THE BREATH OF NEW LIFE!

THE WATERS CHURN ANEW-- AND STILL MORE CHILDREN OF THE MIDWIVES ARE REBORN!
AMONG THEM IS MENALIPPE-- SHE WHOSE ONENESS WITH NATURE SHALL MAKE HER ORACLE OF THE GODS' NEW RACE.
AND AELLA-- WHOSE COURAGE SHALL BE AS THE HAWK'S--
--YET WHOSE HEART IS SO EASILY SWAYED.
BUT THEN, AS THE BLESSED LAKE'S WATERS GROW STILL--
DAUGHTERS! ATTEND ME!
-- A VISION... AND THE NEW-BORN ARE SUDDENLY HUSHED.
YOU ARE A CHOSEN RACE-- BORN TO LEAD HUMANITY IN THE WAYS OF VIRTUE --THE WAY OF GAEA! THROUGH YOU, ALL MEN SHALL KNOW US BETTER-- AND WORSHIP US ALWAYS!
THEREFORE DOES ATHENA GRANT YOU WISDOM, THAT YOU MAY BE GUIDED BY THE LIGHT OF TRUTH AND JUSTICE!
I, ARTEMIS, GRANT YOU SKILL IN THE HUNT! DEMETER SHALL MAKE YOUR FIELDS FRUITFUL!
HESTIA SHALL BUILD YOU A CITY AND WARM YOUR HEARTHS AND IT IS FAIR APHRODITE WHO GRANTS YOU THE GREAT GIFT OF LOVE!
FOREVERMORE, YOU SHALL FIND STRENGTH IN THESE GIFTS. THEY ARE YOUR MOST SACRED BIRTHRIGHT-- THEY ARE YOUR POWER!
"YOU, HIPPOLYTE, SHALL BE QUEEN OVER ALL MY DAUGHTERS!
"ANTIOPE, YOU SHALL RULE BY YOUR SISTER'S SIDE!
"SEE TO IT THAT THESE GIFTS WE GIVE ARE NEVER ABUSED!
"AND WEAR YOU BOTH THESE SYMBOLS OF OUR TRUST-- GAEA'S GIRDLE! NEVER LET IT BE REMOVED!
"NOW GO, MY DAUGHTERS! HENCEFORTH, YOU SHALL FORM A SACRED SISTERHOOD! HENCEFORTH, YOU SHALL BE AMAZONS!
"AND NONE MAY RESIST YOUR POWER!"
10

THE ECHOES OF ARTEMIS' WORDS FADE-- AND THE WINDS OF TIME CARRY THE YEARS AWAY. BUT UPON THE GALE RIDE THE VOICES OF POETS!

LISTEN! *FROM THEIR MOUTHS POUR* WONDROUS *TALES--TALES OF A CITY-STATE GOVERNED SOLELY BY* WOMEN*--OF A PLACE WHERE COMPASSION AND JUSTICE REIGN-- A PLACE THE POETS CALL* THEMYSCIRA! *IN THIS WAY, THE* POWER *AND THE* GLORY *OF THE AMAZONS IS SOON KNOWN* THROUGHOUT ALL GREECE!

YET, KINGS DO NOT LIKE *POPULARITY--NOR DO THEY LIKE* POWER*--UNLESS IT IS* THEIR OWN! *THUS THE RULERS OF* GREECE GROW JEALOUS *OF THE AMAZONS. AND SO THE POETS ARE SEIZED--AND BRIBED--AND THREATENED.*

NOW ARE TALES TOLD OF AMAZON ATROCITIES-- OF MURDERS, WARS *AND* THIEVERY! *NOW DO THE GODESSES* CRY *FROM OLYMPUS' HEIGHTS! FOR THEIR DAUGHTERS HAVE BECOME* OUTCASTS*--REGARDED BY ALL MANKIND AS* DIFFERENT...STRANGE...*AND EVEN* INHUMAN! *NOW, MANKIND* UNDERSTANDS *THE AMAZONS* NOT AT ALL. *AND THAT WHICH MAN DOES* NOT UNDERSTAND, *HE* FEARS!

MY DEAREST *HERACLES--* MUST YOU LEAVE SO *SOON?*

AFTER ALL, IT IS NOT *EVERYDAY* THAT I PLY MY TRADE WITH A *DEMI-GOD!*

MY DALLIANCE WITH *YOU* WAS BUT A *BRIEF RESPITE* FROM THE TASKS MY RULER *EURYSTHEUS* HAS SET ME. I MUST GO.

BUT IN TRUTH, I SHALL BE *GLAD* WHEN MY LABORS ARE DONE. *HERA* HAS SET A *MADNESS* UPON ME WHICH *BURNS MY SOUL*-- AND IT SHALL NOT COOL UNTIL I HAVE DONE *EURYSTHEUS'* WILL!

COME BACK TO BED, MY HERO. EURYSTHEUS CAN *WAIT--*

--AND *SO* CAN THE *AMAZON QUEEN* WHO CALLS YOU *"EURYSTHEUS' TRAINED DOG!"*

SILENCE, WENCH! HERACLES IS NO MAN'S *PET!*

OOOH! SEE HOW HE BARKS AND GROWLS! HIPPOLYTE WAS RIGHT...
...YOU'D LOOK SO HANDSOME ON A LEASH!
I SAID BE SILENT!
NO WOMAN--NOR MAN--CAN SAY SUCH A THING ABOUT HERACLES!
HUSH, MY LOVER-- BE CONTENT!
I MERELY REPEAT WHAT I'VE HEARD... WHAT EVERYONE HAS HEARD...
...FROM THE LIPS OF THE AMAZON QUEEN!
HERACLES, YOUR LEGIONS ARE ASSEMBLED.
THEN LET US RIDE, THESEUS!
NO LONGER DO I DESIRE TO PLEASE WOMEN...
...ONLY TO CONQUER THEM!
"EXCELLENT, MY DEAR, EXCELLENT! YOUR LIES HAVE STIRRED SUCH HATRED WITHIN HIM!
"IRONIC, IS IT NOT? ALMOST LAUGHABLE!
"WHILE HE BURNS WITH HERA'S MADNESS...
"YOUR SOUL BURNS AS MY SPIRIT CONSUMES YOU!
"BUT THEN... YOU HAVE SERVED YOUR PURPOSE."
ARES IS WELL PLEASED!
12

FOOLISH GODDESSES! DID THEY TRULY BELIEVE THAT THEIR AMAZONS COULD KEEP ME IN CHECK?

HERACLES SHALL DECIMATE THEIR RANKS! THEN, NOTHING SHALL STAND BETWEEN THE GOD OF WAR AND ULTIMATE POWER!

ALL I NEED DO... IS WAIT!

FOR HERE, ON THE HILL CALLE AREOPAGUS, NO ONE--NOT EVEN ZEUS--MAY TOUCH ME!
YET, FROM THIS VANTAGE, I MAY WATCH AS MAN'S LUST FOR WAR AND CARNAGE GROWS!
HEAR ME, ARTEMIS! YOUR FEEBLE AMAZONS SHALL NOT RALLY MEN AROUND THE GODS! MAN CRAVES WAR!
AND WITH EACH DROP OF BLOOD HE SPILLS, MAN FEEDS ME! STRENGTHENS ME! WORSHIPS ME!
SOON, MAN SHALL FORGET ALL OTHER GODS--AND ARES WILL RULE SUPREME!

IN TRUTH, HERACLES--NEVER HAVE I SEEN YOU IN GREATER AGONY!
THE CLOSER WE TRAVEL TO THE AMAZONS' CITY, THE HOTTER YOUR MADNESS BURNS!
REMIND ME NOT OF HERA'S CURSE, THESEUS!
I THINK ONLY OF THE HARLOT HIPPOLYTE--AND HER BRASH BOASTS!

FOR THERE AT LAST LIES THEMYSCIRA! SOON SHALL HIPPOLYTE'S AMAZONS KNOW THE PAIN OF UTTER DEFEAT!

YOU SEE, THESEUS? THEY HIDE IN THE TREES LIKE VIPERS!
I AM HERACLES OF THEBES! I DEMAND TO SEE YOUR QUEEN!
INTRUDERS! HALT AND BE RECOGNIZED!

"HIPPOLYTE KNOWS OF YOUR COMING, MIGHTY ONE.

"OUR QUEEN WOULD SPEAK WITH YOU IN YONDER CLEARING."

SO, MENALIPPE--THAT WHICH YOU FORETOLD HAS COME TO PASS! THE ARMY OF HERACLES AWAITS WITHOUT OUR WALLS.
AYE, ANTIOPE--AND I AM FILLED WITH DREAD THIS DAY!
NOT I, ORACLE.

I AM FILLED ONLY WITH LUST FOR REVENGE! MAN HAS HUNTED US FOR TOO LONG! I SAY WE KILL THIS LOT AS A WARNING TO ALL!
HUSH, AELLA... MURDER IS ARES' WAY, NOT OURS!

SO--YOU ARE HIPPOLYTE.
AND YOU ARE THE FABLED HERACLES.
14

MY ORACLE SAYS YOU COME TO WAR UPON US.
THAT WOULD BE FOOLISH. WHY NOT JOIN US INSTEAD, IN PEACE?
LONG HAVE THE AMAZONS DESIRED TO LEAD MANKIND TOWARD A BETTER WAY OF LIFE!
LEAD?!! YOU EXPECT MEN TO FOLLOW WOMEN? HERACLES IS YOUR BETTER, HARLOT QUEEN!
IN TRUTH, HERACLES, NO MORTAL IS YOUR EQUAL IN BRUTE STRENGTH.
YET, IN WISDOM AND THE ART OF BATTLE, I AM YOUR SUPERIOR!
THEN PROVE IT!
AS YOU WISH, MIGHTY ONE!
HEAR YOU THE LAUGHTER OF MY AMAZONS?
NOW I ASK YOU TO END THIS.
I HAVE NO WISH TO HARM YOU!
IT IS YOU WHO ARE IN DANGER OF HARM, HARLOT QUEEN!
I AM THE SON OF ZEUS HIMSELF.

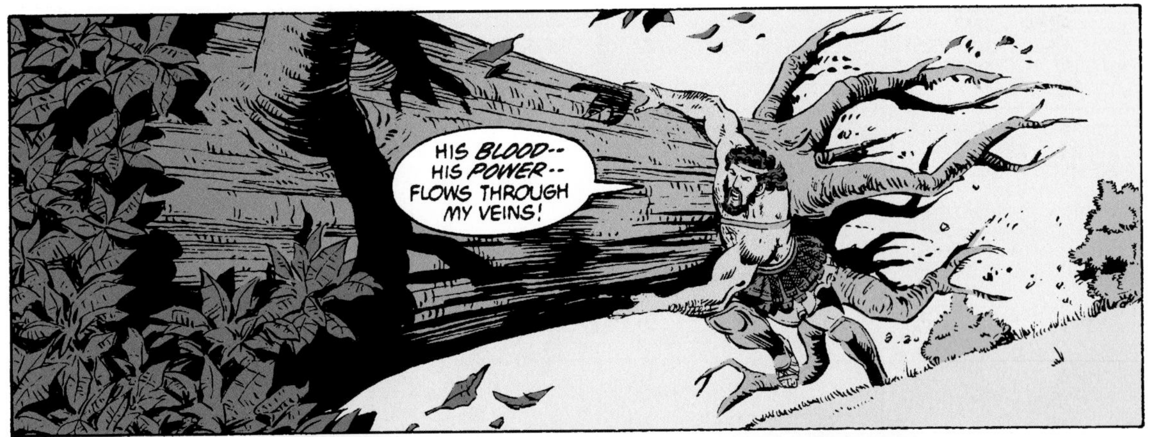
HIS BLOOD--
HIS POWER--
FLOWS THROUGH
MY VEINS!

AYE, HERACLES!
BUT YOUR MOTHER
WAS A MORTAL!
AND
MORTALS
MAKE
MISTAKES!

KRASH

SURRENDER OR DIE!
THE
CHOICE
IS
YOURS!

AND WITH HIPPOLYTE'S WORDS,
A STILLNESS FALLS OVER ALL--
AS WAR OR PEACE RESTS ON
HERACLES' REPLY.

HA! BY
ZEUS, GIRL--
HERACLES IS
IMPRESSED!
THE
AMAZONS
ARE WORTHY
ALLIES
INDEED!
MEN!
LAY BACK!
16

LAUGHTER -- THE UNIVERSAL LANGUAGE. HEALER OF DISCORD. MOTHER OF UNITY.
TONIGHT, ITS SONG DANCES BRIGHTLY BENEATH A FULL MOON...
...RISING MERRILY FROM THE LIPS OF MEN -- AND WOMEN.
THIS GATHERING IS HERACLES' IDEA -- A GESTURE OF GOOD WILL TOWARD THE WOMEN HE NOW CALLS FRIENDS!
YET, NOT ALL AMAZONS ARE CONTENT THIS NIGHT.
THESEUS AND ANTIOPE SEEM SO HAPPY!
BUT, I HAVE READ THE SIGNS. THEY FORETOLD DISASTER ON ON THIS DAY!
"HOW COULD I HAVE BEEN SO WRONG?"
HERACLES... I REJOICE UNTO MY VERY SOUL!
THIS IS HOW MEN AND WOMEN SHOULD FACE ONE ANOTHER -- NOT WITH SWORDS, BUT WITH LOVE, LAUGHTER, AND EQUALITY.
I SHOULD NEVER HAVE LISTENED TO MENALIPPE!
ORACLES SEE ONLY WHAT MIGHT BE. MORTALS CREATE THEIR OWN DESTINIES.
AND WHEN I GAZE UPON YOUR BEAUTY, FAIR HIPPOLYTE...
...I FEEL THAT MY DESTINY MUST BE EVERMORE AT YOUR SIDE!
HERACLES, I --
SPEAK NOT, MY QUEEN. DRINK WITH ME.
TO THE UNITY OF MAN AND WOMAN!
DRINK!
WHY... MY INCOMPARABLE HIPPOLYTE! DOES MY POTION DISPLEASE YOU?
ALLOW GALLANT HERACLES TO RELIEVE YOU...
...OF YOUR MISERY!

SEMI-CONSCIOUSNESS: IT IS LIKE A SEA OF TAR THROUGH WHICH HIPPOLYTE STRIVES TO SURFACE.
AND FROM SOMEWHERE BEYOND THE INKY BLACKNESS, SHE HEARS THE WOEFUL CRIES OF HER AMAZON SISTERS!
THEY WAIL AS HERACLES' MEN TAKE UP ARMS AGAINST THEM!
WAIL AS THEIR HOMES ARE TORCHED, THEIR BODIES RAVAGED, THEIR PRIDE STRIPPED AWAY!
AND FAINTLY, RISING ABOVE THE CHAOS AND BRUTALITY, IS ANOTHER SOUND...
...THE COLD AND DISTANT ECHO OF ARES' LAUGHTER!
I SEE YOU ARE FINALLY COMING TO YOUR SENSES, MY QUEEN!
GOOD!
HOW STUPID YOU HAVE BEEN! DID YOU TRULY BELIEVE I WOULD BE YOUR ALLY?
NO WOMAN IS HERACLES' EQUAL! AND NO WOMAN WITHHOLDS HERSELF FROM HERACLES' EMBRACE--EVEN IF SHE MUST BE READIED BY DRUG AND CHAIN!
NOW, I HAVE MADE YOU A REAL WOMAN!
THIS GIRDLE I TAKE AS A PRIZE--A SYMBOL OF MY CONQUEST!
HOW DEARLY I WOULD LIKE TO BREAK YOU FURTHER...TO SEE YOU BEG AND PLEAD!
ALAS, EURYSTHEUS' MADNESS LEADS ME ON! I LEAVE FOR TROY TONIGHT.
FAREWELL, AMAZON QUEEN! IT HAS BEEN MOST...AMUSING!
GODDESSES OF OLYMPUS! I BEG YOU--FORGIVE ME! I HAVE FAILED YOU!
18

NO, DAUGHTER...
...YOU HAVE BETRAYED ONLY YOURSELF.
EXAMINE YOURSELF, HIPPOLYTE-- EXAMINE YOUR RACE. ONCE, THE AMAZONS DREAMED OF LEADING MANKIND!
BUT YOU CHOSE TO WITHDRAW FROM HUMANITY-- TO IGNORE THE PURPOSE FOR WHICH YOU WERE CREATED-- AND YOU GREW BITTER AND CORRUPT.
HAVE YOU FORGOTTEN THE SOURCE OF YOUR POWER? HAVE YOU FORGOTTEN THE EXAMPLE YOU WERE TO SET?
PLEASE, ATHENA! FREE ME!
I YEARN TO TAKE REVENGE UPON THIS... HERACLES!
BLOODY VENGEANCE IS NOT THE ANSWER, DAUGHTER!
IT IS TIME FOR YOU TO CLEANSE YOUR SOUL-- TIME TO REDEDICATE YOURSELF TO THAT WHICH GAEA GAVE YOU! ONLY THEN SHALL YOU BE FREE!
"LOOK UPON MY FACE, HIPPOLYTE! SEE THERE THE TRUTH OF WHAT I SAY!
"THEN, AS I LEAVE YOU..."
EH?
"...BATHE IN THE LIGHT OF MY WISDOM!"
YOU! AMAZON! WHAT BLASPHEMOUS TRICKERY ARE YOU--
BY THE GODS!
GREETINGS, BROTHER.
THIS IS WHAT YOU DESIRE, IS IT NOT?
THEN YOU SHALL HAVE IT...
...BUT NOT AS YOU IMAGINED!
YOUR KIND SHALL IMPRISON MINE NO MORE!

NOW, SUDDENLY, HIPPOLYTE IS EVERYWHERE--SURPRISING HER CAPTORS--FREEING HER SISTERS--SOUNDING THE CALL TO ARMS! YET, WITH THAT CALL, SHE WHISPERS A CAUTION...
"AMAZONS, REMEMBER THE SOURCE OF OUR POWER--REMEMBER GAEA'S WAY!"
BUT THEY HEED THEIR QUEEN NOT!
FOR THEIR SOULS BOIL WITH RAGE--THEIR WEAPONS, LIKE THE FANGS OF MADDENED DOGS, DRINK DEEP OF THEIR ENEMIES--AND THE GROUND AT THEIR FEET IS SOON COVERED WITH CRIMSON!
AND LIKE SOME CRAZED, BLOODTHIRSTY BEAST, THE BATTLE GROWS OUT OF CONTROL!
THEN DOES HORROR SCREAM WITHIN HIPPOLYTE'S HEAD! FOR HER EYES ARE FILLED WITH SIGHTS OF BLASPHEMY--
--OF SISTERS WHO KILL WITH HEARTLESS PRECISION...
...OF ONE SISTER WHO KILLS...
...WITH EYES OF SPARKLING PLEASURE!
20

WHEN IT FINALLY ENDS -- WHEN THE SCREAMS OF THE ENEMY HAVE BEEN SILENCED --
-- THE VICTORY CRIES OF THE AMAZONS BUFFET HIPPOLYTE LIKE A COLD AND CALLOUS WIND.
WELL DONE, MY SISTERS! NOW LET US RIDE AFTER HERACLES! LET US SACK HIS HOME AND RECLAIM YOUR GIRDLE!
THEN, WE SHALL SLIT HIS ACCURSED THROAT FROM EAR TO EAR!
NO, ANTIOPE. NEVER VENGEANCE -- NEVER AGAIN!
ATHENA HAS SPOKEN TO ME. SHE WAITS FOR US BY THE SHORES OF THE AEGEAN.
ATHENA?!!
WHERE WAS SHE WHEN HERACLES MURDERED HALF MY SISTERS? WHERE WAS SHE WHEN MANKIND SHUNNED US, HOUNDED US -- HUNTED US?
RENOUNCE ATHENA, MY SISTER! AVENGE YOUR AMAZON DEAD!
THAT IS ARES' WAY, ANTIOPE. WE ACHIEVE NO GLORY BY EMBRACING THE DARK GOD'S POWER!
ARE YOU SO NAIVE, MENALIPPE? ARES IS NOT OUR ENEMY! WE NEED THE GOD OF WAR MERELY TO SURVIVE!
HIPPOLYTE, I GIVE YOU MY GIRDLE! FROM THIS DAY FORWARD, I TAKE NOTHING FROM OLYMPUS.
NO, ANTIOPE! I BEG YOU -- COME WITH US!
I CANNOT. MAY THE FATES BE WITH YOU, HIPPOLYTE!
I SHALL ALWAYS LOVE YOU!
THE HOOFBEAT OF ANTIOPE AND HER FOLLOWERS FADE INTO NOTHINGNESS...

...AND THEN, THE LONG WALK TO THE AEGEAN.
MY DAUGHTERS--YOU HAVE FAILED US! YOU HAVE FORGOTTEN THE SOURCE OF YOUR POWER--FORGOTTEN THE TRUST PLACED IN YOU!
FOR THESE FAILURES, YOU MUST DO A PENANCE! ONE IN WHICH THERE IS NEW HONOR--NEW RESPONSIBILITY! WE SHALL SEND YOU TO AN ISLAND--BENEATH WHICH LIES AN UNSPEAKABLE EVIL!
YOU SHALL BE THE JAILERS OF THAT EVIL FOR ALL ETERNITY!
AS LONG AS YOU REMAIN THERE AND SHIRK NOT YOUR NEW CHARGE--YOU SHALL LIVE AS IMMORTALS AND YOUR SOULS SHALL AGAIN BECOME PURE.
22
"YET, YOU MUST EVERMORE WEAR THE SYMBOLS OF YOUR FORMER BONDAGE--AS A REMINDER NEVER TO ERR AGAIN!"
GODDESS--WHERE IS THIS ISLAND?
"WHERE MAN MAY NOT EASILY DISCOVER IT. IT APPEARS A PARADISE! AND SO IT SHALL BE--AS LONG AS YOU GUARD ITS VILE SECRET WELL...
"...AND LET NO MORTAL MAN TRESPASS ITS GROUNDS!
BUT ATTEND YOU NOW!
POSEIDON CLEARS A PATH TO YOUR NEW HOME!"
FOR THIS AID, WE THANK YOU, GOD OF THE SEAS!
ARES DID MURDER MY OWN SON, DEMETER.
I AM GLAD TO HELP!
"BESIDES, THE ORACLES TELL ME THAT YOUR AMAZONS ARE MORE THAN THEY SEEM--THAT UPON ONE OF THEIR KIND RESTS NOT ONLY THE FUTURE OF THE GODS...
"...BUT OF ALL MANKIND!"

THE DAYS BRING FATIGUE, THE NIGHTS ARE BITTER COLD-- AND AT EVERY TURN, THE FOLLOWERS OF HIPPOLYTE FEAR THAT POSEIDON'S TUNNEL WILL SUDDENLY FALTER-- AND COME THUNDERING DOWN AROUND THEM! YET, THROUGHOUT THEIR THREE MONTHS' JOURNEY, THE WATERY PATHWAY HOLDS. AND AS THEIR FEET TOUCH THE SOIL OF PARADISE ISLAND, EACH AMAZON KNOWS THE GIFT OF IMMORTALITY! THEREBY ARE THEY REJUVENATED-- AND SET THEMSELVES, HEART AND SOUL, TO WORK...

...BUILDING...

...CLEARING...

...PLANNING...

...KEEPING THEIR ARTS AND HISTORY ALIVE...

...ERECTING GREAT HALLS OF JUSTICE...

...SCULPTING ICONS TO THE GLORY OF THE GODS!

THUS DO THE CENTURIES PASS AND UPON THE GROUNDS OF PARADISE, THE AMAZON NATION RENEWS ITS SENSE OF PURPOSE AND DISCIPLINE.
FOR THOUGH THE AMAZONS KNOW IMMORTALITY-- THOUGH THEY NEVER AGE OR HUNGER...

... STILL THERE ARE THOSE WHO FALL IN BATTLE! FOR THE EVIL SECRET WITHIN THE ISLAND IS NOT EASY TO CONTAIN!
AND THE BURDEN OF THE AMAZONS' RESPONSIBILITY IS HEAVY INDEED!

OUTSIDE, BEYOND THE SEAS, THE WORLD OF MAN CHANGES. GREAT CIVILIZATIONS RISE AND FALL.

BUT THE AMAZONS KNOW NOTHING OF THIS. THEY HEAR ONLY THE VOICES OF THE OLD GODS GROW MORE DISTANT --AS IF OLYMPUS ITSELF WERE BEING SWALLOWED IN THE CLOUDS!

UNTIL FINALLY, OF ALL WHO DID ONCE COMMUNE WITH THE GODS, ONLY MENALIPPE REMAINS ABLE.

THUS IT IS THAT ON THIS FATEFUL NIGHT, DURING THE 30TH CENTENNIAL OF PARADISE ISLAND, THE ORACLE OF THE AMAZONS DOES WHAT HER QUEEN REQUESTS...

MENALIPPE!

TELL ME--DO THE SIGNS SAY ANYTHING ABOUT THIS FEELING WITHIN ME?
WHAT IS THIS STRANGE YEARNING WHICH HOLDS ME SO?--THAT HAS HAD ME IN ITS GRIP LO THESE MANY MONTHS!
BE AT PEACE, HIPPOLYTE! YOU FEEL THE CALL OF A GREAT DESTINY!

KNOW THAT YOU--AND ALL ORIGINAL AMAZONS--ARE REINCARNATIONS! ALL OF US KNEW LIFE BEFORE THE MIDWIVES PLUCKED US FROM GAEA'S WOMB.
BUT ONLY YOU, MY QUEEN, WERE PREGNANT AT THE TIME OF YOUR DEATH! NOW, YOU HEAR THE CALL OF YOUR UNBORN DAUGHTER!

THIS YEARNING, THEN--IT IS A YEARNING--FOR MY CHILD!!?

"AYE! AND IF YOU WOULD SATISFY IT, FOLLOW ARTEMIS' BIDDING!
"GO AT SUNRISE TO THE SHORE--AND KNEEL THERE!

"THEN, FROM THE CLAY OF PARADISE, FORM YOU AN IMAGE!

"YOUR HEART SHALL RACE WITH ANTICIPATION--BUT STEADY YOURSELF...

"...AND SHAPE THE IMAGE WITH CARE!

"THEN OPEN YOURSELF TO FAIR ARTEMIS--THAT THE MID-WIFE OF ALL OLYMPUS MAY ENTER YOU!"
24

"AND WITH HER GUIDANCE, LET YOUR SPIRIT CRY OUT..."
"...UNTO THE WOMB OF GAEA!"
GODS OF OLYMPUS! IT IS TIME! NOW DOES THE LAST SOUL DEPART!
"I, DEMETER, GRANT HER POWER AND STRENGTH-- LIKE THAT OF THE EARTH IT-SELF!"
"I, APHRODITE, GIVE HER GREAT BEAUTY, AND A LOVING HEART!"
"I, ATHENA, GRANT HER WISDOM!"
"I, ARTEMIS, SHALL GIVE HER THE EYE OF THE HUNTER AND UNITY WITH THE BEASTS!"
"I, HESTIA, GRANT HER SISTERHOOD WITH FIRE--THAT IT MAY OPEN MENS HEARTS TO HER!"
"I, HERMES, GIVE HER SPEED AND THE POWER OF FLIGHT!"
"ALL THIS WILL BE HERS AS SHE GROWS TO WOMANHOOD!
"AND BLESSED, TOO, SHALL SHE BE WITH GREAT GAEA'S GIFT...
"LIFE!"
"THEN SHALL HIPPOLYTE HONOR HER WITH THE NAME OF A GREAT AND HOLY WARRIOR!
"SHE SHALL BE...
"...DIANA!"

DIANA! THE WORD SINGS FROM THE LIPS OF ALL AMAZONS. SHE IS THE ONLY CHILD THEY HAVE TOUCHED IN OVER 30 CENTURIES. AND HER INNOCENCE STIRS THE LOVE OF APHRODITE WITHIN THEM!
SO IT IS THAT THE INFANT PRINCESS KNOWS THE CARE OF A THOUSAND MOTHERS...
...AND THE TEACHINGS OF THE QUEEN'S MOST LEARNED SCHOLARS!
THEY READ HER THEIR HISTORY-- THAT SHE MIGHT BE ONE WITH THEM, HEART AND SOUL!
AND THE MORE SHE MATURES...
...THE MORE SHE EXCELS!
AS FOR HIPPOLYTE, HER HEART GLOWS AS DIANA GROWS MORE BEAUTIFUL DAILY. AND SHE GIVES THANKS IN HER PRAYERS FOR THIS MOST PRECIOUS OF ALL GIFTS: THIS CHILD-- THIS WOMAN--
THIS PRINCESS OF PARADISE!
BUT EVEN INTO PARADISE THERE CAN ONE DAY COME A SERPENT!
AIEEEEE!!
BY THE GODS, PHILIPPUS! THAT SCREAM!
IT CAME FROM THE ORACLE'S CHAMBER!
MENALIPPE! WHAT IS IT?
THE GODS... THEY CRY FROM OLYMPUS! THERE IS... DANGER!
THE QUEEN, PHILIPPUS...
...CALL THE QUEEN!
26

FOOTFALLS ECHO THROUGH THE PALACE. THEN, MENALIPPE TELLS HER TALE -- OF THE GODS CRYING OUT IN TERROR -- OF ARES GONE INSANE -- HIS MIGHT MULTIPLIED A THOUSAND-FOLD -- HIS BEING DRAWN MAGNET-LIKE TO SOME TERRIBLE POWER WITHIN MAN'S WORLD!
THIS "POWER," MENALIPPE -- WHAT IS ITS NATURE?
I KNOW NOT, MY QUEEN!

BUT WITH IT, ARES MAY CONSUME THE VERY EARTH ITSELF -- AND EVEN PARADISE SHALL NOT BE SPARED!
AND WHAT OF THE GODS?
CAN THEY NOT STOP MAD ARES?
NO, I -- I KNOW NOT WHY. BUT WE ARE COMMANDED TO CHOOSE A CHAMPION -- THE VERY BEST AMONG US! SHE SHALL PROVE HERSELF THROUGH TOURNAMENT AND THE TRIAL OF FLASHING THUNDER!
SHE ALONE CAN SAVE US AND SHE ALONE SHALL FACE ARES IN THE WORLD OF MAN!

IF THE GODS WILL IT, IT SHALL BE DONE! PROCLAIM IT THROUGHOUT PARADISE! THERE SHALL BE A TOURNAMENT ON THE 'MORROW!
AND THERE --
-- SHALL A CHAMPION B
BORN!

AYE. A CHAMPION. YET HOW CAN EVEN THE BEST OF US SUCCEED...
...WHERE THE GODS DARE NOT GO?

MOTHER, I -- FORGIVE ME. I OVERHEARD YOU BY YOUR LEAVE, I WISH TO BE INCLUDED IN THIS TOURNAMENT.
NO, DIANA! YOU ARE BUT A CHILD!

I AM AN AMAZON, MOTHER! I WEAR THE MARK, LIKE ALL MY SISTERS!
I HAVE NO INTENSION OF LOSING YOU, DAUGHTER -- EVER! THE ANSWER IS NO!
BUT...

SILENCE!
I AM YOUR QUEEN AS WELL AS YOU
MOTHER! AN
I HAVE SPOK

IT IS SO... UNFAIR! WAS I BORN ONLY TO BE CODDLED LIKE SOME ETERNAL INFANT?
AM I NOT AN AMAZON? AM I NOT A WOMAN?

OH, GODS OF OLYMPUS! THOUGH I LOVE PARADISE, I YEARN FOR MORE FROM MY LIFE...
...I YEARN FOR PURPOSE!

AYE, DIANA! AND PURPOSE YOU SHALL HAVE! THE TIME HAS COME!

MORNING:
OUR HERALDS DID SPREAD THE NEWS SWIFTLY, MY QUEEN! OUR TWO-HUNDRED FINEST WARRIORS HAVE ASSEMBLED...
...TO ACCEPT THE GODS' CHALLENGE! BUT, BY YOUR LEAVE, WHY HAVE YOU COMMANDED THEM TO COME MASKED?
FOR THREE THOUSAND YEARS, THESE AMAZONS HAVE LIVED AS SISTERS! NOW, I CALL UPON THEM TO COMPETE FIERCELY!
NO AMAZON SHALL HESITATE BECAUSE SHE VIES AGAINST A DEAR FRIEND-- OR BECAUSE SHE SYMPATHIZES WITH ANOTHER'S TURMOIL.
THE SALUTE IS GIVEN--
--THE GAMES BEGIN!
ALL THROUGH THE DAY, AMAZONS PROVE THEIR PROWESS IN CONTESTS OF SKILL AND STRATEGY!
EACH KNOWS THE SERIOUSNESS OF THIS TOURNAMENT...
...AND EACH PERFORMS AS ONLY AN ATHLETE OF THREE-THOUSAND YEARS' EXPERIENCE CAN!
BUT ONE THRILLS MORE THAN THE OTHERS. SHE IS KEENEST OF EYE, MOST FLEET OF FOOT..
...AND HER MIGHT IS BEYOND COMPARE!
28

ON THE FINAL DAY THIS AMAZON HAS INDEED BESTED ALL-- AND HER SISTERS ROAR THEIR APPROVAL!
SISTER, YOU HAVE PROVEN YOURSELF CHAMPION THIS DAY. NOW, IF THE GODS BE PLEASED, YOU SHALL PASS THE FINAL TEST-- THAT OF THE FLASHING THUNDER!
I AWARD YOU NOW THESE SILVER BRACELETS!
"BY THEM, ALL SHALL KNOW YOU AS THE MOST WORTHY AMONG US!
"NOW LET US SEE YOUR FACE..."
...THAT WE, AND THE GODS, MIGHT SMILE UPON IT!
GREAT HERA!
IT CANNOT BE!
I'M SORRY, MOTHER-- BUT ATHENA HERSELF SPOKE TO ME AS I SAT BY HER STATUE!
I KNOW THAT WHAT I DO IS RIGHT!
DIANA?!!
NO! I FORBID THIS!
HUSH, MY QUEEN! YOU MUSTN'T!
THE PRINCESS WON HER PLACE RIGHTFULLY. YOU CANNOT FIGHT THE WILL OF THE GODS!
29

NIGHT AT THE TEMPLE OF HADES:
THIS PLACE--IT CHILLS ME, MENALIPPE! WHY HAVE WE COME HERE ?
PRINCESS, IF YOU ARE TRULY THE CHAMPION THAT THE GODS WOULD HAVE...
...THEN IT IS HERE YOU MUST FACE THE FLASHING THUNDER!
OF ALL AMAZONS WHO HAVE SEEN IT, ONLY THOSE BEFORE YOU STILL LIVE! FOR THE FLASHING THUNDER IS A SECRET AND TERRIBLE PART OF OUR PAST. IT IS A GREAT POWER WHICH CAN DESTROY WITH BUT A SINGLE CLAP!
KNOWING THIS, DO YOU STILL DESIRE TO FACE IT?
I AM NOT AFRAID, MENALIPPE!
SO BE IT! PHILIPPUS! ARE YOU READY?
AYE, ORACLE.
THOUGH WE HAVE NOT SEEN THIS ABOMINATION SINCE THE TRAGEDY...
...I BELIEVE I REMEMBER HOW TO DO IT!
I POINT IT LIKE THIS... AND SQUEEZE!
MY PRINCESS! PREPARE YOURSELF--FOR I SHALL NOT MISS!
DIANA, NO!
MOTHER--I DO LOVE YOU--AND MAY THE GODS EVER PROTECT YOU!
PHILIPPUS! I AM READY!
30

GREAT HERA!
BY THE GODS! WHAT IS THAT THING? WHERE DID IT COME FROM?
THIS IS NO TIME FOR TALES OF HORROR, MY DAUGHTER!
YOU ARE ALIVE! THAT IS ALL THAT MATTERS!
BUT MOTHER, I--
HUSH! KNOW THAT THE GODS ARE WITH YOU...
...AS AM I!
NOW IS THE PLAN OF THE GODDESSES CLEAR, DIANA! YOU WERE BORN INTO THIS WORLD TO BE THE MOST HONORED AMONG ALL AMAZONS! HENCE-FORTH, YOUR WARRIOR'S GARB SHALL PROCLAIM YOUR HONOR!
LOOK NOW UPON THE STANDARD FROM WHICH WE SHALL WEAVE THAT GARB...
...THE STANDARD OF THE WARRIOR FOR WHOM YOU WERE NAMED...
...SHE WHO DIED NOBLY THAT THE AMAZON RACE MIGHT LIVE!
"AMAZONS! HEAR YOUR QUEEN! EVEN AS APOLLO'S SUN GIVES BIRTH TO THIS GLORIOUS DAY, I HAVE GATHERED YOU HERE...
"...TO WITNESS A BIRTH OF ANOTHER KIND!
"THE CHAMPION HAS BEEN CHOSEN...
..."THE GODS HAVE BEEN SATISFIED!"
31

THERE IS A MOMENT OF SILENCE. THEN, DIANA RAISES HER BRACELETS... AND SMILES.
FROM A THOUSAND AMAZON THROATS, A MIGHTY CHEER RISES TO THE HEAVENS!
AND ON A MOUNTAIN CALLED OLYMPUS, FIVE GODDESSES KNOW JOY!
ONLY HIPPOLYTE SMILES NOT--FOR HER THOUGHTS ARE OF ARES--AND OF THE WORDS SHE SPOKE JUST DAYS BEFORE...
"HOW CAN EVEN THE BEST OF US SUCCEED... WHERE THE GODS DARE NOT GO?"
AND SO THE QUEEN PULLS HER CLOAK AROUND HER... AND SHIVERS 'NEATH APOLLO'S SUN!

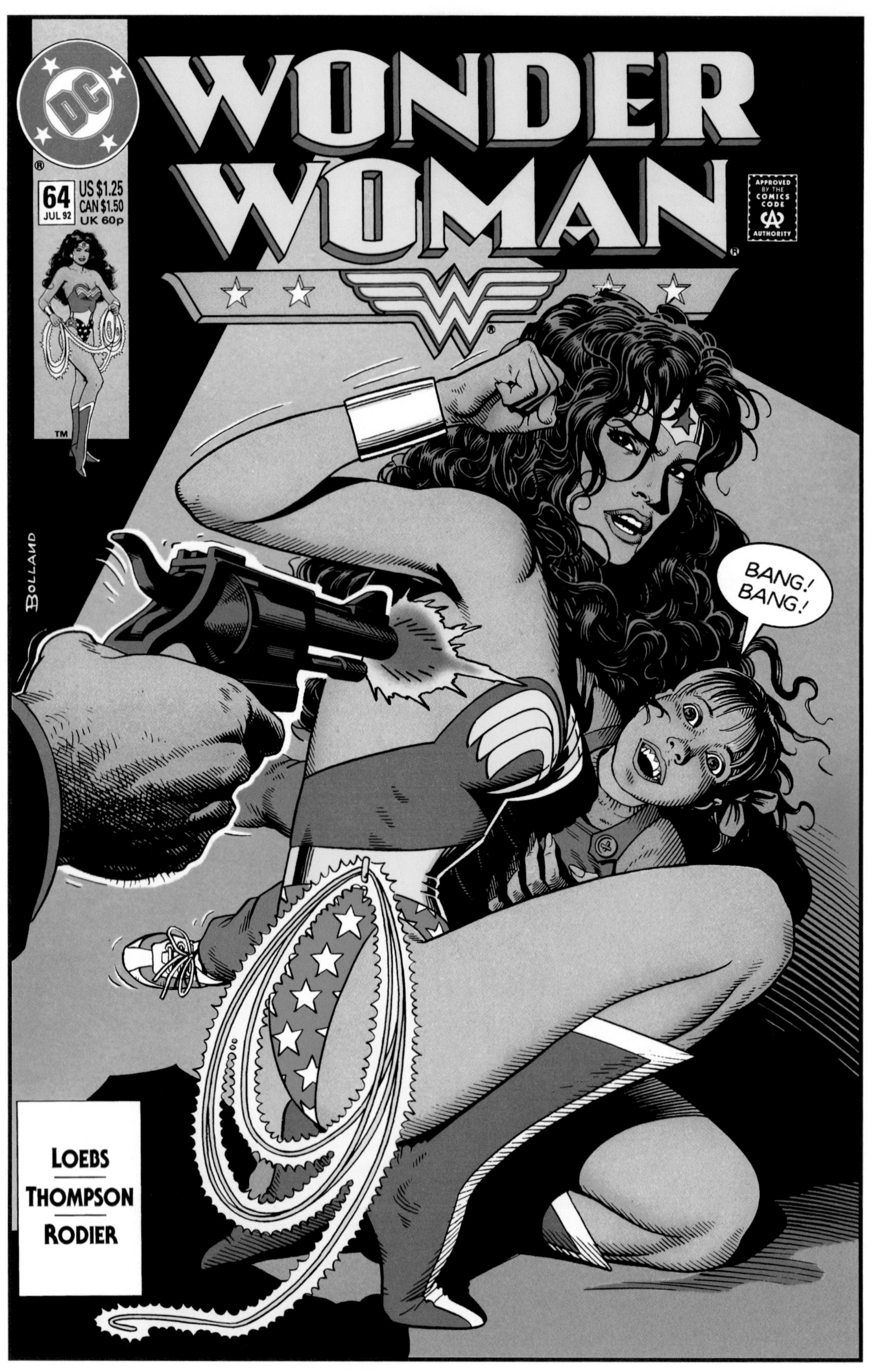
DC
WONDER WOMAN
64 JUL 92 US $1.25 CAN $1.50 UK 60p
APPROVED BY THE COMICS CODE AUTHORITY
BOLLAND
BANG! BANG!
LOEBS
THOMPSON
RODIER

I HOPE I'M NOT TOO LATE!
YOU ARE A LUCKY MAN, INDELICATO. VERY LUCKY.
EXTREMELY LUCKY.
The HEART of the CITY
BILL MESSNER-LOEBS--
Lovelier than Aphrodite
JILL THOMPSON--
Wiser than Athena
DENIS RODIER--
Swifter than Hermes
JOHN COSTANZA--
Brighter than Apollo
NANSI HOOLAHAN--
Stronger than Heracles
DAN THORSLAND--
One of the many secret faces of Ares
WONDER WOMAN
Created By William Moulton Marston

YOU SHOULD BE UP ON DEPARTMENTAL CHARGES. YOU INTERFERED WITH THE ARREST OF THIS WONDER WOMAN...
...ASSAULTED A FELLOW OFFICER...

YOU COULD BE LOOKING AT HARD TIME!
YES, SIR, I...
I'M NOT FINISHED YET, DETECTIVE!

HOWEVER, MR. SMITHERS FROM INTERNAL AFFAIRS HAS REQUESTED WE OFFICIALLY IGNORE AS MUCH AS WE CAN ABOUT THE RECENT PAST.
FRANKLY, THE MYSTICAL ELEMENTS OF THE UM... EVENTS IN QUESTION WOULD MAKE PROSECUTION A NIGHTMARE.

SO, ENNYWAY, HERE'S Y'R BADGE.

MY BADGE? REALLY, CAPTAIN? I'M A COP AGAIN? OH, JOY! DOES THIS MEAN I GET TO STAND IN THE RAIN FOR HOURS WHILE BUMS VOMIT ON MY SHOES?
AND I C'N DRINK COLD COFFEE AND SPEND HALF MY LIFE DOING PAPER-WORK? AND I GET TO HAVE PEOPLE SHOOT AT ME?

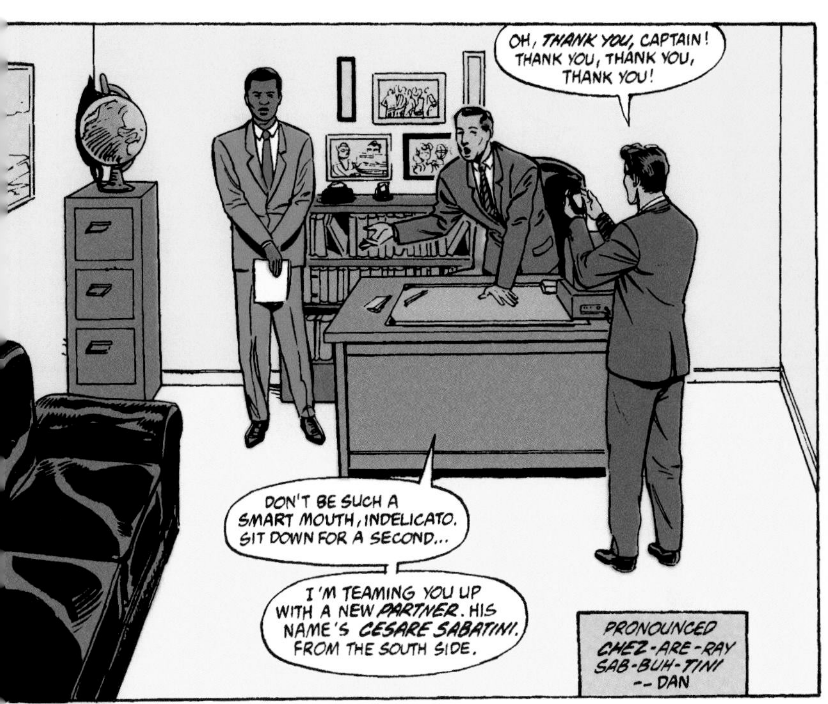
OH, THANK YOU, CAPTAIN! THANK YOU, THANK YOU, THANK YOU!
DON'T BE SUCH A SMART MOUTH, INDELICATO. SIT DOWN FOR A SECOND...
I'M TEAMING YOU UP WITH A NEW PARTNER. HIS NAME'S CESARE SABATINI. FROM THE SOUTH SIDE.
PRONOUNCED CHEZ-ARE-RAY SAB-BUH-TINI --DAN

CESARE, HUH? GOOD OLD ITALIAN NAME. AND FROM THE SOUTH SIDE...
HOPE HE'S NOT TOO MUCH OF A HARD CASE. I DON'T MIND 'EM TOUGH, BUT...

HI. I'M CHES. YOU MUST BE ED. WHAT'S YOUR SIGN?
!
HA HA! THAT WAS A JOKE! SO I GUESS WE'RE GOING TO BE BREATHING EACH OTHER'S AIR FOR A WHILE, HUH?

UH, CAPTAIN? I THINK THEY SHOULD BE ALONE...?
GOOD IDEA.
UM...
I HOPE THAT SUIT'S NOT WOOL. BEING EVEN THIS CLOSE TO WOOL MAKES ME BREAK OUT.
BUT I LOVE THE CUT. THE SHAPELESS LOOK IS IN.
CAPTAIN, WE HAVE TO TALK...!
WHY DON'T YOU GUYS GO HAVE LUNCH ON THE DEPARTMENT... GET TO KNOW EACH OTHER?
CAPTAIN...?
LATER, INDELICATO!

SO, DO YOU THINK THIS LUNCH SHOULD GO UNDER "GIFTS" OR "INCOME"?
IF IT'S 'INCOME' THEN... IT'S HER!
HER WHO?
AND YOU WANT THIS MADE OUT TO "KEN, WITH ALL MY LOVE, DIANA"?
ARE YOU REALLY REALLY A PRINCESS?

HER HER!
WO-WO-WONDER W-W-W-HER!

YES, I'M A PRINCESS. REALLY.
BUT, DO YOU GET TO EXECUTE PEOPLE?
FUND RAISERS
Chocolate Bars

HEY, IT'S DIANA! HEY, DIANA!
INSPECTOR INDELICATO! I CAME FOR YOUR HEARING! AM I LATE?
NAH, IT GOT CALLED ON ACCOUNT O' SANITY! LEMME TAKE YOU OUT T' LUNCH INSTEAD!

SHE...SHE'S GOING W-W-
YEAH. THAT OKAY WITH YOU?
PRINCESS DIANA... THIS IS CHES SABATINI... HE'S MY NEW PARTNER.

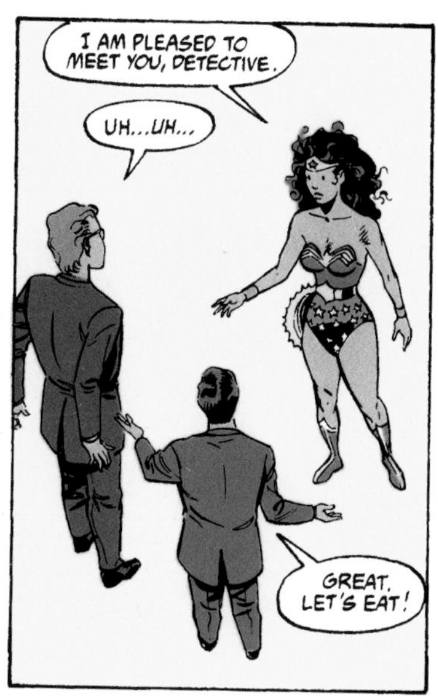
I AM PLEASED TO MEET YOU, DETECTIVE.
UH...UH...
GREAT. LET'S EAT!

WE DON'T HAVE MUCH TIME...OR MONEY...
HEY, I KNOW! THAT GUY HAS THE BEST HOTDOGS IN BOSTON!
MR. RED HOT'S

I'LL BET YOU NEVER HAD AN AUTHENTIC RED HOT!
WHY, NO.

YOU KNOW, UMM, PRINCESS WONDER, I READ ABOUT YOUR ADVENTURES EVERY MONTH...
THAT'S NICE, BUT ACTUALLY THAT'S NOT MY LI...
WHIIIIINNE

DID SHE EVER SHOW YOU THIS PURPLE RAY THING, EDDIE? IT'S GREAT STUFF!
YOU SEE, THEY JUST MAKE UP THOSE STORIES. AT FIRST IT WAS A PUBLICITY GIMMICK, BUT THEN...
Wonder Woman

...AND THAT EGG FOO! I LOVE THAT GUY!
OH, WELL...
MNCH
Wonder Woman

SO, ANYWAY, EDDIE... DID I MENTION MY MOM DRESSED ME LIKE A GIRL TILL I WAS 13?
WHAT?
Wonder Woman

IT WASN'T SO BAD, BUT IT SURE GIVES YOU A DIFFERENT PERSPECTIVE ON THINGS, Y'KNOW?
URRRK
NOT REALLY...
YAP!
Wonder Woman

I GUESS THERE COULD'VE BEEN WORSE THINGS THAN BEING KICKED OFF THE FORCE!
FAUGH... I CAN STILL TASTE THE CHEMICALS!
Wonder Woman

SO, YOU'VE BEEN FULLY REINSTATED? YOU WERE SO BRAVE TO HELP ME! I'D HATE TO THINK YOU WERE PUNISHED FOR IT!
I'M HERE TO SERVE, PRINCESS. BESIDES...
ARE YOU POLICEMEN? YOU'VE GOT TO HELP ME!

MY HUSBAND JUST STOLE MY LITTLE GIRL!
YOU'VE GOT TO FIND HIM!
OH... UMM... WELL, MA'AM, WE DON'T HANDLE... DOMESTIC DISPUTES.
HE STOLE YOUR DAUGHTER?
UHH... YES, AND BESIDES, SHE PROBABLY HASN'T BEEN GONE 48 HOURS...

BUT WE HAVE TO HELP HER!
HEY, PARTNER! WAIT UP!
SEND HER IN TO THE DESK, DIANA. THEY'LL ROUTE 'ER THROUGH!
CAN'T YOU HELP ME? YOU ARE WONDER WOMAN, AREN'T YOU?
YES, AND I'LL DO ANYTHING I CAN...

THANK YOU. JOHN, MY HUSBAND, IS A GOOD MAN. HE'S GOT A RESPONSIBLE JOB AT HIS BANK...
BUT LATELY HE'S BEEN SHORT-TEMPERED... FIGHTING WITH EVERY-ONE...WITH ME.
WE GOT A TRIAL SEPARATION YESTERDAY... WHEN I GOT TO THE DAY CARE CENTER, HE'D ALREADY PICKED HER UP. HE TOLD THEM HE WAS GOING OUT OF TOWN...!

DIANA'S A SWEET KID, BUT...
... SHE DOESN'T UNDERSTAND HOW TOUGH WE HAVE TO BE ON THE STREETS. RIGHT, EDDIE?
INSPECTOR! COME ON!

WE'RE GETTING NOISE OUT OF THE FERGUSSON BUG!
THE DRUG RUNNER... YOU FINALLY MANAGED TO PLANT A WIRE IN THE ROOM?

"THERE'S SOME JOKER FROM A BANK THERE TOO. MIGHT HAVE A MONEY LAUNDERING CHARGE ON TOP OF IT ALL..."
THIS IS MY LAST PICK-UP, GUYS. I'M FADING FROM THIS SCENE. I OWE TOO MANY PEOPLE MONEY 'ROUND HERE.
MUH GUN IS THE ONLY LAW YEW'LL EVER SEE, YA POLECATS!
MONEY'S A BAD THING, MAN... NOT! HA HA!
THIS MONEY WE GOT FROM A PRIVATE SOURCE... AND AFTER TONIGHT, WE'LL HAVE A LOT MORE.

BANG-BANG, DADDY!
TAKE THAT! Y'MANGY...

REMEMBER, WASTE 'EM ALL! NO WITNESSES!
I HEARD THAT!
CA-CHUKA
THOOM THOOM THOOM
THOOM
BAM

JANEY! LOOK OUT!
BANG! BANG! OH!

KA-BLAMM KA-BLAMM AHHHH!

CA-CHUKA THOOM
CA-CHUKA THOOM

CA-CHUKA THOOM AIIEEE!
IT'S GONE SOUR!

WOO WOO WOO WOO WOO
SIRENS! IT'S THE COPS, MAN! WHAT ABOUT THE BREAD!?
FORGET IT! SIMPSON AIN'T PAYIN' ENOUGH T' BURN FOR!

A PASSING FIRE TRUCK SPOOKED THEM! LET'S GET OVER THERE!

UHHH!

THE MONEY! THEY FORGOT THE MONEY! AND EVERYBODY ELSE IS DEAD!

MAYBE THIS IS OUR BIG CHANCE, JANEY...

ED! CHESTER...? WHAT IS IT? HAS SOMETHING HAPPENED?
EVERYTHING'S HAPPENED, PRINCESS, AND UNLESS I MISS MY GUESS, THE CITY'LL SOON BE ON FIRE!

THEN I HAD BETTER FIND THAT LITTLE GIRL SOON!
GO FOR IT, DIANA!

WHERE TO, FIRST?
FIRST WE HAVE TO GET TO THE SCENE AND SEE WHAT HAPPENED.

SOMETIMES I THINK ED LIKES SAYING THINGS LIKE "THE CITY WILL SOON BE ON FIRE" EVEN MORE THAN HE LIKES SOLVING CRIMES.
TO TRACK THIS MAN, TIM JANCOSKY, I MUST FIRST KNOW HIM--

"--MUCH AS A HUNTER KNOWS ITS PREY."
BUS
DRINK more CO

GILLESPIE...? WHAT ARE YOU...?
MR. SIMPSON SENT US OUT TO WATCH WAYS OUT OF THE CITY.

AND, WHAT A SURPRISE... I FIND *YOU* HITTIN' THE *HIGH ROAD!*
LOOK, I... OH, WHAT THE HELL. YOU'RE JUST GONNA KILL ME, NO MATTER *WHAT* I SAY, RIGHT?

WRONG!
SMAK

DAD'Y... BANG-BANG...?
IT IS NOW, SWEETIE.

BUS
DRINK more CO

"THEY'LL BE WATCHING THE AIRPORTS AND TRAIN STATIONS TOO. GOTTA FIND SOMEPLACE SAFE..."
SO NOW WE GOT A ROOM FULL OF DEAD GUYS AND A TRAIL OF BLOOD, INSPECTOR.
DO YOU THINK THE GUY WHO WALKED AWAY IS THE SAME TIM JANCOSKY WONDER WOMAN IS LOOKING FOR... THE ONE WITH THE KID?
THAT'S THE WAY I'M BETTING. WHICH IS ONE MORE REASON TO FIND HIM QUICK.
DEVON APT.
1300

SHE DOESN'T KNOW THAT HE'S GOT A SATCHEL FULL OF DIRTY MONEY, AND HALF THE WISEGUYS IN BOSTON ARE AFTER HIM.
SHE BELIEVES IN MERCY AND HOPE. SHE DOESN'T KNOW THOSE THINGS DON'T APPLY IN THE HEART OF THE CITY.

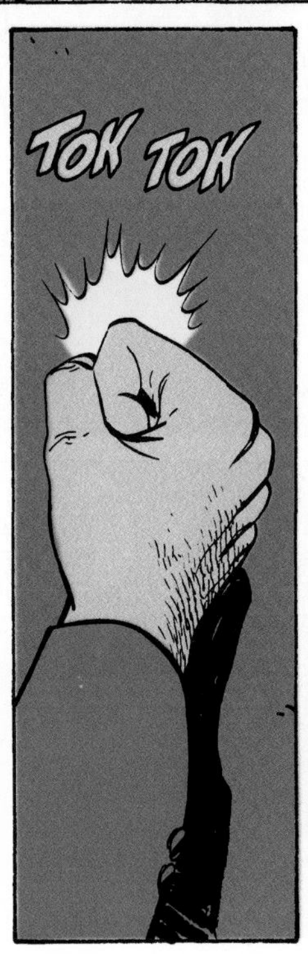
TOK TOK

YES?
POLICE, SIR. ARE YOU THE ARNOLD NEAL WHO'S MANAGER OF THE FIRST NATIONAL BANK...?

SURE YOU ARE.
LOOK, MR. NEAL, I'M TRYING TO FIND ONE OF YOUR EMPLOYEES, TIM JANCOSKY. I THINK THE MOB MAY BE AFTER HIM, AND YOU KNOW WHY!
WHAT CAN THE SEAMY PROBLEMS OF AN ASSISTANT MANAGER HAVE TO DO WITH ME? IF HE'S GOTTEN MIXED UP WITH DRUGS OR SOMETHING...

DO I LOOK LIKE I TAKE STUPID PILLS?
WE KNOW YOUR BANK HAS BEEN LAUNDERING DRUG MONEY. WAS JANCOSKY THE BAG MAN... THE ONE WHO COLLECTED FROM THE BENT NOSE BRIGADE?

WE... THE BANK... MADE INJUDICIOUS INVESTMENTS DURING THE EIGHTIES. WE HAD TO GET LIQUID ASSETS FROM SOMEWHERE...
TIM... KEPT TRACK OF... CERTAIN FUNDS FROM... DONALD SIMPSON AND HIS ASSOCIATES.

WE DIDN'T HAVE A CHOICE! THERE WAS SO MUCH MONEY, AND WE JUST NEEDED IT FOR A WHILE...

DONALD SIMPSON...?
GREAT. THE KID COULDN'T JUST TAKE MONEY FROM ANY MOBSTER. WE BETTER FIND HIM QUICK.

CLICK

HELLO, MR SIMPSON ARNOLD NEAL HERE...

"I THINK I'VE DISCOVERED WHO TOOK YOUR MONEY..!"
THEN YOU AND YOUR WIFE WERE FOSTER PARENTS TO TIM JANCOSKY, MR. ASTOR?

ME AN' ABOUT A HUNNERT OTHERS. THE KID WAS NO GOOD. ALWAYS RUNNIN' OFF, BREAKIN' THINGS. ROTTEN FROM THE TIME HE WAS FOUR OR FIVE.

THAT'S WHY I GOT OUTTA THE FOSTER BUSINESS AFTER ANNIE DIED. MOST OF THESE KIDS TODAY ARE LIKE ANIMALS...
THEY'RE BORN CRIMINALS.

AN' THE STATE WON'T LET YOU PROTECT YOURSELF FROM THEM NEITHER. ALL I WANTED TO DO WAS GIVE 'EM A LITTLE PRIVACY AN'...
SYLVIA IS good help me Be good

THE CLOSET? YOU WOULD LOCK THOSE CHILDREN IN THE CLOSET?

HEY, LADY, DON'T TAKE A TONE WITH ME!
I WASN'T THE ONE SPOILIN' THOSE KIDS. ANNIE'S SISTER, SYLVIA, WOULD ALWAYS PROTECT HIM, KEEP HIM FROM BEIN' A MAN!
NO WONDER HE'S IN TROUBLE, WITH THE COPS, TH' MOB AN' YOU LOOKIN' FOR HIM!

HE IS IN TROUBLE, WITH THE POLICE AND THE UNDER-WORLD?

"SURE, I GOTTA POLICE-BAND, SEE? LEMME FILL YOU IN ON LITTLE TIMMY..."
LOOK, I DON'T KNOW ANYTHING ABOUT THIS TIM.
STICK MEN
YOUR NAME WAS IN HIS ROLODEX. I THINK HE USED YOU TO SET UP MEETS FOR HIM WITH SIMPSON'S BOYS.

NAHH. HE DID ALL THAT THROUGH THE BANK. WE WERE JUST FRIENDS. WE WERE RAISED IN THE SAME FOSTER...

BUDDABUDDABUDDABUDDABUDDA
SSCREEEEEEEEE

THEY'RE SHOOTING AT US! THEY'RE SHOOTING AT US!
PANG
TING
KTANG
I KNOW! I KNOW! I'M HERE!

"I THINK THEY'RE COMING BACK!"
IT WAS GOOD OF YOU TO SEE ME, MRS. HORTON.
TIM WAS ALWAYS SPECIAL TO ME. I TRIED MY BEST TO SAVE HIM FROM MY SISTER AND THAT DREADFUL HUSBAND OF HERS.

I AM LOOKING FOR A PLACE THAT MIGHT BE SPECIAL TO HIM... A PLACE HE WOULD GO IN TIME OF TROUBLE.
HAVE A COOKIE... I WISH TIM CAME HERE MORE OFTEN.

PERHAPS MY OLD APARTMENT ON WILFRED STREET. THE NEIGHBORHOOD'S GONE TO HELL, BUT HE USED TO LOVE IT THERE.

HERE, LET ME SHOW YOU SOMETHING.

HE GAVE THIS TO ME A COUPLE OF YEARS AGO. IT'S ALL HIS PAPERS, HIS AWARDS...
math 1st PLACE
W-NNER

IT MEANS I WON, DOESN'T IT? HE LOVED ME, AND HE DID NOT LOVE THEM!
"WON"?

NO WONDER HE STOPPED VISITING HER. I BELIEVE HER LOVE CAME AT A *PRICE*.
AND YET SHE DID THE BEST SHE COULD.

JEEZ, THOSE GUYS WERE TRYIN' TO *WHACK* ME.
YEAH, WELL, THEY'RE *THUGS*. IT GOES WITH THE *JOB DESCRIPTION*.
ODDS ARE THEY WANT TO KEEP YOU QUIET, IN HOPES THAT THEY FIND JANCOSKY BEFORE *WE* DO...

BUT I ALREADY *TOLD* THEM WHERE HE IS. TIM WANTED ME TO DELIVER A COUPLE OF TICKETS TO *RIO* TO AN OLD APARTMENT HOUSE ON WILFRED. MEBBE THEY DIDN'T BELIEVE ME...
YOU *TOLD* THEM?
WE BETTER GET OVER THERE *FAST!*

POOR SCHMUCK. I HOPE WE BEAT THE WISE GUYS HERE.

IT LOOKS LIKE NOBODY'S LIVED HERE FOR YEARS.
MAYBE WE BEAT JANCOSKY.

OR EVERYBODY'S IN THERE ALREADY... WITH GUNS OUT AND ITCHING.
DID I MENTION I HAVE A LITTLE PROBLEM WITH *STRESS*, INSPECTOR?

IS THERE *ANYTHING* YOU *DON'T* HAVE A... DAMN.
SCREEE
DUCK.

BUDDABUDDABUDDA

CRASH
POW POW POW POW
CALL FOR *BACK UP* AND FOLLOW ME IN!

GUNFIRE. I'M NOT... SAFE... HERE...
BANG-BANG! BANG-BANG!
KRAAW
BANG
KPING
BLAM
BLAM
BLAM

LEG HURTS SO BAD... IF ONLY I C'D REST FOR A SEC...

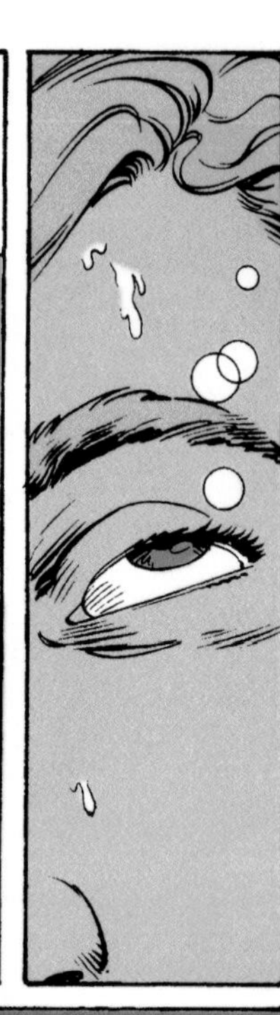

DAD'Y?

DAD'Y HURTS?

OOOH. BANG-BANG!

TAKE THE DOWNSTAIRS. WE GOTTA SWEEP THIS PLACE IN A HURRY!
RIGHT, CHIEF!

NO TELLING HOW MANY PRIVATE SHOOTERS ARE INVOLVED NOW.

THIS IS THE *HEART* OF THE CITY...

WHERE ONLY THE *STRONG* SURVIVE! WHERE THERE'S NO ROOM FOR *MERCY* OR *FEAR*...
WHERE THE *SLIGHTEST* HESITATION IS THE DIFFERENCE BETWEEN *LIFE* AND *DEATH*...

THERE'S *BLOOD* ON THAT DOOR...

"SOMEHOW, THE HITTERS GOT HERE AHEAD OF ME..."

BANG-BANG!
NO...!

NO... THEY'RE WAITING... IT'S AN AMBUSH!

BLAM

SKRRATTCRASS

CLICK
CLICK
CLICK
CLICK
CHTINNG

OH GOD
OH GOD
OH GOD...
IN THE HEART OF THE CITY, THERE'S NO TIME FOR MERCY, NO ROOM FOR HOPE... BUT SOMETIMES, IF YOU'RE LUCKY, YOU GET THEM ANYWAY...

DC
WONDER
WOMEN
93
JAN 95
$1.50 US
$2.10 CAN
70p UK
LOEBS
DEODATO
APPROVED BY THE COMICS CODE AUTHORITY
MIKE DEODATO JR.
DC
UNIVERSE

"Most great beginnings are, in their own way, violent, creating, as they do, a powerful change. Seen in a certain light, birth is violent. But, we must ask, violence to what end?" LONDRA CHAPPEL RANDOLPH, REFLECTIONS
THESE SANDALS WERE LEFT TO US BY THE LORD HERMES HIMSELF. THEY WILL ENABLE YOU TO FLY AGAINST EVIL. THESE BRACELETS ARE THE GAUNTLET OF ATLAS. THEY WILL GIVE YOU THE STRENGTH OF TEN!
WILLIAM MESSNER-LOEBS WRITER MIKE DEODATO, JR. ARTIST JOHN COSTANZA LETTERER
VIOLENT BEGINNINGS
PATRICIA MULVIHILL COLORIST JASON HERNANDEZ-ROSENBLATT ASSISTANT EDITOR PAUL KUPPERBERG EDITOR
WONDER WOMAN created by WILLIAM MOULTON MARSTON
HERMES? A GOD LEFT YOU HIS SANDALS? AMAZING. I'VE NEVER HEARD THAT STORY.
NEITHER HAVE I.
ARTEMIS, NOW THAT YOU HAVE PROVEN YOURSELF WORTHY TO CARRY OUR MESSAGE OF PEACE AND LOVE INTO PATRIARCH'S WORLD, I ALSO ACCEPT YOU INTO MY HEART, AS A SISTER--AND A DAUGHTER.

REMEMBER, AS YOU GO INTO BATTLE AGAINST BRUTALITY AND OPPRESSION, ALL THE SHADES OF ALL THE AMAZONS WHO HAVE DIED FOR FREEDOM GO WITH YOU!
OH MOTHER ...YOUR NEW DAUGHTER ISN'T EVEN LISTENING TO YOU!
IT'S ALL TRUE! I CAN FLY! I CAN FLY!
SHE'S STILL SUCH A SAVAGE.
AND SHE'S NOT THE ONLY ONE. I'VE NEVER SEEN THE PRINCESS SO ANGRY.
A LITTLE LATER...
I'M GLAD YOU AGREED TO TALK TO ME, DIANA. NOW THAT THE BURDENS OF REPRESENTING US AS "WONDER WOMAN" HAVE PASSED FROM YOU, WE NEED TO DISCUSS YOUR FUTURE!
YES, MY FUTURE...
YOU'LL BE STAYING HERE, OF COURSE...TO BATTLE IN THE WISDOM OF AMAZONIAN WAYS. AND BE GROOMED FOR YOUR OWN QUEENSHIP.
I BROUGHT A PRESENT FOR YOU, MOTHER.
ANTIOPE! MY SISTER!
YES. YOUR EXILED, DEAD SISTER.

I LOOK LIKE HER. ONE OF THE MANY LITTLE FACTS YOU'VE NEGLECTED TO MENTION OVER THE YEARS.
WHY ARE YOU LOOKING AT ME THAT WAY? WHAT LIES HAVE YOU BEEN TOLD?
"LIES," MOTHER? YES, WHAT LIES HAVE I BEEN TOLD?
I CAN HONOR YOU AS A QUEEN, I CAN EVEN LOVE YOU AS A SISTER... BUT I CAN NEVER, EVER TRUST YOU!
NO... NO! THAT'S ALL A VILE FALSEHOOD! AN EVIL FABLE!
WHAT IS, MOTHER? HOW DO YOU EVEN KNOW WHAT I'M TALKING ABOUT?
GAEA ...IT'S ALL TRUE.
WAIT... I CAN EXPLAIN...
JUST TELL ME THIS... WAS HERAKLES MY FATHER?... NO, DON'T BOTHER TO ANSWER. WHATEVER YOU SAID, I WOULDN'T BELIEVE YOU.
AND, LATER STILL...
YOU'RE FLYING LIKE A LUNATIC, LITTLE PRINCESS. WHAT'S WRONG?
I JUST WANT TO GET HOME, ARTEMIS. I JUST NEED TO BE--

"--HOME!"
BOSTON, ONE WEEK LATER.
GET IN TIGHTER. I WANT TO SEE THE BLOOD!
KABRAKKABRAKKABRAKKABRAKKAKA
PCHOW!
KBLAMM
CLOSER. I CAN'T SEE THE STEAM FROM THOSE FROST GUYS.
BOSS... I LOVE YA, BUT SHOVE ME ONE MORE TIME AN' THAT HAND IS HISTORY.
ZZARK
WHAT THE HELL ARE YOU DOING HERE?
BPD
TAPING THE END OF THE WORLD FOR THE SIX O'CLOCK NEWS, INSPECTOR. ARE YOU HERE TO ARREST IT?

"THE WALKING ICICLES ARE PAULIES, COURTESY OF THE WHITE MAGICIAN, EVERY-BODY'S FAVORITE CRAZED DEMI-GOD."
ZZZRAKKK
WHAT'S THIS ALL ABOUT, INSPECTOR?
"NOBODY KNOWS WHERE SAZIA'S GETTING HER TROOPS, BUT..."
HEADS UP! HERE THEY COME!
APPARENTLY, IT'S A JURIS-DICTIONAL SQUABBLE, BETWEEN PAULIE LONGO AND SOME-BODY NEW... MAYBE THE WIDOW SAZIA.

BLAAMM! BLAAMM! BLAAMM! BLAAMM!
DAMN! DAMN! NOTHING STOPS HIM! IF ONLY...
EEEYAAAGH
THANK GOD! IT'S...
WHOINHELLIS THAT?

THANKS FOR THE HELP, TWIST, BUT THERE'S NO ROOM HERE FOR INDIES! GOOD...
KRUNK
...BYE.
WHY, YOU LOUSY...! I'LL CUT YOU IN...
FOOLS.
BUDDA BUDDA BUDDA
BOOM

EARTHQUAKE
IN BOSTON?
RRRRRRRRRMMMMMMMBBBBBBBB
CRUUSSHHH YOOUU...
KKRMMBLE
IT'S SOME KIND OF THING, MADE OUT OF THE EARTH!

WHAM!
I HATE IT WHEN THEY WEAR BLACK. IT KEEPS THROWING THE EXPOSURE OFF!
IT'S DIANA!

< YOU CERTAINLY TOOK YOUR TIME, LITTLE PRINCESS. >
< YOU'RE WELCOME. >
< GAEA! IT'S SOME KIND OF IN-COMPLETE ENCHANT-MENT, GOING TO ROT NOW THAT ITS LINK TO ITS SORCERER IS BROKEN. >
< AND THERE'S ONLY ONE SORCERER I KNOW OF IN BOSTON! >
COULD YOU TWO PLEASE SPEAK ENGLISH? AND TELL US IF IT'S OVER?
LOOK IT'S GOING TO PIECES!
WELL, THAT CERTAINLY WAS EXCITING.

I ONLY WISH THE FIGHT HAD SETTLED SOMETHING. I COULD FIND NO TRACE OF THE WHITE MAGICIAN, AND THESE MOB BATTLES ARE TEARING THE CITY APART.
HOW ARE YOU FEELING, JULIA?
PARALYZED. OTHERWISE FINE.
EXCEPT I'M WORRIED ABOUT NESSIE. SHE'S SPENDING SO MUCH TIME HERE, HER GRADES ARE SUFFERING. AND I HAVE TO FIND SOMEONE TO STAY WITH HER AT THE HOUSE -- SOCIAL SERVICES IS GIVING ME FLAK.
THAT'S DREADFUL. IF THERE'S ANY-THING I CAN DO...
YOU NEARLY RIPPED BOSTON APART TO SAVE HER FROM THE WHITE MAGICIAN. DON'T THINK I'VE FORGOTTEN THAT. THIS IS MY WORRY.
TODAY I GOT A PHONE CALL. THEY'RE THREATENING TO CUT OFF MY INSURANCE.
THAT'S... UNSPEAKABLE. THERE MUST BE SOME-THING...

TA-DAA!
I SWORE I WOULD ALWAYS DO BATTLE UNDER THE INSIGNIA DIANA ROCKWELL TREVOR WORE WHEN SHE SAVED THEMYSCIRA.* NO MATTER WHAT THE UNIFORM, I WILL HONOR THAT PLEDGE.
OUR BELOVED LANDLADY ASKED ME TO HAND THIS TO YOU. THE RENT IS DUE.
DONNA! ETTA! WHAT...?
WE'VE PUT THE FINISHING TOUCHES ON YOUR COSTUME.
I STILL DON'T UNDERSTAND WHY YOU'RE STILL USING THE LOGO.
*Wonder Woman Annual #2. --PAUL
THEN I'LL FIND A WAY OF PAYING IT.
YOU WOULDN'T BE HAVING TROUBLE IF YOU WEREN'T INSISTING ON TRYING TO PAY MY RENT TOO.
YOU HAVE THE LITTLE ONE TO THINK OF... AND YOU'RE MY FRIEND. PEOPLE WILL SOON BE HIRING YOU AGAIN, DONNA.
YEAH, RIGHT. THERE'S NOT MUCH MARKET FOR AN ATTORNEY WHO'S ADMITTED SHE WORKED FOR ORGANIZED CRIME. THEY'RE AFRAID I'M BEING WATCHED. AND I AM.

I'VE GOT TO GET DONNA BACK HOME AND THEN I'VE GOT A CHARTER AT FIVE. SEE YOU GUYS.
DIANA?
IT ALL COMES DOWN TO MONEY, DOESN'T IT? BECAUSE I HAVE NONE, I MUST WATCH MY FRIENDS SUFFER.
WE'RE PROUD OF YOU, DIANA. YOU'VE CHOSEN NOT TO EXPLOIT YOUR POWERS FOR MONEY.
THAT P.I., MICAH RAINS, WANTED TO USE YOU FOR HIS PATHETIC DETECTIVE AGENCY, TO EXPLOIT YOUR NAME. BUT THAT WAS AGAINST THE AMAZONIAN CODE...
YES, THE AMAZONIAN CODE. THE CODE MY MOTHER TAUGHT ME. THE CODE THAT KEEPS ME FROM HELPING ANYONE, INCLUDING MYSELF!
THERE IS ONLY ONE THING I CAN DO, NOW...

NEW YORK CITY:
"... AND IT'S THE RIGHT THING TO DO."
LIVING HERE? I'M NOT SURE. IT IS SO LARGE. I HAVE NEVER SEEN SO MANY PEOPLE!
THAT'S WHY YOU NEED US, ARTEMIS. YOU NEED TO BE CLOSE TO THE LEVERS OF POWER. THAT'S NEW YORK.
BUT THIS APARTMENT, ALL THESE CLOTHES, THE COMPUTERS, THE LABORATORY...
YOU NEED TO ESTABLISH A PRESENCE!
Danial and Dickie Brassalton
META-PROMOTIONS
YOU WANT TO GET YOUR MESSAGE OUT QUICKLY, RIGHT? YOU NEED TO BE ABLE TO ADDRESS WORLD LEADERS AS AN EQUAL. WELL, THAT'S WHAT WE'RE GOOD AT.
BUT WHAT DO YOU GET OUT OF...?
HEY, BABE. ALL YOU HAVE TO WORRY ABOUT IS BEING GOOD ENOUGH! WE DON'T WANT TO WASTE OUR TIME BAILING YOU OUT IF YOU CAN'T CUT IT!

DO NOT WORRY. I AM GOOD ENOUGH.
LADIES AND GENTLEMEN, THE NEW WONDER WOMAN!

HOW WILL YOUR REIGN AS WONDER WOMAN DIFFER FROM THAT OF YOUR PREDECESSOR...?
I WILL SUCCEED. UNFOR-TUNATELY, MY... SISTER ALLOWED HERSELF TO BECOME ENMESHED IN PERSONALITY CONFLICTS AND SIDE ISSUES. I WILL NOT.
THAT SOUNDS AS THOUGH YOU HAVE A PROBLEM WITH DIANA.
I HAVE NO PROBLEM. SHE HAS BEEN WORKING IN A FAST FOOD RESTAURANT FOR SEVERAL MONTHS WHILE THE WOMEN OF THIS PLANET LABOR UNDER OPPRESSION AND VILLAINY. I THINK PERHAPS SHE DOES NOT UNDERSTAND THE SERIOUS-NESS OF THE SITUATION.
FROM THIS DAY FORTH, I WILL FIGHT TO END THE OPPRESSION OF WOMEN, THE DESTRUC-TION OF CHILDREN...
...AND SINCE AGGRESSION AND HATRED TOWARDS WOMEN IS GREAT EVIL...

...MY FIRST PRIORITY WILL BE TO END THE VIOLENCE THAT MARS THE WORLD SOCIETY...
SKRAKK
OKAY, PEEPER... YOU READY TO GIVE BACK THE PAPERS YOU SWIPED? YOU READY TO TELL US WHO YOU TOLD?
GO TO HELL.
TOUGH GUY.
WHOKK!

MICAH!
THE WONDER WOMAN!
DON'T WORRY. SHE AIN'T GONNA *ATTACK* US. THAT WOULD BE REVENGE. SHE DON'T *BELIEVE* IN REVENGE. AND SHE AIN'T EVEN THE WONDER WOMAN ANYMORE.
WE'RE JUST WALTZING OUT OF HERE PEACEFUL AS CAN BE, AND WE'LL CALL IT A *DRAW*, RIGHT, SWEETHEART?
SOMEHOW, YOU HAVE GOTTEN THE *WRONG IDEA* ABOUT ME. I SHOULD *CORRECT* THAT.

TH-WAAAK!
KRUNCH
OOF!
WHUMP
KRAM

GRONCH!
NO... DON'T UNNSTAN'! I'M... NOT FIGHTIN'...
KRAK
GOOD.
IF YOU... UNTIE ME, PRINCESS, I'LL APPLAUD.

HAWKMAN!
YOUR FRIEND THERE LEFT A MESSAGE WITH ORACLE ABOUT DISCOVERING A CRIMINAL CON-SPIRACY. I CAME TO HELP, BUT IT SEEMS I'M TOO LATE.
THERE IS, HOWEVER, SOMETHING I COULD USE YOUR HELP WITH. SOME UNDERCOVER WORK.
I HAVE TO GET HIM TO THE HOSPITAL. THEN I'M ALL YOURS.
PRETTY TERRIFIC... BACK THERE, PRINCESS. I KNOW HOW YOU'VE SAID YOU DON'T WANT TO WORK FOR ME FULL-TIME, BUT...
FIFTY-FIFTY.
HUH?

WE WILL RENT A REAL OFFICE, WITH A REAL TELEPHONE AND WE WILL SHARE IN IT 50-50. I WILL RECEIVE AN ADDITIONAL 20% OF ANY NEW REVENUES I GENERATE FOR THE AGENCY.
WE WILL EACH CONTRIBUTE 10% TOWARDS THE FUNCTIONING OF THE AGENCY, WHICH WILL NOT BE CALLED "THE WONDER WOMAN AGENCY" OR ANYTHING FOOLISH LIKE THAT.
WE ARE GOING TO HIRE MY FRIEND DONNA MILTON TO BE OUR ATTORNEY AND OFFICE MANAGER. ANY QUESTIONS?
BUT I'M STILL IN CHARGE, RIGHT?
YES, MICAH. YOU ARE STILL IN CHARGE...
The End...
...BUT THE SAGA OF DIANA AND WONDER WOMAN CONTINUES EVERY MONTH IN
WONDER WOMAN

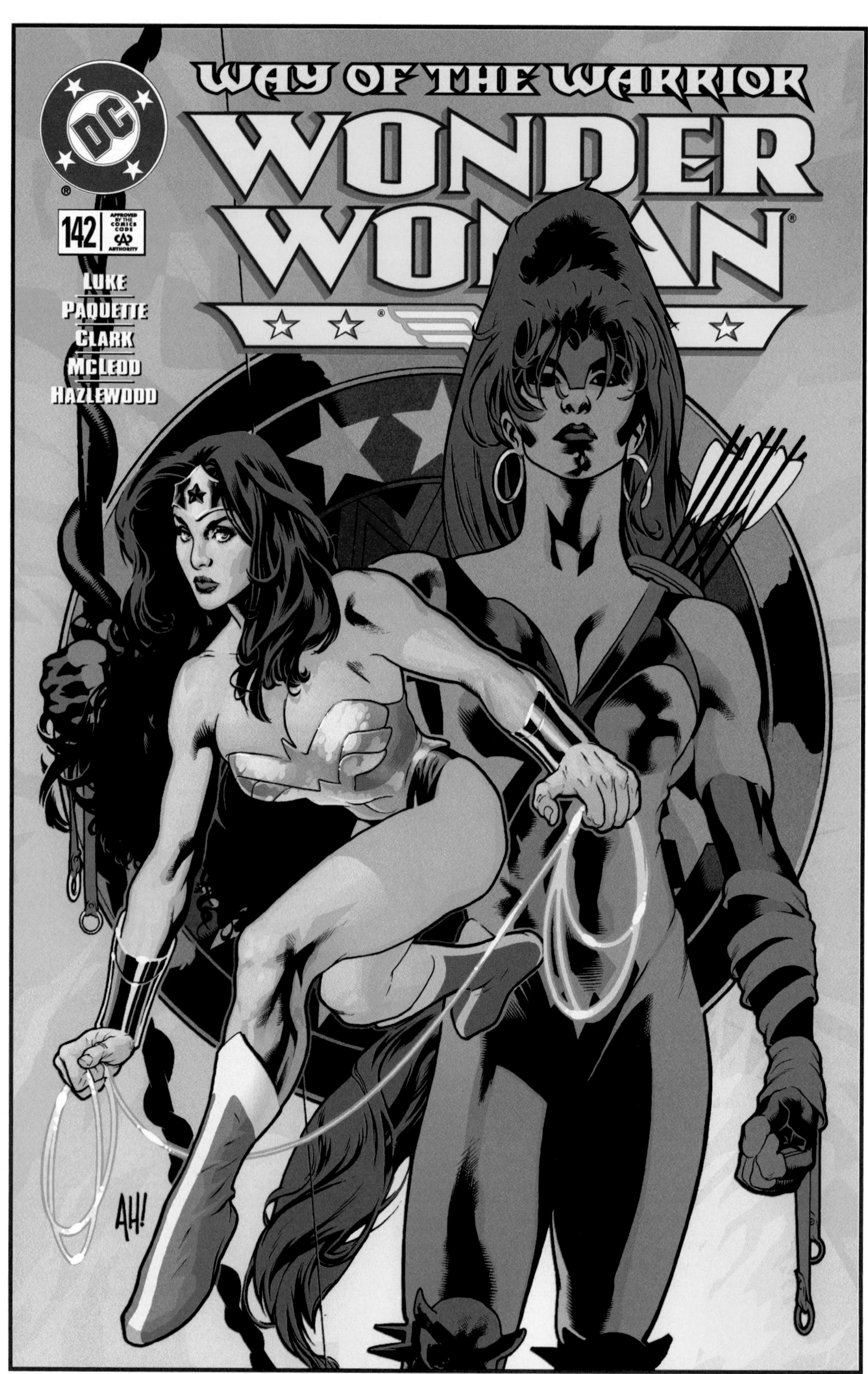
WAY OF THE WARRIOR
WONDER WOMAN
142
APPROVED BY THE COMICS CODE AUTHORITY
LUKE
PAQUETTE
CLARK
McLEOD
HAZLEWOOD
AH!

LONG AGO, A LINE WAS DRAWN IN THE SAND. THE MEN ON EACH SIDE OF THE LINE PROCLAIMED THE LINE UNJUST.
BOTH SIDES RECENTLY PURCHASED RETIRED GULF WAR ORDNANCE ON THE INTERNATIONAL BLACK MARKET.
AGING F-117A STEALTH BOMBERS AND F-4G WILD WEASEL AIRCRAFT STRIKE WITH ANTIRADAR MISSILES.
AH-1 COBRA HELICOPTERS FIRE MISSILES LASER-GUIDED TO TANKS BY GROUND OBSERVERS.
A7 MS18
BUT IT'S STILL JUST A LINE IN THE SAND.
<TARGET IN RANGE! WE HAVE THEM!>
* Translated.
<WHAT IN THE NAME OF...!>

A SECOND AGO, SHE HAD NO RADAR PRESENCE.
NOW SHE SHINES LIKE A BEACON.
HER WORDS FLOAT UPON THE AIR.
THEY RING OUT CLEAR IN ANY LANGUAGE.
<STOP THIS WAR!>
<STOP THIS WAR!>
<STOP THIS WAR!>

THESE MEN HAVE HEARD OF THE WESTERN SUPER-HEROES...
...HOW THEY INJECT THEMSELVES INTO THE AFFAIRS OF OTHERS.
THEIR ANSWER IS CLEAR.
THIS...WOMAN... SHOWING HER NAKED SKIN TO THE WORLD...
...PRESUMES TO INTERFERE IN THE WARS OF MEN.
OVER THE TANK FIRE, A WHISPER BEGINS TO SHAKE THE GROUND...

...AND THUNDER BREAKS OPEN THE SKY.
"I have a deep sympathy with war, it so apes the gait and bearing of the soul."
Henry David Thoreau
1817-62

The Bearing of the Soul
ERIC LUKE–writer
YANICK PAQUETTE and
MATTHEW CLARK–pencils
BOB McLEOD and
DOUG HAZLEWOOD– inks
JOHN COSTANZA–letters
PATRICIA MULVIHILL –colors
PAUL KUPPERBERG and
MAUREEN McTIGUE–edits
Wonder Woman
created by
William Moulton Marston

THE MADNESS OF THE GENERALS INFECTS THE MEN.
HATRED OVER-COMES REASON
NO! DO NOT KILL THEM! I WILL NOT PLAY THEIR GAME!
LET'S SEE HOW YOU FIGHT WITHOUT YOUR TOYS!
WHY WON'T YOU LISTEN? ARE YOU ALL MAD?

THERE ARE OTHER WAYS TO RESOLVE THIS!
YOU MUST FIRST BEGIN TO TALK! AND TO TALK, THE FIGHTING MUST STOP!
IF I HAVE TO I WILL DESTROY EVERY LAST ONE OF YOUR WAR MACHINES! THEN WE WILL TALK...
"...OF PEACE!"

AS MY USELESS WORDS RING IN MY EARS...
I SLIP BACK IN TIME...
YESTERDAY...I CALLED MY FRIENDS TOGETHER FOR THE LAST TIME...
OFFICER SCHORR, YOU'RE HERE TOO?
THIS LITTLE THING SHOWED UP AND STARTED TALKING WITH DIANA'S VOICE, TOLD ME TO FOLLOW IT.
ONE CAME FOR EACH OF US.
HEY, LOOK!
IT MUST BE FROM DIANA!
I THINK WE'RE ABOUT TO FIND OUT.
MAN, LOOK AT THIS CITY. I DON'T EVEN RECOGNIZE IT.
DIANA SURE TOOK THIS HARD.
BUT IT WASN'T HER FAULT.

SHE JUST LIVES HERE. THINGS HAPPEN TO HER.
BIG THINGS. SHE TOOK ALL THE BLAME.
AS SHE DOES WITH EVERYTHING THESE DAYS.
HER EYES ARE DIFFER-ENT.
I CAN'T REMEMBER THE LAST TIME I SAW HER SMILE.
THERE IT IS!
THE NEWS IS CALLING IT THE WONDER-DOME.
WOW, WE'RE FINALLY GOING INSIDE!
WHY AM I SO NERVOUS?
MAYBE BECAUSE IT FLATTENED MOST OF THE CITY?
OR BECAUSE SHE'S BEEN UP HERE THREE WEEKS AND WE HAVEN'T SEEN HER THE WHOLE TIME?
SHE SAID SHE HAD SOME HARD DECISIONS TO MAKE. I JUST HOPE SHE CAME THROUGH OKAY.
C.P.

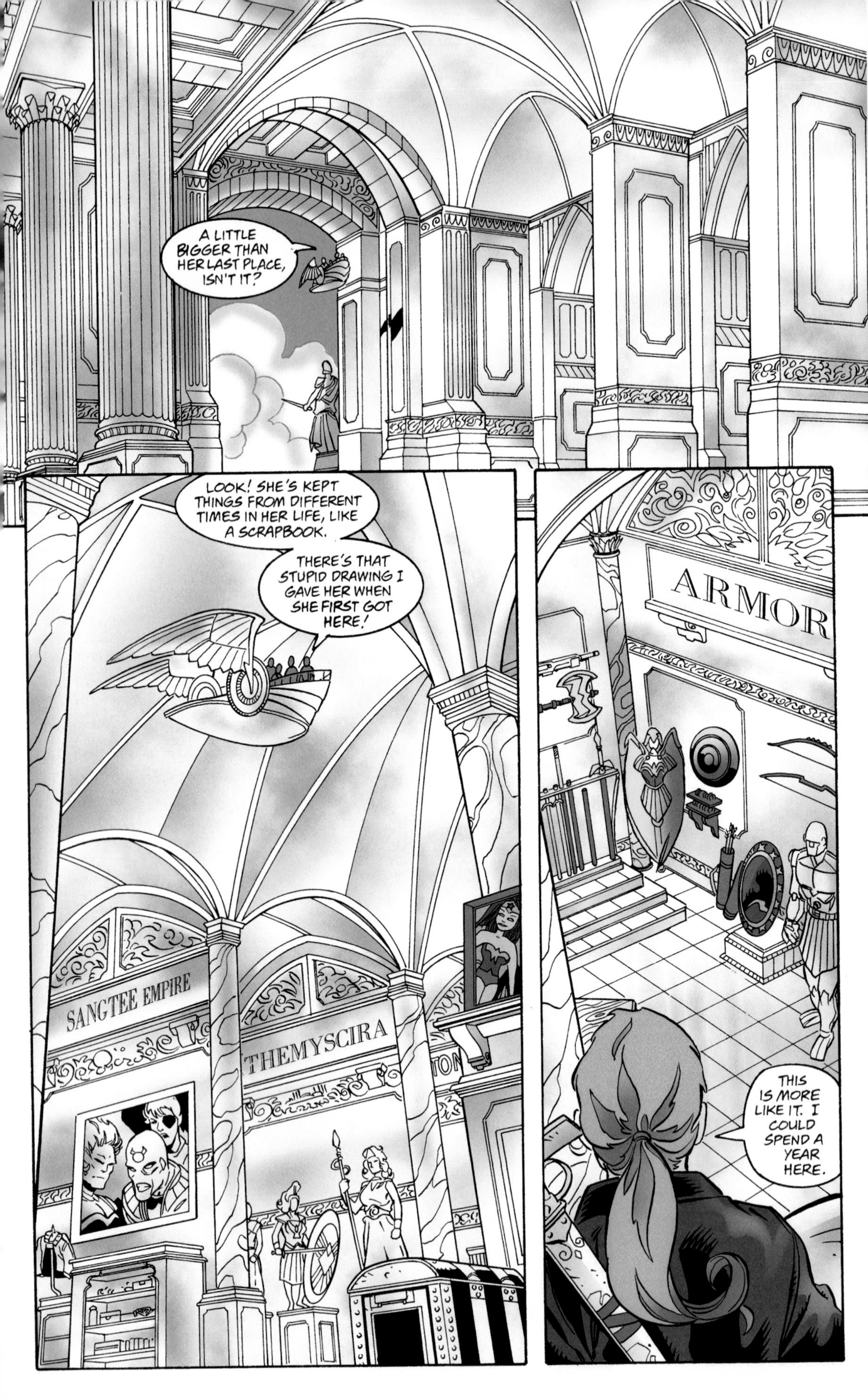
A LITTLE BIGGER THAN HER LAST PLACE, ISN'T IT?
LOOK! SHE'S KEPT THINGS FROM DIFFERENT TIMES IN HER LIFE, LIKE A SCRAPBOOK.
THERE'S THAT STUPID DRAWING I GAVE HER WHEN SHE FIRST GOT HERE!
SANGTEE EMPIRE
THEMYSCIRA
ARMOR
THIS IS MORE LIKE IT. I COULD SPEND A YEAR HERE.

IT'S KIND OF WEIRD.
LIKE A MUSEUM OF HER LIFE.
WHO ARE THESE GUYS, OFFICER SCHORR?
THE JUSTICE SOCIETY, CASSIE. IF YOU WANT TO STAND ON THE SHOULDERS OF GIANTS, LOOK NO FURTHER.
THIS GARDEN... THESE FORMS KEEP CHANGING, ALMOST LIKE A REFLECTION OF HER SUB-CONSCIOUS...
HEY, IS THAT SUPERMAN?
CASSIE!
GARDEN OF DREAMS

GREAT HERA! SHE HAS COLLECTED THE SURVIVING CREATURES OF MYTH!
THERE IS PEGASUS, WHO SPRUNG FROM MEDUSA'S NECK! AND THE REST, CASSIE? REMEMBER YOUR LESSONS!
MENAGERIE
UH... LADON, THE DRAGON FROM THE GARDEN OF HESPERIDES? AND THE CHIMERA WHO FOUGHT BELLEROPHON AT LYCIA!
AND THAT'S GOT TO BE THE SPHINX!
AND CHIRON, THE WISEST CENTAUR, WHO TAUGHT THE HEROES IN HIS CAVE ON MOUNT PELION.
SEEMS WE'VE REACHED JOURNEY'S END.
DIANA?

MY FRIENDS, I'M SORRY I COULDN'T GREET YOU. THERE'S BEEN A CRISIS...
DIANA! THIS PLACE IS AMAZING!
CPD
I'M WORRIED ABOUT YOU ALL ALONE UP HERE. THE WONDERDOME IS GREAT, BUT... ARE YOU OKAY?
I'M GOOD, CASSIE, THOUGH THINGS WILL BE DIFFERENT NOW. YOU'VE SEEN WHAT MY MERE PRESENCE DID TO GATEWAY.
I CAN'T LIVE AMONG YOU ANY-MORE.
BUT I DON'T WANT YOU TO GO!
CASSIE, IT IS TIME FOR YOU TO TAKE THE NEXT STEP. IF THE WORLD CALLS ME WONDER WOMAN, IT IS GOING TO CALL YOU WONDER GIRL. BUT YOU AREN'T READY YET.
I FEAR YOU ARE A CHILD OF YOUR AGE: YOUR MIND IS LIKE A TELEVISION SHOWING ALL CHANNELS AT ONCE. YOU NEED TO BE CLEAR.
THE NATIVE PEOPLE OF AMERICA HAVE A TRADITION CALLED A VISION QUEST. ON THEMYSCIRA WE CALL IT THE WORLD GAUNTLET.

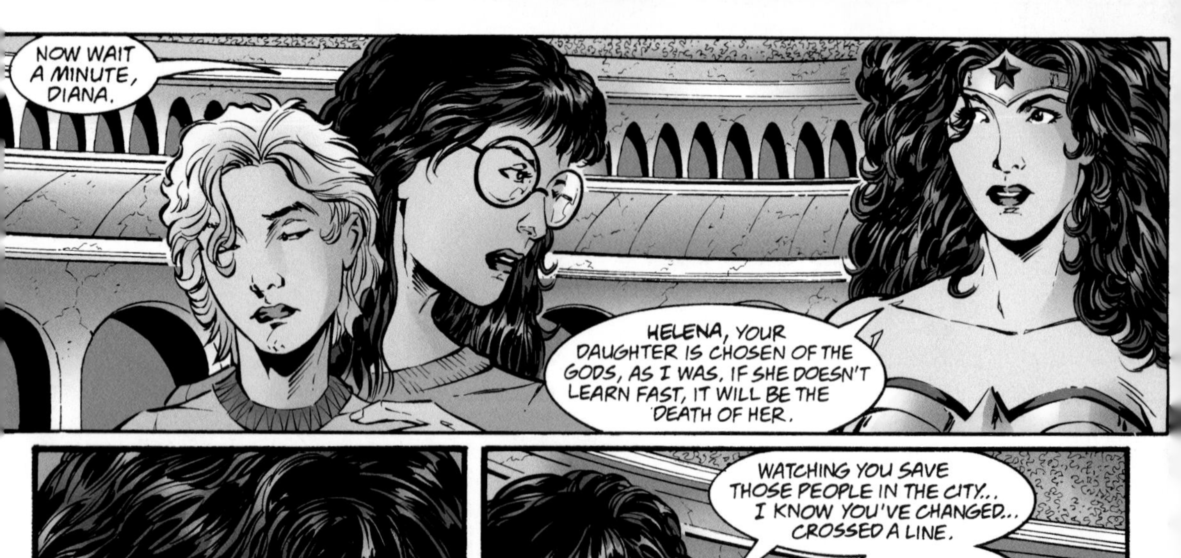

NOW WAIT A MINUTE, DIANA.
HELENA, YOUR DAUGHTER IS CHOSEN OF THE GODS, AS I WAS. IF SHE DOESN'T LEARN FAST, IT WILL BE THE DEATH OF HER.

WATCHING YOU SAVE THOSE PEOPLE IN THE CITY... I KNOW YOU'VE CHANGED... CROSSED A LINE.
YOU'RE GOING TO BE A HERO NOW.

I HAVE ASKED ARTEMIS TO BE YOUR GUIDE AND MENTOR.

THAT IS MY PLEDGE, LITTLE SISTER. OUR JOURNEY BEGINS WITH A SINGLE STEP, BUT IT WILL TAKE US TO *METROPOLIS*... AND TO *GOTHAM*.

WE'RE GOING TO WALK ALL THE WAY TO--!

CASSIE, I WANT YOU TO STUDY AT THE FEET OF THE *WORLD'S FINEST*. ONE WILL TEACH YOU HOW TO FIND THE TRUTH IN THE PAST, AND THE OTHER WILL SHOW YOU THE HOPE FOR THE FUTURE.

I PROMISE I'LL TRY, DIANA. IT'S JUST, LIKE, SO HUGE!

REMEMBER, YOU ARE BORN OF *WONDER* ...NOW MAKE WONDER OF YOUR *LIFE.*

BUT DIANA, WHERE WILL *YOU* GO?

AFTER SO LONG, MY MISSION IS CLEAR.

I'M GOING TO FLASHPOINTS, PLACES THE WHOLE WORLD IS WATCHING, AND I'M GOING TO SHOW THEM HOW TO RESOLVE THEIR DIFFERENCES.
WITHOUT WAR.

LET ME COME WITH YOU, DIANA. I'LL SHOW THEM A PEACE THEY'LL NEVER FORGET!
THANKS ALL THE SAME, SISTER. ETERNAL REST IS NOT THE PEACE I SEEK FOR THEM. TAKE CARE OF CASSIE.

"OH MOM, I'M WORRIED ABOUT HER. SHE LOOKS SO LONELY."

I AWAKE TO THE FEELING OF BEING LIFTED INTO THE AIR.
MY FIRST THOUGHT IS THAT I'M BEING TAKEN UP INTO OLYMPUS.
BUT IT IS MY GUARDIAN, MY WONDERDOME PROTECTING ME.
BY THE GODS... IT IS TIME TO FINISH THIS.
BUT WHEN MEN NEED TO DIE FOR THEIR CAUSE...
... WHAT WILL BRING AN END TO WAR?
IN THE END, IT IS THE DREAM OF MY FRIENDS AND ALL I HOLD PRECIOUS...THE FARE-WELL TO EVERYTHING I'VE SACRIFICED FOR PEACE...MY HOME...COMPANIONSHIP.. LOVE..
THAT SHOWS ME THE ANSWER.

PRESIDENTIAL BUNKER, CAPITAL CITY.

YOU...YOU DARE TRESPASS HERE! WEARING THE COLORS OF THE UNITED STATES! THIS IS AN OUTRAGE! AN INTERNATIONAL INCIDENT! YOU... A HALF-NAKED WOMAN!
YOUR WORDS ARE MEANINGLESS! THE SONS OF YOUR COUNTRY ARE BLEEDING TO DEATH ON YOUR BATTLEFIELDS!
COME WITH ME.

THREE HUNDRED MILES ACROSS THE BORDER, THE ROYAL PALACE.

I DO SOMETHING THAT ANGRY YOUNG PEOPLE HAVE DREAMED OF THROUGH-OUT HISTORY.
I LOCK THE LEADERS IN A ROOM...
AND LET THEM SORT IT OUT.
THE HATRED OF GENERATIONS HANGS IN THE AIR.
THEIR COMMON FEAR IS NO BOND.
IT IS THE DEATH OF THEM.

UNFORTUNATELY, I NEED THEM.
THEIR PEOPLE LOOK TO THEM AS LEADERS.
SO I ROPE THEM LIKE ANIMALS...
THE LASSO IS A CONDUIT OF TRUTH, SECRETS FLOWING LIKE BLOOD FROM ONE HEART TO THE OTHER.
AND SUDDENLY THERE ARE NO SECRETS.
THE TERRIBLE DETAILS OF THEIR SORDID LITTLE LIVES...
...THE LONELINESS... ISOLATION... THE ABUSE OF A FATHER ...THE SUICIDE OF A MOTHER...
... BRING THEM TOGETHER.
TWINS OF PAIN.

AFTER FIFTY YEARS OF FIGHTING, THE ARMISTICE IS HEARD ROUND THE WORLD.
MY INVOLVEMENT IS IMPLICIT. THE HEROISM OF PEACE IS CHAMPIONED.
12
OF COURSE, I SHOULD KNOW BY NOW...
PEACE IS A DREAM.
12
LIVE
LIVE
12
«ALL TRAITORS MUST DIE!»
I FIGHT TO MAKE THE DREAM COME TRUE...
THOUGH MY HANDS ARE COVERED WITH BLOOD
I FEEL THE STARS WATCHING, WAITING. NO, NOT THE STARS...
THE DARKNESS BETWEEN.

WONDER
WOMAN
#177
JIMENEZ
LANNING
AH!

PARADISE FOUND
IT'S OVER.
CLANNG
Phil Jimenez Story & Pencils
Andy Lanning Inks
Trish Mulvihill Colors
Heroic Age Separations
Comicraft Letters
Tom Palmer jr. Assistant Editor
Eddie Berganza Editor
Wonder Woman Created By William Moulton Marston

GET BACK! I SAID GET BACK!
RICKY, SHE AIN'T BACKIN' DOWN. WE'RE DUST!
BAM BAM

CLNKG
CLNKG
CLNKG
WELL, YOUR LITTLE OPERATION HERE CERTAINLY IS.

RUN!!
WHERE THE HELL ARE WE GONNA GO? THAT'S WONDER WOMAN!

BABOOM
Ah, NO!

I SAID THIS WAS OVER...

...AND I MEANT IT.

YOU CAN'T BREAK THE LASSO OF HESTIA, OR DEFY ITS *POWER...*
...SO DON'T TRY.

YOU'VE USED YOUR LITTLE NETWORK HERE TO *DEFRAUD* THOUSANDS OF INNOCENTS IN THE WAKE OF THE ALIEN WAR, HAVEN'T YOU?
HAVEN'T YOU?!

Y-YES... WE SET UP THE HOTLINES AND THE *FALSE* INSURANCE CLAIMS...
TOLD PEOPLE WE'D FIND THEIR LOST LOVED ONES FOR CASH-- THEY WERE SO *DESPERATE,* AND THEY PAID SO MUCH MONEY...

HOW *DISGRACEFUL.* AND HOW *SICK.*
WHERE DOES IT COME FROM, THIS IDEA YOU SEEM TO HAVE-- THAT TREATING OTHER HUMAN BEINGS IN SUCH A MALIGNANT WAY IS SOMEHOW *ACCEPTABLE...?*

THAT'S WHAT I *LOVE* ABOUT YOU, DIANA. TO THIS DAY, IT STILL *AWES* YOU THE DEPTHS TO WHICH THE SOULS OF THOSE IN PATRIARCH'S WORLD CAN *SINK.* EVEN AFTER ALL YOUR YEARS HERE.
IT REALLY *IS* ONE OF YOUR GREAT CHARMS.
NOW, WHEN YOU'RE DONE *"PLAYING"* WITH YOUR NEW FRIENDS, DROP THEM OFF WITH THE CLOSEST AUTHORITIES AND COME WITH ME.
I HAVE SOMETHING TO *SHOW* YOU.

ARTEMIS? WHERE ARE WE GOING?
JUST KEEP YOUR EYE ON THE STEERING WHEEL, LITTLE SISTER. AND FOLLOW THE COORDINATES I'VE SET FOR YOU.
WHAT DO YOU THINK OF THE NEW INVISIBLE JET?
IT FLIES LIKE A DREAM-- BUT I'M NOT SURE I UNDERSTAND. WHO CRAFTED ITS CURRENT DESIGN? WHY AM I FLYING IT?
AND THE COORDINATES YOU'VE SET-- THERE'S NOTHING THERE.
SIGH.
A LITTLE FAITH WOULD BE NICE.
BUT THE BERMUDA TRIANGLE?
TRUST ME, DIANA. FLY THROUGH THE VEIL OF CLOUDS--
--AND KEEP YOUR BLUE EYES PEELED.
GREAT HERA!
IS THAT THEMYSCIRA?!

GAEA!
IT'S... UNBELIEVABLE!

WHAT'S HAPPENED HERE?
HOW IS THIS POSSIBLE?

PHILLIPUS? IS THAT YOU?
HELLO, DIANA.

I GUESS YOU COULD SAY, AS THEMYSCIRA HAS TRANSFORMED, SO HAVE I.
I'M JUST SO THRILLED TO SEE YOU.

BUT YOU HAVE TO TELL ME HOW THIS ALL HAPPENED!
WHY DON'T YOU ASK THEM?
GREAT HERA!
HERA BRINGS YOU HER GREETINGS, DEAR DAUGHTERS. AS DOES GAEA HERSELF.
AS DO WE, LADY ARTEMIS...
...THE GODDESSES OF THE AMAZONS OF BANA-MIGHDALL.
I HAVE HEARD YOUR PRAYERS, DIANA. I APOLOGIZE FOR NOT ANSWERING THEM SOONER.

FORGIVE MY IMPERTINENCE, LADY ARTEMIS--
--BUT *WHERE* HAVE YOU BEEN?
"DEFENDING OLYMPUS, AND WORLDS BEYOND, DAUGHTER.
"FOR *ARES, SEKHMET, SKANDA,* AND OTHERS-- THE GODS OF BLOODY WARFARE, FOUND POWER BEYOND IMAGINING DURING THE COMING OF *IMPERIEX.* IT TOOK NEARLY ALL OUR POWER TO STOP THOSE RAMPAGING GODS FROM CONQUERING THE HEAVENS AND THE UNIVERSE BELOW.

"WITH THE HELP OF HIS BROTHER HADES, LORD ZEUS FINALLY *CAPTURED* HIS SON, BINDING HIM IN *TARTARUS*--
"--ALONG WITH ARES' FOUL CHILDREN.
"BY THE TIME WE COULD REFOCUS ON OUR *WORSHIPERS*-- YOU AND YOUR SISTER AMAZONS-- THEMYSCIRA HAD ALL BUT BEEN *DESTROYED* BY IMPERIEX AND THE SYNTHETIC ALIEN *BRAINIAC 13.*
"THE GODDESSES OF THE THEMYSCIRAN AMAZONS AND THE GODDESSES OF THE AMAZONS OF BANA-MIGHDALL GATHERED IN THE HALLS OF MIGHTY OLYMPUS, TO DISCUSS THE *FUTURE* OF THEIR MOST DEVOTED WORSHIPERS.
"WE KNEW THAT WE COULD NOT ABANDON YOU...
"...NOT AFTER YOU AND YOUR SISTERS *SACRIFICED* SO MUCH TO *SAVE* OUR UNIVERSE.
"SO WE USED OUR POWERS TO *REINVIGORATE* THEMYSCIRA..."

...THAT YOU MIGHT ONCE MORE TRANSFORM IT INTO *PARADISE!*

A TRUE *HOME* FOR THE AMAZONS...
WITH A SECOND CHANCE TO FORM ONE MIGHTY *NATION.*
WITH ALL DUE RESPECT, LADY ATHENA -- WILL THIS BE A NATION THE AMAZONS CAN DEVELOP *THEMSELVES?* WITHOUT GODLY LIMITS AS TO DEVELOPMENT OR PROGRESS?

DIANA --!
PHILLIPUS, ARTEMIS -- I HAVE AN *IDEA.* WITH THE GODS' *BLESSING,* I THINK THEMYSCIRA CAN BE TRANSFORMED *UTTERLY...*

...IN A WAY THAT WILL GIVE BACK TO THE AMAZONS FUNCTION... AND *PURPOSE.*
SO?

WHAT DO YOU SAY, GODS OF OLYMPUS AND HELIOPOLIS?
ARE YOU GAME?

AND SO, IN THE DAYS AND WEEKS THAT FOLLOW, NEGOTIATIONS BEGIN TO TAKE PLACE BETWEEN THE TWO TRIBES OF AMAZONS AND THEIR GODDESSES...

I KNOW IT SOUNDS *TERRIFYING,* BUT MANY OF US HAVE SEEN WHAT PATRIARCH'S WORLD HAS TO OFFER. IT'S NOT SIMPLY WAR AND FILTH...

...BUT SCIENCE AND MEDICINES AND TECHNOLOGIES MANY OF US HAVE ONLY *DREAMED* ABOUT, FROM THIS WORLD AND A THOUSAND OTHERS.

WE CAN *DO* THIS. WE CAN TAKE THE VERY BEST WE'VE SEEN, AND COMBINE IT WITH THE BEST *WE* HAVE TO OFFER...
AND MAKE A THEMYSCIRA LIKE NONE WE'VE EVER SEEN!

AND SOON, THE INVISIBLE JET GOES FORTH ACROSS THE GLOBE...

...HANDING OUT INVITATIONS TO SOME OF THE GREATEST MINDS AND POWERS ON THE PLANET...

...TO CONTRIBUTE TO THE TRIUMPHANT REBUILDING OF THE AMAZONS' ISLAND HOME.

ARCHITECT **HENRI CLAUDE TIBET...**

...HARVARD PROFESSOR **JULIA KAPATELIS,** SPIRITUAL DAUGHTER OF THE AMAZON PYTHIA...

...J'ONN J'ONZZ, THE **MARTIAN MANHUNTER,** AND KIMIYO HOSHI, KNOWN TO SOME AS DOCTOR LIGHT...

DECORATED PILOT AND ENGINEER **STEVE TREVOR,** AFTER WHOSE MOTHER DIANA WAS NAMED...

...ALL COME TOGETHER WITH IDEAS, TECHNOLOGIES, AND POWERS, UNDER THE AMAZON MASTER DESIGNER **KALEEZA FASHED.**

...INCLUDING ONE FINAL BEING:
YOUR GIFTS TO ME HAVE ALWAYS BEEN EXTRAORDINARY, DOME.

PLEASE -- GRANT THEM TO ME ONCE MORE.
THERE ARE MANY BEYOND THE SHORES OF THEMYSCIRA WHO BELIEVE WE'RE A DYING RACE -- PLAGUED BY WAR AND ANTIQUATED IDEAS. BEFORE US LIES AN EXTRAORDINARY OPPORTUNITY...

...TO CHANGE THAT PERCEPTION.
SO LET'S TAKE IT. FOR THE GLORY OF GAEA.
FOR ALL OF US.

USING SECRETS GLEANED FROM THE ALIEN **WONDERDOME'S** TECHNO-BIOLOGY, THE AMAZONS WHO CHOOSE TO STAY ON THEMYSCIRA, ALLIED WITH THEIR OUTWORLD COMPANIONS, BEGIN TO DESIGN THEIR NEW WORLD. INCORPORATING RADICAL ARCHITECTURE, ALIEN SCIENCE, OTHERDIMENSIONAL ENERGIES, AND ANCIENT PHILOSOPHIES ABOUT HARMONY AND NATURE...

...BUILDING...

...CLEARING...

...PLANNING...

...KEEPING THEIR ARTS AND HISTORY ALIVE...

...ERECTING GREAT HALLS OF JUSTICE...

...SCULPTING ICONS TO THE GLORY OF THE GODS!

AND THEN:

I, *DEMETER,* GRANT THESE ISLANDS *ETERNAL FERTILITY* -- THAT THE SOIL AND FIELDS WILL PROVIDE ENDLESS BOUNTY!

I, *ISIS,* ENCHANT THESE ISLANDS WITH *MAGIC,* AND THE MAGIC POSSIBILITY!

I, *MAMMITU,* BIND THESE GIFTS TO THEMSYCIRA, WITH AN OATH OF *COMMITMENT* NO GOD OR MORTAL SHALL DEFY WITHOUT SWIFT *RETRIBUTION!*

I, *ARTEMIS,* ENDOW THE FORESTS AND THE STREAMS WITH GAME AND FISH, TO HUNT, TO FEED, AND TO TRAIN!

I, *NEITH,* GRACE THEMYSCIRA WITH THE NURTURING SPIRIT OF *MOTHERHOOD* AND ITS FEROCIOUS PROTECTION!

I, *HESTIA,* SANCTIFY EACH HOME WITH *WARMTH* OF THE *HEARTH,* AND THE *FIRES* OF *SECURITY!*

AND I, *APHRODITE,* BLESS THESE ISLANDS WITH SUCH LOVE AND COMPASSION THAT *NO WEAPONS* WILL WORK ON THEM, SAVE ONE!

"FOR *THIS* THEMYSCIRA...

"...MAY TRULY CHANGE THE WORLD!"

"TO ALL OF OUR HONORED GUESTS-- DIGNITARIES FROM BEYOND OUR SHORES, FELLOW AMBASSADORS OF PEACE AND GOODWILL-- THE AMAZONS BID YOU WELCOME...

"...AND ASK YOU TO PARTAKE IN OUR HOME, AND MARVEL AT IT AS WE DO.

"YOU HAVE BEEN ASKED HERE TO JOIN US IN OUR NEW VENTURE..."

DONNA, WOULD YOU LOOK AT THIS!
I KNOW-- IT'S LIKE A DREAM!

LOIS!
TOGETHER AGAIN, Eh, DIANA?

I WOULDN'T MISS IT.
NO EVIL APPLES TO SCREW THIS ONE UP, I HOPE.
DIANA, THIS IS MY MOTHER, ELLA.
IT'S A PLEASURE TO MEET YOU, DIANA. I'M VERY SORRY TO HEAR ABOUT YOUR MOTHER...

"...AND TO BEAR WITNESS AS THEMYSCIRA IS RECONCEIVED."

DIANA..
TREVOR? I'M SO... HONORED YOU COULD COME HERE.

THE U.N. OFFICIALS YOU'VE INVITED ARE OFFICIALLY WOWED, DIANA. INCLUDING ME.
YES, WELL...

...CHANCELLOR PHILLIPUS IS ABOUT TO BEGIN SPEAKING AT THE INAUGURATION.
PERHAPS YOU'D CARE TO JOIN ME...?

-- NO LONGER A "PARADISE ISLAND" FOR A SHRINKING RACE FROM A LOST AGE...
...BUT AN INSTITUTION-- A UNIVERSITY-- FOR NOTHING LESS THAN THE UNFETTERED EXCHANGE OF IDEAS AND INFORMATION FROM ACROSS THE MULTIVERSE.
VISITORS OF EVERY GENDER AND SPECIES WILL BE WELCOMED HERE, TO DEBATE THEORIES, TO CRAFT TREATIES, TO CREATE ART AND LITERATURE: TO DEVISE MEDICINES: TO CRAFT TECHNOLOGIES: AND TO WORSHIP WITHOUT FEAR IN THE MANNER THAT THEY CHOOSE.
A TRULY DEMOCRATIC SOCIETY WHICH WILL DEPEND ON THIS COMPETITION OF IDEAS...
...IN A SPACE THAT WILL BE FIERCELY PROTECTED BY THE VERY BEST OUR RACE HAS TO OFFER.
AS BEFORE, AN AMAZON WILL REPRESENT US IN THE OUTER WORLD-- SET FORTH WITH THE TASK OF REPRESENTING US AND SPREADING OUR HIGHEST IDEALS.
THE NOTIONS OF PEACEFUL COEXISTENCE, OF EQUALITY, OF LOVE AND RESPECT. THIS AMAZON TRULY IS THE VERY BEST OUR NATION HAS TO OFFER...
GASP!
AND SHE WILL ONCE AGAIN WEAR AS PART OF HER GARB A GOLDEN CORONET. A TIARA, WHICH, STRIPPED OF ITS ROYAL SIGNIFICANCE, NOW HAS A NEW MEANING...
...AS A CONSTANT SYMBOL OF OUR NATION, AND OF OUR HOPE AND DREAMS.
WE KNOW THIS AMBASSADOR OF PEACE AS THE DAUGHTER OF A QUEEN. OUR DEAREST DIANA...
...BUT MANY MORE OF YOU HAVE COME TO CALL HER-- WONDER WOMAN!
YOU GO, SIS!
CLAP CLAP CLAP
CLAP CLAP

THE TEMPLE OF HIPPOLYTA, ON THE ISLE OF REMEMBRANCE:
SO IS IT TRUE, CHANCELLOR PHILLIPUS? YOU'VE GIVEN UP YOUR ROLE AS A SOLDIER? AS A WARRIOR?
THERE ARE MANY WAYS TO FIGHT A WAR, DIANA.
AFTER ALL THE DEATH I'VE SEEN, THOUGH -- I'M NOT SURE I EVER NEED TO WIELD MY SWORD AGAINST ANOTHER.
DON'T LET MOTHER HEAR YOU SAY THAT. YOU WERE HER GREATEST GENERAL.
Oh, I WON'T LET HER GO SOFT ON US, LITTLE SISTER. I PROMISE YOU THAT. AND DON'T YOU GO SOFT ON US, EITHER.
WE NEED YOU OUT THERE IN PATRIARCH'S WORLD AS OUR REPRESENTATIVE. PYTHIA KNOWS I WAS NO GOOD AT IT. EVEN YOUR MOTHER KNEW IT --
-- AND YES, IT TOOK THE AMAZONS A LITTLE TIME TO REALIZE IT. BUT THINGS WERE SO RAW AFTER THE CIVIL WAR...
WE MADE A MISTAKE IN REJECTING YOU AND YOUR HELP. WE'RE TRYING TO RECTIFY THAT NOW.
SO DON'T TAKE TOO LONG DECIDING TO PUT THAT TIARA BACK ON YOUR HEAD. THERE'S A WORLD OUT THERE THAT NEEDS YOU.
YOU AND THAT DAMNED OPTIMISM OF YOURS.
DID YOU HEAR THAT, MOTHER?
A WORLD THAT NEEDS ME; A BEACON OF CIVILITY. A PERFECT EXAMPLE OF HUMANITY.
IF ONLY THEY KNEW HOW WRONG THEY WERE.
I NEED YOU SO MUCH, MOTHER.
I NEED YOUR HELP.
I NEED TO TELL YOU HOW SORRY I AM...

DIANA...
GREAT HERA...
MOTHER?
IT'S YOU, ISN'T IT? IT'S NOT CIRCE, OR SOME DREAM --!
THANK GAEA, IT'S YOU!
MOTHER, I'LL PETITION LORD HADES -- I'LL FREE YOUR SPIRIT AND THEN YOU CAN COME BACK AND RULE THE NEW THEMYSCIRA. I'LL BE A DAUGHTER YOU CAN BE PROUD OF -- SUBMIT TO YOUR LOVING RULE...
DIANA, YOU WERE NEVER GOOD AT SUBMITTING TO ME OR ANYONE. HOW OFTEN DID YOU DEFY THE GODS, FOR GAEA'S SAKE?
DIANA, YOUR WILL IS INDOMITABLE. IT IS ONE OF YOUR GREATEST ASSETS. ONE OF THE THINGS I'M MOST PROUD OF.

INDEED. SOME WOULD SAY IT'S THE STRONGEST TRAIT YOU INHERITED FROM ME.
AUNT ANTIOPE?!

HEY, WHAT AM I, CHOPPED LIVER?
NICE TO SEE YOU, DI.
ATHENA HELP ME. DIANA TREVOR--?!

WELL, WE CERTAINLY DO LOOK ALIKE, DON'T WE?
HIPPOLYTA HAD TOLD ME AS MUCH, BUT TO SEE IT IN PERSON...

IT'S AN HONOR TO FINALLY MEET YOU, NIECE.

HEY, KIDDO-- HOW YOU DOING? YOU'VE BEEN PUTTING MY NAME TO GOOD USE, Eh?
YOUR MOM AND I HAVE BEEN PLAYING A LOT OF CATCH-UP. YOU KNOW, I COULDN'T TELL YOU THIS BEFORE, BUT IT WAS YOUR MOM WHO INSPIRED ME TO BE A PILOT...

I MISS YOU SO MUCH.
IF I CAN'T FREE YOU, THEN I'LL COME WITH YOU. I WANT SO BADLY TO BE WITH YOU.

DAUGHTER, YOU ARE EXACTLY WHERE YOU NEED TO BE.
YOU HAVE A SACRED MISSION. IT'S WHAT YOU WERE BORN TO DO, AND YOU'RE NOT DONE YET.

YOU *ARE* WONDER WOMAN. YOU MUST GO FORTH AND REPRESENT OUR IDEALS AND HOPES AND DREAMS. OUR NATION HAS PLACED ITS FAITH IN YOU-- FOR YOU ARE ITS BEST OPPORTUNITY TO HELP *TRANSFORM* THIS WORLD.

SWEETHEART, DO YOU KNOW HOW MANY PEOPLE LOOK UP TO YOU AND THINK THEY CAN DO IT IF THEY CAN BE MORE LIKE YOU? YOUR MOM *INSPIRED* ME TO FLY, YOU'LL DO THE SAME FOR SO MANY OTHERS... THERE'S SO MUCH *FLYING* FOR YOU TO DO.

THERE ARE *OTHER* AMAZONS OUT THERE. DESCENDANTS OF MY TRIBE, OTHER OFFSHOOTS-- DIANA, YOU MUST SEEK THEM OUT, AND GUIDE THEM-- AND REPRESENT THEM IN THE WORLD OF MAN.

YOU ARE THE *BEST* OF US, DIANA. THE BEST OF OUR RACE. YOU MAY HAVE FORGOTTEN THAT, BUT I NEVER HAVE.

YOU HAVE MUCH TO DO OUT THERE, BEYOND PARADISE. LIVES TO MAKE BETTER, TO CHANGE, INCLUDING YOUR *OWN.*

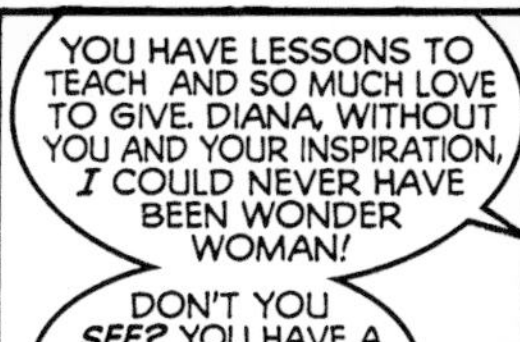
YOU HAVE LESSONS TO TEACH AND SO MUCH LOVE TO GIVE. DIANA, WITHOUT YOU AND YOUR INSPIRATION, *I* COULD NEVER HAVE BEEN WONDER WOMAN!

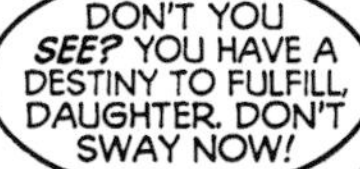
DON'T YOU *SEE?* YOU HAVE A DESTINY TO FULFILL, DAUGHTER. DON'T SWAY NOW!

BUT *HOW* WILL I GO ON *WITHOUT* YOU?

WE'LL BE THERE FOR YOU, DARLIN'!
GUIDING AND PROTECTING YOUR SPIRIT.

IT IS TIME, AMAZONS.

WE HEAR YOU, *LORD HADES.*
WE KNOW THE DRILL.
BE GOOD, DIANA. BE STRONG.

I'M SORRY I COULDN'T HAVE BEEN A BETTER MOTHER TO YOU.
NO! I'M SORRY I COULDN'T HAVE BEEN A MORE THOUGHTFUL, LOVING DAUGHTER TO YOU. A BETTER PRINCESS FOR HER QUEEN.

I'LL HEAR NONE OF THAT NONSENSE. NOW, PLACE THAT TIARA UPON YOUR HEAD AND WEAR IT AS YOU SHOULD.
YOU'VE BEEN HONORED BY OUR NATION AS ITS GREATEST CHAMPION AND REPRESENTATIVE.

YOU'LL WEAR THAT HONOR PROUDLY.
NOW THAT'S MY GIRL.
YOU ARE MY PRIDE AND JOY, DIANA OF THEMYSCIRA. WISE AS ATHENA, BEAUTIFUL AS APHRODITE, SWIFT AS HERMES AND STRONGER THAN HERACLES. A LEADER, A TEACHER -- A HERO -- TO GENERATIONS DESPERATE FOR THE VERY IDEALS YOU EMBODY. WHAT MORE COULD ANY MOTHER HAVE ASKED FOR?

MY TIME WITH YOU WAS THE GREATEST GIFT OUR LOVING GODDESSES COULD BESTOW UPON ME.
I WILL ALWAYS CHERISH YOU, DIANA. CHERISH YOU BEYOND IMAGINING.

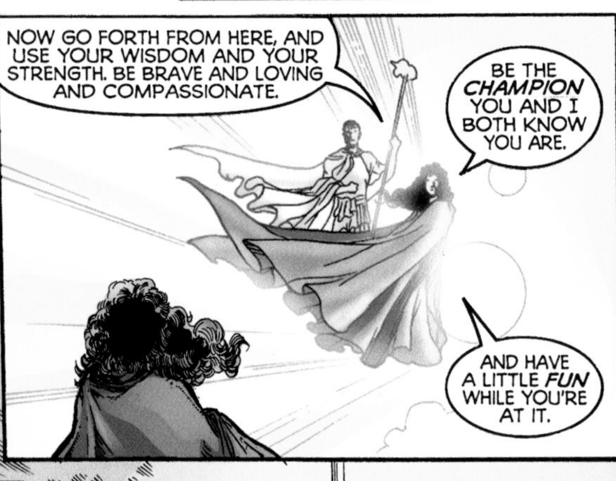
NOW GO FORTH FROM HERE, AND USE YOUR WISDOM AND YOUR STRENGTH. BE BRAVE AND LOVING AND COMPASSIONATE.
BE THE CHAMPION YOU AND I BOTH KNOW YOU ARE.
AND HAVE A LITTLE FUN WHILE YOU'RE AT IT.

THE GLORY OF GAEA BE WITH YOU, MY DAUGHTER.
I LOVE YOU, MOTHER! I LOVE YOU SO MUCH!

AND I LOVE YOU, DIANA.
I WILL ALWAYS LOVE YOU.

DAYS LATER...

EUDIA, VENELIA, I'LL MISS YOU BOTH SO MUCH. BUT IF YOU NEED ANYTHING, PLEASE-- CONTACT MY *FOUNDATION.*

WE'LL BE FINE, DIANA. YOU CAN'T IMAGINE HOW *EXCITED* WE ARE!
TRAVEL *SAFELY,* MY DEAR FRIENDS.
DIANA?

HELLO, TREVOR...
I JUST WANTED TO *CONGRATULATE* YOU ON ALL OF THIS...
...EVERYONE THE WORLD OVER IS ABUZZ WITH THE POSSIBILITIES OF THIS PLACE.
WELL, THANK YOU. I...

AND I JUST...
...I'VE *CHANGED MY MIND.* I WAS HOPING IT MIGHT NOT BE TOO LATE TO TAKE YOU UP ON YOUR *DINNER INVITATION.*

Oh? AND WHAT'S BROUGHT THIS CHANGE OF HEART? DECIDED I MIGHT BE *WORTH* IT...?
NO, IT'S NOT LIKE THAT AT ALL. I'VE JUST *SEEN* SOME THINGS--

WAIT A MINUTE.
OF COURSE, J'ONN! YES, OF COURSE--! I'LL GATHER MY ARMOR AND WEAPONS AND BE THERE AT THE SPEED OF HERMES!
I HAVE TO GO. MANGATRON'S ATTACKING JAPAN AGAIN.*
*MANGATRON ATTACKED DIANA AND AQUAMAN IN JLA #5.

BUT I'LL BE BACK IN NEW YORK IN TWO WEEKS-- CALL ME AT THE EMBASSY AND WE'LL ARRANGE A TIME FOR THAT DINNER. AND *YOU'RE* BUYING!
BUT WHAT ABOUT YOUR UNIFORM--? HOW WILL YOU--?

Oh, I'LL JUST USE A LITTLE TRICK MY MOTHER TAUGHT ME.
"WHAT IS THIS STUFF OF LEGENDS?
"THE STUFF OF LEGEND IS THE REALITY OF TODAY: A DEAD CAVEWOMAN'S UNBORN CHILD SURVIVES THE RAVAGES OF TIME, AND A POWERFUL SOCIETY OF WOMEN WHOSE GREATEST CHAMPION LEAVES THE SANCTITY OF HOME TO VENTURE INTO A WORLD THEY CANNOT DREAM EXISTS.
"BORN A PRINCESS ON AN ISLAND HIDDEN IN SPACE AND TIME, SHE HAS BECOME ONE OF EARTH'S GREATEST WARRIORS.
"THIS, THEN, IS THE STUFF OF LEGENDS. THIS...

"...IS
WONDER WOMAN

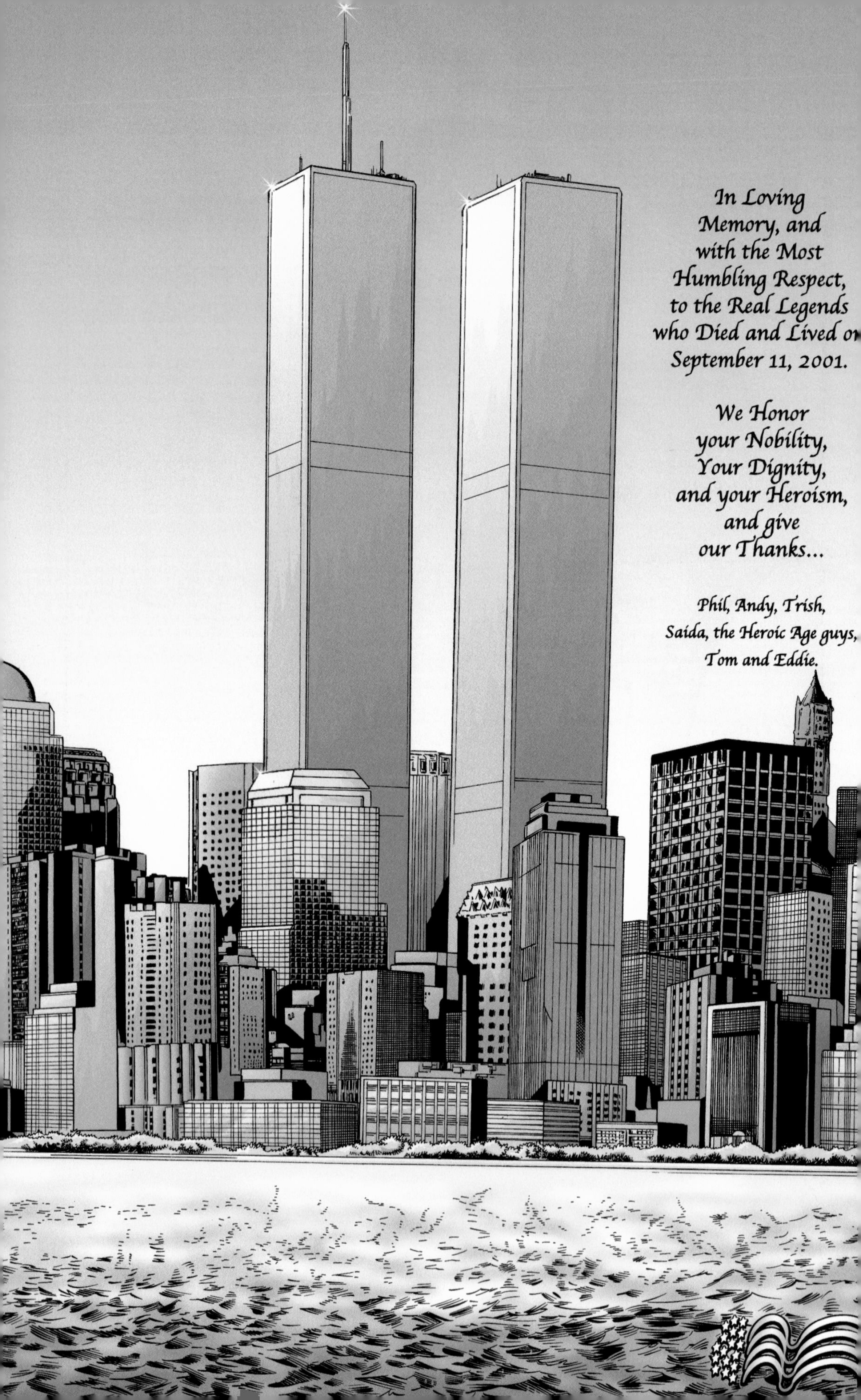
In Loving Memory, and with the Most Humbling Respect, to the Real Legends who Died and Lived on September 11, 2001.
We Honor your Nobility, Your Dignity, and your Heroism, and give our Thanks...
Phil, Andy, Trish, Saida, the Heroic Age guys, Tom and Eddie.

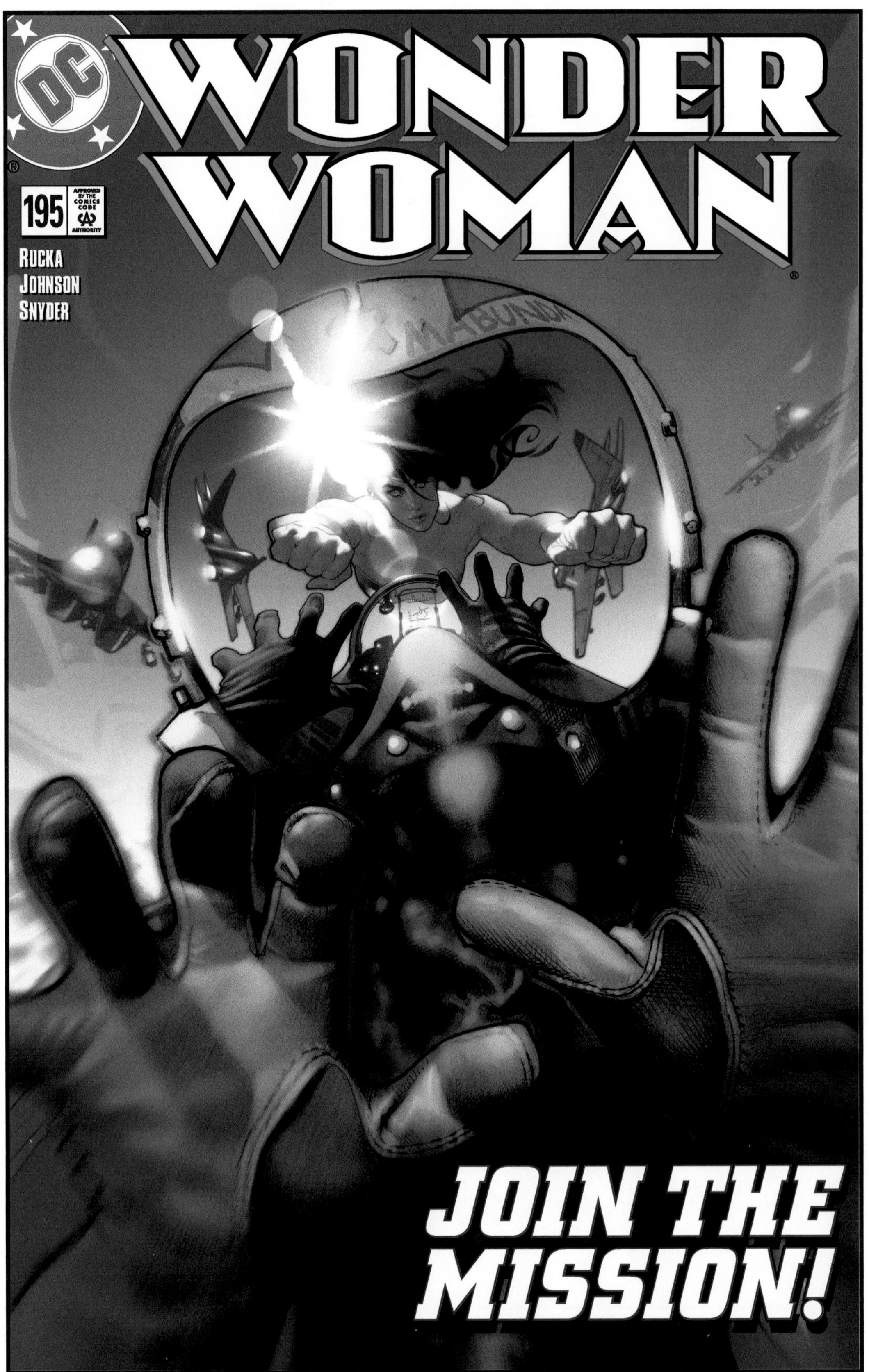
WONDER WOMAN
195
APPROVED BY THE COMICS CODE AUTHORITY
RUCKA
JOHNSON
SNYDER
JOIN THE MISSION!

"GOOD MORNING, MISTER McCARTHY. I'M ALANA DOMINGUEZ, THE AMBASSADOR'S SECRETARY. PLEASE, HAVE A SEAT."
"THANK YOU."
"WE DON'T STAND ON TOO MUCH FORMALITY HERE. PLEASE, CALL ME ALANA."
EVALUATION: A0887 51874511
INCOMING OBJECT STATUS: UNIDENTIFIED EL: 12489 SP: M 1.6
"NICE TO MEET YOU, ALANA. I'M JONAH."
"THAT'S WHAT IT SAID ON YOUR RÉSUMÉ."
"THAT'S A JOKE, JONAH, YOU'RE FREE TO LAUGH."
"AH."
"DON'T BE NERVOUS, YOU'VE ALREADY GOT THE JOB...
"...THIS IS SIMPLY YOUR ENTRY INTERVIEW."
"IT'S A LITTLE... IT'S A LITTLE OVERWHELMING, THAT'S ALL."
"YOU'LL GET OVER IT, TRUST ME."
"REALLY?"
"NO, NOT REALLY..."

...SHE'S THE WONDER WOMAN, AFTER ALL.
YOU NEVER GET OVER IT, BUT YOU GIVE IT SOME TIME, YOU MIGHT GET USED TO IT.
...IS SHE HERE?
THE AMBASSADOR HAD SOME BUSINESS THIS MORNING ON BEHALF OF THE U.N., BUT SHE SHOULD RETURN LATER THIS AFTERNOON.
YOU'RE IN FOR A TREAT WHEN SHE GETS BACK.
I'M SORRY, A TREAT?
IT'S A SURPRISE, YOU'LL SEE.
STANFORD... HARVARD LAW...DONE SOME WORK WITH THE SOUTHERN POVERTY LAW CENTER AND AMNESTY INTERNATIONAL...
HOW OLD ARE YOU, JONAH?
I'M TWENTY-NINE.
DO YOU SLEEP AT ALL?
NOT MUCH.
YOU'LL FIT RIGHT IN. NOW LET'S TALK ABOUT THE JOB. YOU'LL HAVE SEVERAL DUTIES...

...ASSISTING RACHEL KEAST IN LEGAL, SPECIFICALLY IN MATTERS OF INTERNATIONAL LAW AND U.N. PROCEDURE, AS WELL AS WORKING WITH PETER GARIBALDI IN MEDIA AFFAIRS.
OCCASIONAL TRAVEL WITH THE AMBASSADOR AS HER HANDLER. YOU'LL HAVE TO APPEAR AT FUNCTIONS WITH THE PUBLIC, OTHER DIGNITARIES, SOMETIMES A HEAD OF STATE.
THESE ARE PEOPLE WHO WANT A LOT OF THE AMBASSADOR'S TIME, AND SHE'S THE KIND OF PERSON WHO WOULD HAPPILY GIVE IT TO THEM.
YOU'LL BE THE ONE WHO HAS TO SAY NO, TO KEEP HER ON TARGET.
YOU'RE ON CALL TWENTY-FOUR SEVEN. DURING A CRISIS YOU COULD BE HERE IN THE OFFICE FOR THIRTY, FORTY HOURS AT A STRETCH, OFTEN WITH HER ABSENT.
SHE DISLIKES YES-MEN. WHEN SHE IS HERE, SHE'LL EXPECT YOU TO OFFER INPUT ON POLICY, TO SPEAK YOUR MIND, AND TO DEFEND YOUR ARGUMENTS.
I UNDERSTAND.
DO YOU ALSO UNDERSTAND THAT THE AMBASSADOR REGULARLY DEALS WITH THINGS MOST PEOPLE CONSIDER EXTRAORDINARY?
ALIEN INVASIONS. GIANT KILLER ROBOTS. MYTHICAL BEASTS FROM HADES TRYING TO RIP HER INTO PIECES. THE IMMINENT DESTRUCTION OF THE EARTH.
IT CAN GET A LITTLE STRESSFUL.
I READ THE PAPERS.
IT DOESN'T PAY WELL, JONAH, ESPECIALLY FOR NEW YORK.
THIRTY-TWO K A YEAR PLUS BENEFITS. TWO WEEKS ANNUAL VACATION YOU'LL NEVER HAVE A CHANCE TO TAKE.
THAT'S FINE.
ALL RIGHT. TELL ME WHY YOU WANT THE JOB.
BECAUSE SHE MAKES A DIFFERENCE.

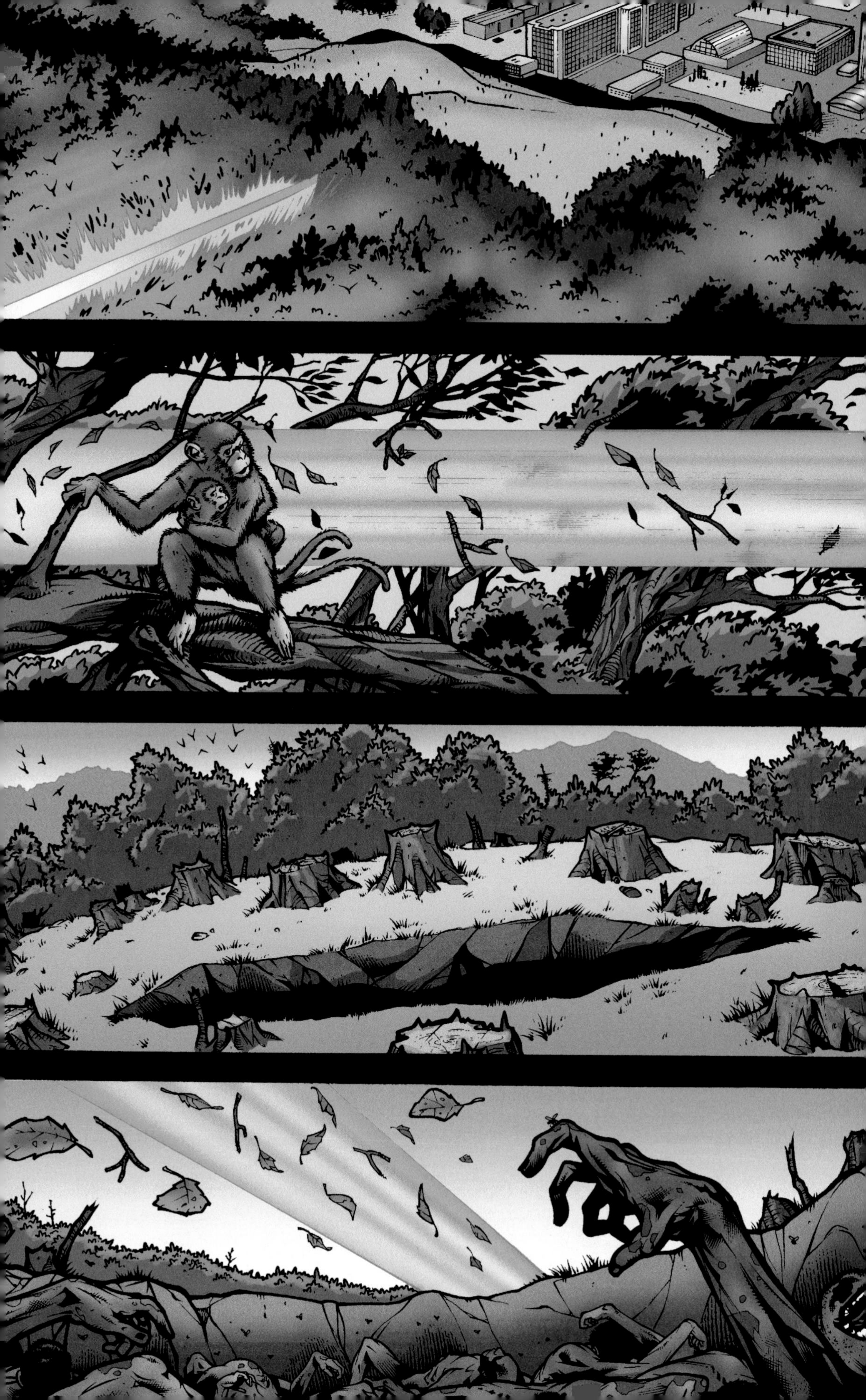

RACHEL? GOT SOMEONE FOR YOU TO MEET, HERE...
...THIS IS JONAH McCARTHY, HE'LL BE HELPING YOU OUT--
NOT NOW.
NO, I'M NOT SPEAKING TO YOU, BRIAN...YES, YES, WE DID, AND I'M GONNA TELL YOU WHAT I TOLD YOUR ASSOCIATE...
...SELF-INCRIMINATION AND LYING ARE TWO DIFFERENT THINGS...
...OF COURSE I UNDERSTAND A RIGHT TO COUNSEL, BUT THEY DON'T HAVE TO ANSWER HER, BRIAN! WE'RE NOT TALKING ABOUT THE LASSO!
...YES... NO, NOT AT ALL, BUT FRANKLY, I'D HAVE EXPECTED BETTER FROM THE A.C.L.U.
BRIAN KUHN?
THE SAME. HE'S GRAND-STANDING, TRY-ING TO GRAB A HEADLINE.
YOU, NEW GUY, YOU'RE A LAWYER?
UH, YEAH--
WHAT DO YOU MAKE OF THIS?
IT LOOKS LIKE A COURT PETITION FOR AN INJUNCTION, TO PREVENT THE AMBASSADOR FROM QUESTIONING SUSPECTS APPREHENDED DURING THE COMMISSION OF A CRIME.
whereas the Ambassador of
Themyscira has no legal
jurisdiction in any
ON THE NOSE.

FIFTH AMENDMENT ISSUE?
THEY'RE ARGUING THAT DIANA, BY HER NATURE, COMPELS A SELF-INCRIMINATORY ANSWER FROM WHOEVER SHE QUESTIONS.
THAT'S ONLY IF SHE USES THE LASSO, RIGHT?
BY HER NATURE, NEW GUY.
IT'S NEXT TO IMPOSSIBLE TO LIE TO DIANA AT THE BEST OF TIMES.
YOU CATCH THE NEWS?
NOT IN THE LAST HOUR.
SHE'S IN ITARI AIRSPACE. THEY SENT MIGS UP TO STOP HER.
PITY THE PILOTS.
STILL GIVING THE TOUR?
WE'RE INTERRUPTING IT. GARIBALDI AND I HAVE A MEETING WITH THE EDITORS AT CARELTON.
JONAH'S GONNA JOIN US.
MAKE SURE HE MEETS FERDINAND WHEN HE GETS BACK.
5TH STREET BAGEL CO.
WHO'S FERDINAND?
THE CHEF.

CGP
I WAS HOPING DIANA WOULD JOIN US, PETER.
NICE TO SEE YOU, TOO, NITA.
DIANA'S OUT OF THE COUNTRY RIGHT NOW. SHE ASKED ME TO HANDLE THIS FOR HER.
NEW YORK TIMES BESTSELLER Matt Idelson THE CAB DRIVER "TERRIFYING!" Fletcher Chu-Fong USA Today
WELL, WHEN YOU SEE HER, PLEASE TELL HER I'M STILL WAITING FOR THE GALLEY PAGES WITH HER FINAL CHANGES.
WE'RE HOPING TO GO TO PRESS BY THE END OF THE MONTH.
SHE'S ASKED A FRIEND TO GIVE THE MANU-SCRIPT A FINAL LOOK, YOU SHOULD HAVE IT BACK BY TOMORROW.
CHAD FLETCHER
DAN JOLLEY REDEEMER'S LAW
The Color of BLOOD Moose Bauman
ETHAN AND TOM HERE HAVE A COVER DESIGN WE'RE HAPPY WITH. I'LL LET THEM EXPLAIN.
THANK YOU, NITA.
Carelton Group CGP Publishing
THE PROBLEM WAS, OF COURSE, HOW TO PROMOTE THE BOOK WITHOUT APPEARING EXPLOITATIVE.
WE'VE SETTLED ON A COVER THAT WE THINK SAYS TO THE WORLD, THIS WOMAN IS A GODDESS, AND THESE ARE HER WORDS.
WE WANTED TO SHOW WHO SHE IS, HER THOUGHTS, HER EMOTIONS...
Carelton Group CGP Publishing
SHASTA COLLEGE ART DEPT
...AND HER PASSIONS!

Wonderful Words
A GODDESS SPEAKS
VOILA!
By Princess Diana of Themyscira
WHAT DO YOU THINK?
Wonderful Words
A GODDESS SPEAKS
By Princess Diana of Themyscira
IT'S...
...IT'S CERTAINLY ONE DIRECTION WE COULD TAKE IT, YEAH.
MY LIFE WITH ROBOTS
T.O. MORROW
FORTUNATELY, DIANA ASKED AN ARTIST FRIEND OF HERS TO DO A MOCK-UP OF

THIS IS THE COVER SHE WANTS, AND THE TITLE.
REFLECTIONS
A Collection of Essays and Speeches
by Diana of Themyscira
ALL THE ART FILES ARE ON THE CD.
I'LL LOOK FORWARD TO SEEING THE PROOFS.
MISTER GARIBALDI--
CHAD FLETCHER
BLOOD
Moose Bauman
IT'S NOT OPEN TO DISCUSSION, NITA. IT'S WHAT SHE WANTS, AND IF SHE DOESN'T GET IT, SHE'LL TAKE THE BOOK ELSEWHERE.
IT'S REALLY AS SIMPLE AS THAT.
WE'LL HAVE THE PROOFS SENT TO THE EMBASSY BY MONDAY MORNING.
THANKS.

YOU BELIEVE THAT?
SADLY, YES.
THEY'RE STILL ASKING THAT THE AMBASSADOR TOUR.
I'VE DISCUSSED IT WITH HER, AND SHE SEEMS AMENABLE.
ARELTON · GROUP · PUBLISHING
YOU KNOW DIANA, ANY CHANCE TO SPREAD THE MESSAGE.
JONAH, YOU GOT SOMETHING TO WRITE WITH?
I'VE GOT MY P.D.A.
GOOD...
4410 BROADWAY
...I WANT YOU TO START LINING UP BOOK STORES FOR DIANA TO SIGN AT. PREFERABLY INDEPENDENTS, RATHER THAN THE BIG BOX CHAIN STORES.
WE'RE LOOKING AT THIRTY CITIES, SHE'LL START THE WEEK AFTER THE BOOK IS RELEASED.
WAIT, THIRTY?
TAXI
WE'LL SCHEDULE THIRTY, BUT THE WAY THINGS WORK AROUND WONDER WOMAN, SHE'LL END UP HAVING TO CANCEL HALF THE DATES.
EITHER U.N. OR LEAGUE OR SOMETHING ELSE, GOD KNOWS WHAT.
NERVOUS?
OH, YEAH.
GOOD.

<WE SHOULD RUN.>
<GENERAL ABAKU HAS ORDERED ALL DESERTERS TO BE SHOT.>
<WE SHOULD STILL RUN-->
<FIRE! OPEN FIRE!>
KRAK!

CHAKCHAKCHAKCHAKCHAK
BUDDABUDDABUDDABUDDABUDDA
TINK
TINK
TINK
TING
TINK
CHAKCHAKCHAKCHAKCHAK

MISS DOMINGUEZ?
THEMYSCIRA HO
MINI
YVETTE FROM THE SECRETARY-GENERAL'S OFFICE IS ON LINE THREE.
TELL HER I'LL BE RIGHT THERE.
JONAH, IF YOU WANT TO WAIT HERE, THIS SHOULDN'T BE MORE THAN A MINUTE OR TWO.
FINE.
AESOP'S FABLES
TK-TK

YOU MUST BE NEW. I'M SUPERMAN.
YOU'RE...?
I'M... UH...
...UH...
AESOP'S FABLES
...I THINK I'VE FORGOTTEN MY NAME...
IT HAPPENS.
IF YOU COULD GIVE THIS TO DIANA WHEN SHE GETS BACK, I'D BE GRATEFUL.
I'VE MARKED THE PAGES THAT I THINK COULD USE ANOTHER PASS, BUT FOR THE MOST PART I THINK IT'S VERY STRONG.
I WILL, I'LL DO THAT.
JONAH? SORRY ABOUT THAT...

...LET'S TAKE YOU TO MEET FERDINAND NOW.
GOOD AFTERNOON, SUPERMAN.
MS. DOMINGUEZ, NICE TO SEE YOU.
AND NICE TO MEET YOU, TOO, JONAH.
COME ON. YOU CAN LEAVE THE MANUSCRIPT ON THE TABLE.
WE'RE GOING THIS WAY.
THAT WAS SUPERMAN. I JUST MET SUPERMAN.
THAT HARVARD EDUCATION IS REALLY PAYING OFF FOR YOU, ISN'T IT?
NO, I MEAN THAT WAS SUPERMAN, HE JUST DROPPED BY, HE JUST--
YES, I KNOW. HE'S BEEN DOING IT QUITE OFTEN OF LATE, AND FREQUENTLY UNANNOUNCED.
OF LATE?
SINCE MISS TROY DIED.
HOW'S SHE...IT MUST BE HARD FOR HER.
THEY SHARED AN APARTMENT, BUT THE AMBASSADOR SOLD IT.
SHE'S MOVED BACK INTO HER ROOMS HERE.
DOES SHE TALK ABOUT IT?
NO. AND NEITHER SHOULD YOU.
FERDINAND, THIS IS JONAH McCARTHY...

JONAH, THIS IS FERDINAND...
...HE'S JUST JOINED THE AMBASSADOR'S **STAFF**.
HI THERE.
...HE RUNS THE **KITCHEN**.

YOU'LL HAVE TO **FORGIVE** HIM.
HE JUST MET SUPER-MAN.
THAT EXPLAINS IT.
YOU'RE A...
...YOU'RE A **MINOTAUR**.
NOT "**A**," BOY. "**THE**."

AND NO, I'M **NOT**, ACTUALLY. WE'RE **RELATED**, BUT THE ONE YOU'RE THINKING OF IS FROM **MINOS**.
I GREW UP OUTSIDE KITHIRA, SO I SUPPOSE THAT MAKES ME A KITH-O-TAUR.

YOU STAYING FOR **DINNER?**

STAY BACK! STAY BACK, YOU HAVE NO AUTHORITY THE UNITED NATIONS HAS NO AUTHORITY--
KRAK KRAK KRAK
TING
PING
PKOW
YOU'RE UNDER ARREST, GENERAL.

SHEPHERD
SORRY IT TOOK SO LONG.

THERE WAS *RESISTANCE.*
BUT NO *LOSS* OF *LIFE?*
NONE.

THEN IT TOOK *JUST* LONG ENOUGH, AMBASSADOR.
THANK YOU.
SHEPHERD

AS FOR *YOU,* GENERAL, YOUR *PRESENCE* HAS BEEN REQUESTED IN THE *HAGUE.*
THERE ARE SEVERAL *CHARGES* THE *WORLD* WOULD HAVE YOU *ANSWER.*

I'M CONSTANTLY AMAZED AT WHAT YOU CAN DO WITH TOFU, FERDINAND.
MORE CHIPS THAN COOKIE
MTA
87

ONE MAKES DO.
ARE ALL THE MEALS VEGETARIAN?
DIANA DOESN'T EAT MEAT.

WOULD YOU IF ANIMALS COULD TALK TO YOU?
NO, I GUESS NOT.
THAT'S NOT THE ONLY REASON SHE DOESN'T-- MARTIN, LEAVE YOUR BROTHER ALONE.

DON'T EAT TOO MUCH, JONAH.
YOU'LL RUIN YOUR TREAT.
THERE'S A SPECIAL WELCOME- ABOARD DESSERT?

NOT QUITE.
ROBBY, SIT BACK DOWN. FERDINAND DOESN'T NEED YOUR HELP.

FERDINAND DOESN'T MIND, DO YOU--
JONAH.

I HOPE THE ORIENTATION WENT WELL.
I'M VERY GLAD YOU'LL BE JOINING THE STAFF.
IT'S AN HONOR TO BE HERE.
THE HONOR IS IN THE WORK.
COME UP TO THE ROOF WITH ME.
YOU'LL WANT YOUR COAT.
GO ON, JONAH. YOU DON'T KEEP HER WAITING.
NEW GUY.
TELL ME ABOUT IT.

WAS IT A GOOD DAY, JONAH?
IT WAS AN INTERESTING DAY, MADAME AMBASSADOR.

DIANA, PLEASE.
TURN AROUND.

UH...IS THIS THE THING EVERYONE'S BEEN HINTING ABOUT?
YES.
JUST RELAX, REMEMBER TO BREATHE.

WELCOME ABOARD.

THE MISSION

Greg Rucka: Writer
Drew Johnson: Penciller
Ray Snyder: Inker
Trish Mulvihill: Colorist
WildStorm FX: Separator
Todd Klein: Letterer
Ivan Cohen: Editor
Wonder Woman created by William Moulton Marston

IT'S 1962 AND BEING POLITICALLY CORRECT MEANS YOU'RE A DEMOCRAT. SHE'S A WOMAN OF DISTINGUISHED ENDEAVORS, BUT THIS TIME THE AMAZON PRINCESS OUTDOES HERSELF. JOIN US AS OUR RAVEN-HAIRED WARRIOR BECOMES ***"THE MOTHER OF THE MOVEMENT!"***

Wonder Woman and Black Canary

Script: D.Cooke Art: J.Bone
Color: D.Stewart Letters: J.Fletcher
ASST EDITOR: IAN SATTLER
EDITOR: DAN DIDIO

YOU'LL FEEL THAT IN THE MORNING, YOU DOG!

POUND!

JEEZ, DIANA, ***RELAX.*** MAYBE YOU SHOULD GET A MASSAGE OR SOMETHING.

KRUNCH
HONESTLY, WHAT'S YOUR PROBLEM?
MY PROBLEM IS THESE TWO-LEGGED PIGS THEY CALL MEN!

LOOK AT THEM. FIVE MINUTES AGO THEY WERE LAUGHING AT THE THOUGHT OF TWO WOMEN TRYING TO STOP THEM.
EVERY TIME THEY OPEN THEIR COWARDLY MOUTHS, THEY SAY SOMETHING MEANT TO SUBJUGATE US.
PLEASE-- MY KIDNEYS...
SNIFF

WHAT A SOCIETY. WOMEN SUBJUGATED AS HOMESLAVES WHILE THESE HAIRY BRUTES RUN AMOK.
AND IT'S NOT JUST THE VILLAINS. POLITICIANS, POLICE, JOURNALISTS TOO! AN UNHOLY CABAL MEANT TO KEEP OUR GENDER OPPRESSED.
HERE WE GO AGAIN.

EVEN THE MAGAZINES! LOOK AT THIS THING.

HERA HELP US.
A TRULY BOVINE DISPLAY.
HUH. I THINK I WENT TO MIDDLE SCHOOL WITH HER.

WILL YOU LOOK AT THE HUMILIATION THESE WOMEN ENDURE-- FORCED TO SERVE MEN IN CLUBS DRESSED UP LIKE RABBITS.
YEAH, UH...RABBITS. THOSE CLUBS ARE ALL THE RAGE ACROSS THE COUNTRY.
THERE'S ONE OPENING IN GOTHAM CITY NEXT WEEK.

HERE'S A CHANCE TO STRIKE A REAL BLOW FOR EQUALITY. I WILL GO THERE AND WIN OVER THESE MISGUIDED MEN WITH A MESSAGE OF AMAZONIAN LOVE.
AND IF THAT DOESN'T WORK?
--MERCY, PLEASE--

I WILL BEAT THEM UNTIL THEY CRY FOR THEIR SAINTED MOTHERS.
OY.
I'D BETTER TAG ALONG.
SWAT!

MERCURY'S CODPIECE!

THIS PLACE IS EVEN SLEAZIER THAN I THOUGHT.
AND WHY IN HEAVEN ARE YOU WEARING YOUR COSTUME? I THOUGHT THE IDEA WAS TO BLEND IN?
HA!
TAKE A LOOK AROUND. I'M NOT THE ONE WITH A BLENDING PROBLEM.

IT'S LIKE A WHO'S WHO OF DEGENERATES IN HERE--HERA'S GIRDLE!
WHAT NOW?

--JUST HAPPY YOU COULD MAKE IT.
ARE YOU MAD? I WOULDN'T MISS THIS CHICKFEST FOR--
BRUCE WAYNE!

WHAT ARE YOU DOING HERE?
DIANA! DINAH! I'M UH... I'M TRAILING A VILLAIN!

IMAGINE! THE CAD SNUCK INTO THIS HORRIBLE PLACE. NO CHOICE BUT TO FOLLOW HIM.
JUSTICE, AND ALL THAT, RIGHT?

WHOOPS! THERE HE GOES. I'D BETTER GET AFTER HIM.
G'NIGHT, LADIES!

WHAT A WORLD WE LIVE IN. EVEN THE GOOD GUYS ARE DOGS.
GOOD EVENING, CATS AND KITTENS.

THE MINGUS TRIO WILL BE BACK FOR ANOTHER SET SOON, BUT IN THE MEANTIME I WANTED TO THANK YOU ALL FOR MAKING TONIGHT'S OPENING SUCH A SCENE.
I COOKED UP A SWINGIN' LITTLE CAKE TO HELP US CELEBRATE.

BUT THIS ISN'T ANY ORDINARY CAKE. THIS CRAZY PASTRY HAS A SECRET INGREDIENT--
HOLLYWOOD SEXBOMB JAYNE MANSFIELD!
THIS HAS GONE FAR ENOUGH. C'MON!

--MY BABY JUST CARES FOR ME--

YIIIII!
TAKE A HIKE, HUSSY!

NOW TO DELIVER THESE MEN A MESSAGE OF LOVE AND EQUALITY.
SHOULD BE INTERESTING.
RIP

WHOO HOO HOO
JAYNE JAYNE JAYNE
WOOT

JAYN
HUH?
MEN OF AMERICA, **FOR SHAME.**
I'VE COME HERE TO TALK WITH YOU ABOUT THE OPPRESSIVE YOKE OF OBJECTIFICATION AND THE HEALING POWER OF EQUALITY.
WHAT TH'?

TOGETHER WE CAN MAKE A BETTER DAY, WHERE WOMEN ARE TREATED WITH RESPECT AND JUDGED BY THE BEAUTY OF THEIR SOULS AS WELL AS THEIR BODIES.
THOSE WHO WOULD JOIN ME, ***RAISE YOUR GLASSES!***

NOT EXACTLY WHAT I HAD IN MIND.
GET OFF THE STAGE!
WELL, THE LOVE NUMBER DIDN'T SWING.
SO, NOW WITH THE BEATING?

HOLA, DOGS!
IT'S FOR THEIR OWN GOOD.

SNAP!
FIGHT!
FRACTURE!

S-STAY BACK, YOU SHE DEVIL! IT'S TIME YOU REALIZED THAT IT'S A ***MAN'S WORLD.***

IT TICKLES.
FWOOM

LET THIS BURNING BREASTPLATE SERVE NOTICE OF YOUR VILLAINY--

KLANG!
AND BEAR WITNESS TO YOUR ***DESTRUCTION!***

EVEN IN DEFEAT THESE SWINE SMILE AND SLOBBER.
MAYBE YOU SHOULD PUT YOUR TOP BACK ON.

OUR SISTERS ARE INSPIRED. WE'VE STRUCK A ***MIGHTY BLOW*** FOR WOMEN'S RIGHTS THIS FINE NIGHT.
YOU REALIZE ALL THE PRESS HERE ARE MEN, AND YOU'VE BEATEN THEM STUPID. I DON'T THINK WE'LL BE READING ABOUT THIS ANY TIME SOON.
WHATCHA WRITIN' THERE, GLORIA?
END

PART IV: 2011-PRESENT
THE WARRIOR

The history of the DC Universe is made of permanent recreations. In 2011, FLASHPOINT, written by Geoff Johns and drawn by Andy Kubert, put this post-Crisis history to an end and brought in a new continuity: the DC Comics New 52.

New creative team Brian Azzarello and Cliff Chiang relaunched the title in November 2011, adding new twists to Wonder Woman's origins. In this new reality, what Diana thought was true (she was made from clay by her mother Hippolyta and blessed with life by the gods) wasn't. Now Diana was the illegitimate child of Hippolyta and Zeus. This revelation led to a scathing reunion with the "stepfamily." With Zeus nowhere to be found, his children fought for his succession. Meanwhile, Diana needed to protect Zola, another woman pregnant with Zeus' seed, from Zeus' scorned wife Hera.

Wonder Woman's identity quest brought her new allies and friends: Lennox, her half-brother, Hermes, messenger of Olympus, and Orion, New God of New Genesis. Some new foes also rose: Hades, God of Hell, and the First Born, a son of Zeus and Hera, abandoned and held captive for thousands of years. This rough and bloody saga ends with Diana, more powerful than ever, becoming the new Goddess of War. Following Azzarello and Chiang's departure, the WONDER WOMAN main title was helmed by all-star couple Meredith and David Finch, who reintroduced former Wonder Girl Donna Troy to the DC Universe.

At the same time, Geoff Johns and Jim Lee delivered the first issues of the new JUSTICE LEAGUE series. Wonder Woman and Superman were, of course, founding members of the team. The two teammates began a secret, turbulent romance. This relationship blossomed in a new series, SUPERMAN/WONDER WOMAN, written first by Charles Soule, then Peter Tomasi, and drawn by Tony Daniel and Doug Mahnke. In this series, readers learned that being part of the most powerful couple on Earth isn't exactly a walk in the park.

Finally, as further proof of the character's vital role in the DC pantheon, two new Wonder Woman titles debuted in 2015: SENSATION COMICS FEATURING WONDER WOMAN, featuring short stories by sought-after creators, and WONDER WOMAN '77, which takes place during the 1970s television series.

And in 2016, the Amazon hero's 75th birthday has been celebrated with two tales offering alternate versions of her: WONDER WOMAN EARTH ONE by writer Grant Morrison and artist Yanick Paquette and the nine-issue limited series THE LEGEND OF WONDER WOMAN by Renae De Liz and Ray Dillon. Not to mention, of course, the character's big-screen debut in *Batman v Superman*, brought to life by actress Gal Gadot who will also star in the hero's first-ever solo film in 2017.

THE NEW 52! #0
DC COMICS™
WONDER WOMAN®
BRIAN
AZZARELLO
CLIFF
CHIANG

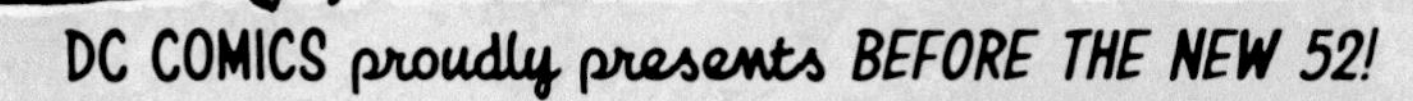

INCONCEIVABLY CONCEIVED ON A MYSTERIOUS ISLAND VOID OF MEN THAT WOMEN CALL PARADISE, SHE IS KNOWN AS *PRINCESS DIANA*--DAUGHTER OF THE MIGHTY *QUEEN HIPPOLYTA*, RULER OF THE AMAZONS! BUT HER MOTHER HOLDS A SECRET--THAT DIANA'S FATHER IS *ZEUS*--THE KING OF THE GODS! NO ONE KNOWS THIS--NOT EVEN US, WHO CALL HER...**WONDER WOMAN**!

THE LAIR OF THE MINOTAUR!

*THE MONTHLY MONSTER STRIKES AGAIN! RATHER THAN GIVE **WONDER WOMAN'S MERRY MEN** THEIR MARCHING ORDERS, WE DUG UP A STORY FROM **WONDER WOMAN'S** PAST! MAY YOU ENJOY THIS MAGNIFICENT MISSIVE THAT ORIGINALLY APPEARED IN **"ALL-GIRL ADVENTURE TALES FOR MEN #41"***

story & art by
BRIAN "*KISS MY*" AZZARELLO & CLIFF "*CHUMP*" CHIANG

coloring
"*MUDDY*" MATT WILSON
lettering
"*JITTERY*" JARED FLETCHER
assists
"*CORNY*" CHRIS CONROY
editor
"*MALIGNANT*" MATT IDELSON

WONDER WOMAN *created by* WILLIAM MOULTON MARSTON

SUDDENLY, FEAR STRIKES-- FROM ABOVE!
GET AWAY FROM MY BABIES!

I KNOW WHO YOU ARE! DIANA--PRINCESS OF THE AMAZONS!
DO YOU KNOW WHAT DAY IT IS, YOU OLD HARPY?

AYE--IT'S THE DAY I CLAW YOUR EYES OUT!

?
WRONG, BIRD BRAIN!
IT'S MY BIRTHDAY.

AND THIS EGG SHALL MAKE MY CAKE!

THE PLUCKY PRINCESS PLUNGES INTO THE ICY WATER, LEAVING THE HORRIBLE HARPY HAPLESS!
SPLOSH

AS HER YOUNG LUNGS ARE ABOUT TO BURST, DIANA SWIMS TOWARD AN UNDERWATER CAVE KNOWN ONLY TO HER...

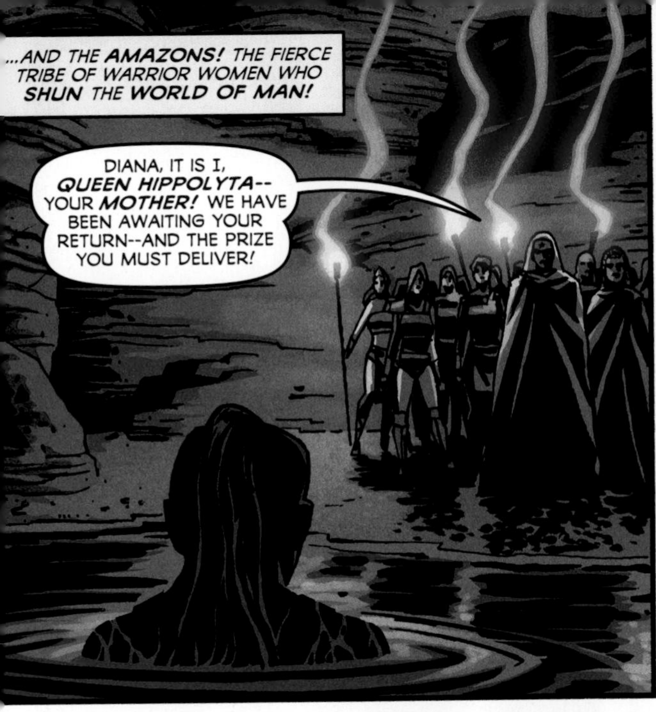
...AND THE AMAZONS! THE FIERCE TRIBE OF WARRIOR WOMEN WHO SHUN THE WORLD OF MAN!
DIANA, IT IS I, QUEEN HIPPOLYTA--YOUR MOTHER! WE HAVE BEEN AWAITING YOUR RETURN--AND THE PRIZE YOU MUST DELIVER!

QUEEN HIPPOLYTA'S TONE MASKS HER CONCERN...FOR SHE KNOWS THAT MANY YOUNG AMAZONS FAIL IN THEIR QUESTS...
TODAY IS YOUR BIRTHDAY...

AS IS OUR CUSTOM, YOU NEED TO PRESENT ME WITH A SUITABLE PRESENT, OR THE PASSING OF YOUR YEAR WILL NOT BE ACKNOWLEDGED.
MY QUEEN, FORGIVE ME. ALL I COULD FIND...

...IS A HARPY'S EGG!

HOORAY FOR PRINCESS DIANA!

FROM THE SHADOWS AN OMINOUS FIGURE DRAPED IN VULTURE PLUMES STANDS IN WATCH...
THE GIRL EXHIBITS SKILLS FAR BEYOND HER YOUNG AGE...

PERHAPS SHE IS THE ONE...

LATER THAT NIGHT, THE AMAZON CITY OF **THEMYSCIRA** CELEBRATES THEIR PRINCESS'S BIRTHDAY WITH A GRAND FEAST--COMPLETE WITH **GAMES OF MARTIAL SKILL!**

AN ODD REQUEST IS MADE...
MY QUEEN, MAY THE PRINCESS AND I DEMONSTRATE WHAT WE'VE LEARNED IN OUR TRAINING EXERCISES?
BUT...WE ARE NOT OLD ENOUGH FOR THE GAMES!

METHINKS I WOULD LIKE THAT, **ALEKA**--BUT WITH WOODEN SWORDS. I DO NOT WANT TO SEE ONE OF YOU INJURED.

PITY THAT BE **EXACTLY** WHAT THE QUEEN WILL SEE...

THE COMBAT **BEGINS!**

GREAT HERA!

ALEKA IS COMING AT ME WITH **ALL HER MIGHT!**

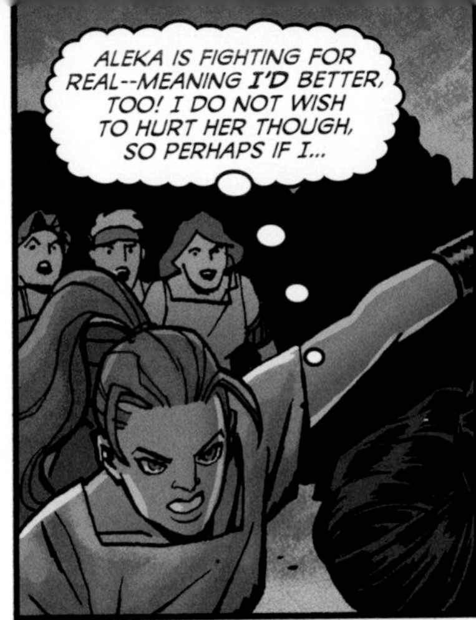
ALEKA IS FIGHTING FOR REAL--MEANING **I'D** BETTER, TOO! I DO NOT WISH TO HURT HER THOUGH, SO PERHAPS IF I...

THWACK

YIELD?
NEVER! I AM A **TRUE AMAZON WARRIOR!**
NOT **YET** YOU'RE NOT!
WELL, YOU WILL **NEVER** BE...

CLAY!
THE MUD **STINGS,** BUT NOT AS MUCH AS ALEKA'S WORDS...

...WORDS THAT SEND THE PRINCESS **INTO A RAGE!**
TAKE IT **BACK!**
DAUGHTER, **STOP!** YOU'RE **HURTING** HER!
KOFF
YIELD!
KOFF

I--

I'M SORRY!

DIANA RUNS INTO THE FOREST AS FAR AS HER LEGS WILL CARRY HER BEFORE FALLING ON THE BANKS OF A SILENT STREAM...
WHAT DID I DO TO DESERVE SUCH A FATE? TO BE FORMED FROM CLAY-- TO NOT HAVE REAL PARENTS-- TO NEVER FIT IN!!*
*DIANA DOESN'T KNOW THAT SHE DOES HAVE A MOTHER AND A FATHER--QUEEN HIPPOLYTA AND ZEUS, KING OF OLYMPUS! -MALIGNANT MATT

I MAY LOOK LIKE MY SISTERS, BUT I WILL NEVER BE LIKE THEM-- AND THEY WILL ALWAYS KNOW THAT IN THEIR HEARTS!

WHY MUST I BE DIFFERENT?

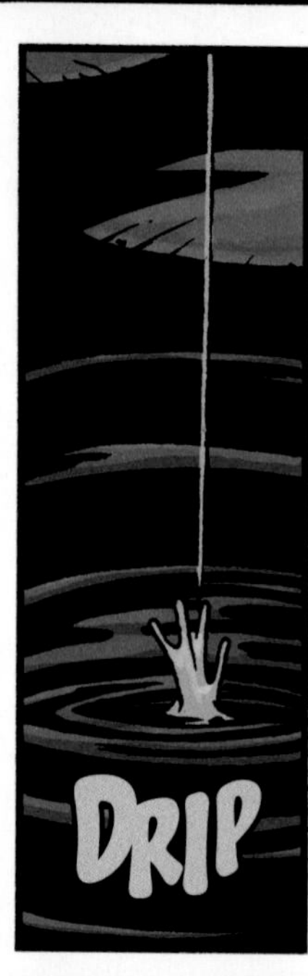
DRIP

PERHAPS, PRINCESS...

HEARING A STRANGE VOICE, DIANA RESPONDS AS HER AMAZON TRAINING HAS TAUGHT HER!

...IT IS A GIFT TO BE DIFFERENT.

WHO ARE YOU TO SAY SUCH A THING?

HA! HAST THOU SPENT ALL THY TIME IN THE ARENA AND NONE IN THE TEMPLE? TRULY THOU ART AFTER MINE OWN HEART!
LITTLE ONE, I BE AN OLYMPIAN. I BE THE SETTLER OF DISPUTE. I BE BLOOD! I BE GUTS! I BE IRON!
I BE WAR!

AND I BE HERE WITH AN OFFER...
THOU HAST BEEN TRAINED BY AMAZONS-- BRAVE WARRIORS, TRUE--BUT THERE IS MORE TO LEARN. WARRIOR WAYS, THAT ONLY A GOD CAN TEACH.
I WANT TO LEARN!

EXCELLENT! HERE IN THE FOREST BEYOND YONDER WALLS EACH FULL MOON, I WILL MAKETH THE GREATEST WARRIOR THE WORLD HAS SEEN OUT OF THEE!

AND SO EVERY MONTH, DIANA MEETS THE OLYMPIAN UNDER THE FULL MOON. THERE HE TEACHES HER TO HARNESS HER BODY...

AND HER SPIRIT...

TO BE ONE WITH THE WAYS OF WAR!
SPLENDID, LITTLE ONE!

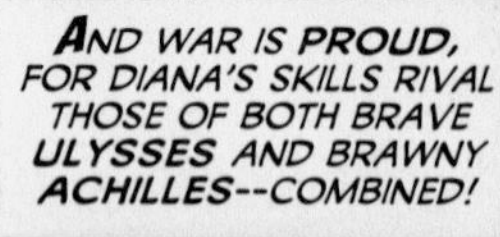
AND WAR IS PROUD, FOR DIANA'S SKILLS RIVAL THOSE OF BOTH BRAVE ULYSSES AND BRAWNY ACHILLES--COMBINED!

SHE BRINGS THE IMMORTAL SOMETHING AKIN TO JOY, AND FOR A BRIEF MOMENT HE ALLOWS HIMSELF TO DREAM OF REST, AND OF ONE DAY PASSING ON THE MANTLE.

ALL THE WHILE, DIANA NEVER NEGLECTS HER TRADITIONAL AMAZON STUDIES.

SHE PROVES HERSELF STRONGER AND FASTER THAN THE OTHER GIRLS HER AGE.

AS WELL AS SOME OF HER AMAZON TEACHERS!

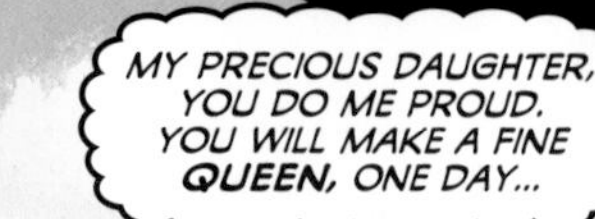
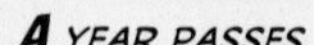

MY PRECIOUS DAUGHTER, YOU DO ME PROUD. YOU WILL MAKE A FINE QUEEN, ONE DAY...
A YEAR PASSES.

THOU DID WELL TONIGHT. WE'LL CELEBRATE AS WARRIORS, WITH MEAD FROM MARKISAN-- TRULY THE FINEST FERMENTER FROM THIS OR ANY ERA!
I WANT TO USE A BLADE.
EH?

WOOD IS FOR CHILDREN.
LITTLE ONE...STEEL IS REAL. A BLADE IN ONE'S HAND IS TRUTH--AND LIKE IT, MUST BE USED AS SUCH.
IT MUST BE RELENTLESS, UNERRING, AND UNFORGIVING.
THOU KNOW NOT WHAT YOU ASK.

I DO. I WANT TO USE REAL BLADES.

SIGH SO BE IT. THIS IS THY CHOICE. THE NEXT MOON, WE FIGHT...

...TO THE DEATH!
WHAT!?
DO NOT PICK UP A SWORD AGAINST A MAN UNLESS YOU MEAN TO PUT HIM DOWN WITH IT. THAT IS THE WARRIOR'S WAY.
UNDERSTOOD?

I UNDERSTAND.

THE BATTLE IS JOINED! IT LASTS FOR HOURS!
LATER, THE AMAZONS WOULD SPEAK OF UNEXPLAINABLE LIGHTNING FLASHING FROM THE MOUNTAINTOP-- SO FIERCE IS THE CLASH OF REAL ON STEEL!

THIS IS HARDER THAN I THOUGHT! PERCHANCE AN OLD TRICK...
KLANG
BUT WILY WAR HAS OLD TRICKS OF HIS OWN!

CLEVER, GIRL...

BUT A CLEVER WARRIOR DISARMED...

...KNOWS TO USE THEIR OPPONENT'S WEAPON AGAINST THEM!
I...

I'M READY TO DIE BY YOUR HANDS.
DIANA'S WORDS SHAKE WAR TO HIS CORE!

PRINCESS... WHILE A WARRIOR KNOWS THAT DEATH BE THE PRICE OF WAR, A WARRIOR NEVER ACCEPTS DEATH...

A WARRIOR FIGHTS TO THE DEATH...

...BUT NOT ON THIS NIGHT, LITTLE ONE.

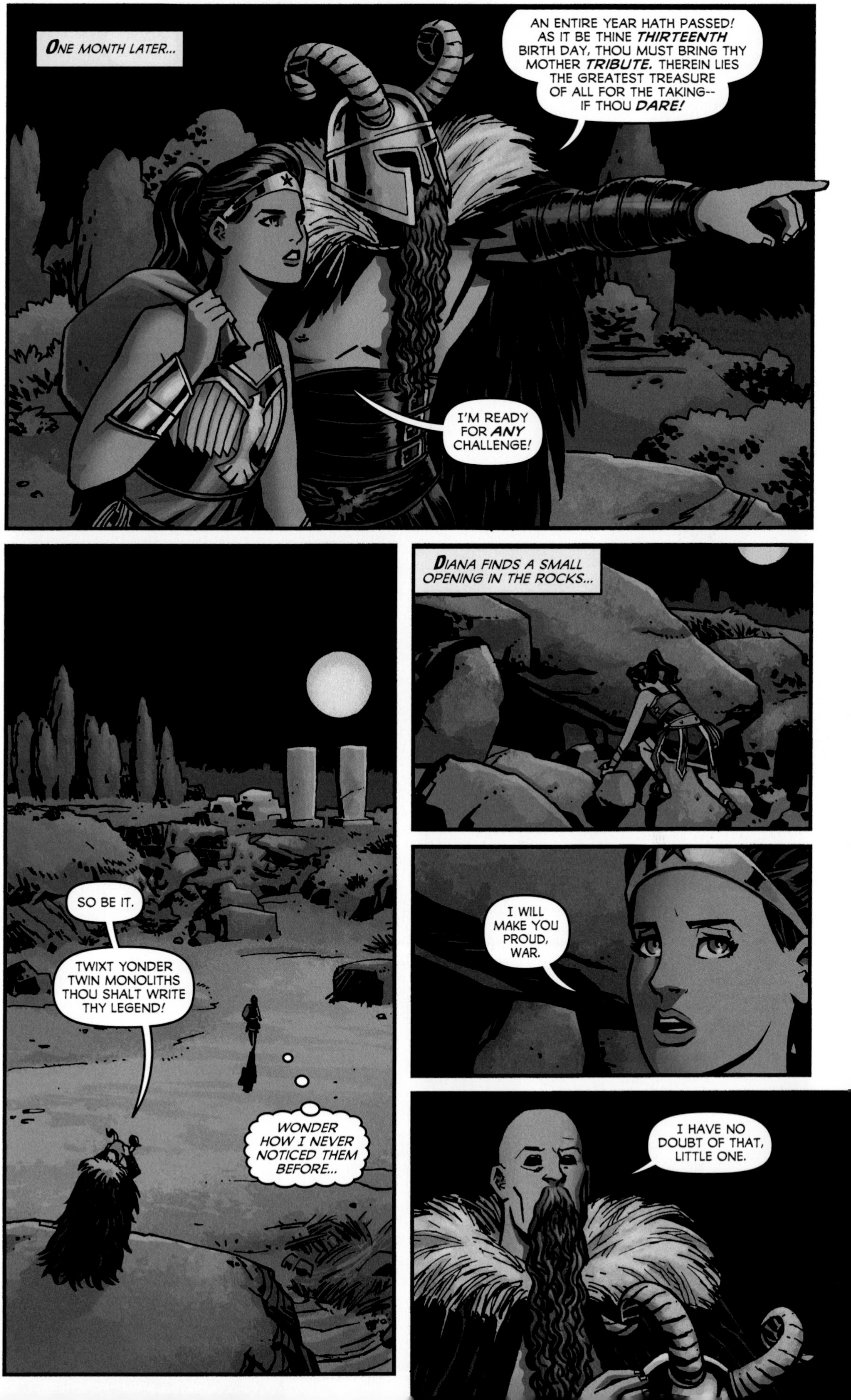

ONE MONTH LATER...

AN ENTIRE YEAR HATH PASSED! AS IT BE THINE ***THIRTEENTH*** BIRTH DAY, THOU MUST BRING THY MOTHER ***TRIBUTE.*** THEREIN LIES THE GREATEST TREASURE OF ALL FOR THE TAKING-- IF THOU ***DARE!***

I'M READY FOR ***ANY*** CHALLENGE!

SO BE IT.
TWIXT YONDER TWIN MONOLITHS THOU SHALT WRITE THY LEGEND!
WONDER HOW I NEVER NOTICED THEM BEFORE...

DIANA FINDS A SMALL OPENING IN THE ROCKS...

I WILL MAKE YOU PROUD, WAR.

I HAVE NO DOUBT OF THAT, LITTLE ONE.

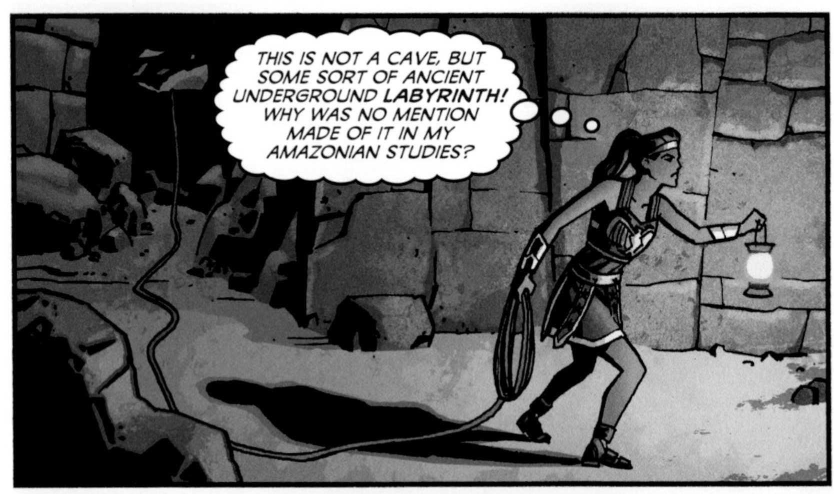

THIS IS NOT A CAVE, BUT SOME SORT OF ANCIENT UNDERGROUND LABYRINTH! WHY WAS NO MENTION MADE OF IT IN MY AMAZONIAN STUDIES?

GREAT HERA!

AS THEY GROW ACCUSTOM TO THE DANK DARKNESS, DIANA'S EYES ANSWER HER QUESTION! HER HAIR STANDS ON END-- THIS IS A PLACE OF **GREAT DANGER!**

A PLACE WHERE THOSE WHO ENTER...

NEVER LEAVE!

GOOD THING I TIED MY MAGIC LASSO TO A ROCK AT THE OPENING, SO I CAN FIND MY WAY OUT!

THE BRAVE YOUNG PRINCESS TRAVELS DEEPER AND DEEPER INTO THE TWISTING MAZE...
THE AIR GETS FOULER WITH EACH STEP I TAKE...

NOTHING BUT DUST AND COBWEBS. WAR SAID I'D FIND TREASURE HERE...

WHAT COULD HE HAVE MEANT?

CLOP

WHEN DIANA TURNS, THE BLOOD IN HER VEINS GOES ICIER THAN THE SEA SHE PLUNGED INTO A YEAR AGO!

RRRRGGGRR
GREAT HERA!
THE MINOTAUR!

YES!--THE MINOTAUR--THE MOST FEARSOME BEAST KNOWN TO MAN, WOMAN, OR GOD!
WAR MUST HAVE TRANSPORTED US TO CRETE! THAT EXPLAINS WHY I'D NEVER SEEN THE MONOLITHS BEFORE!

IT BE FURY IMPOSSIBLE TO TAME! MURDEROUS RAGE IN ITS PUREST FORM!

ITS LIFE'S MISSION--TO KILL!
OOF!
NO--MY LANTERN!

KRAK

BWAARGH
FWOOOM
THAT WAS THE PROVERBIAL LUCKY BREAK...

KKIIIILLLL!

IT'S TOO STRONG... SURELY I CANNOT BEST THE BEAST IN COMBAT!

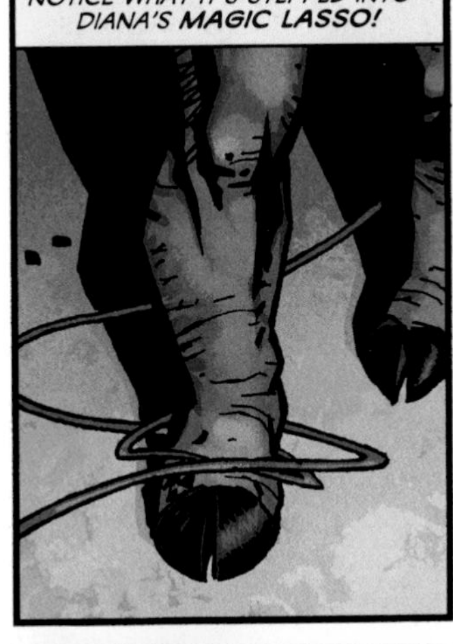
IN ITS BLIND RAGE, THE RAVENOUS MINOTAUR DOESN'T NOTICE WHAT IT'S STEPPED INTO-- DIANA'S MAGIC LASSO!

GOT YOU!

CRASH

IT'S NO USE! I'M JUST MAKING HIM ANGRIER!

WAIT! THAT'S IT!

A CLEVER WARRIOR...
...USES HER OPPONENT'S WEAPON...

RRRAAOOOW
...AGAINST THEM!

AS THE MINOTAUR CHARGES, DIANA LEAPS AWAY--CAUSING THE BERSERK BRUTE TO HURL HEAD-FIRST INTO THE HARD STONE WALL SHE'D BACKED UP AGAINST!
SMAAAACH

IT WORKED! HE'S DAZED!

TIME TO FINISH THE JOB!

WHUMP

I DID IT! I VANQUISHED THE MIGHTY MINOTAUR!
YOU HATH, AND WORDS CANNOT EXPRESS THE ADMIRATION I FEEL...

METHINKS THEY WILL FAIL THY MOTHER AS WELL, WHEN YOU PRESENT HER WITH THE FINEST TREASURE IMAGINABLE.
WHAT TREASURE, WAR?
WHY, THE ONE AT THY FEET...

THINE ENEMY'S HEAD, OF COURSE.

NOW STRIKE.
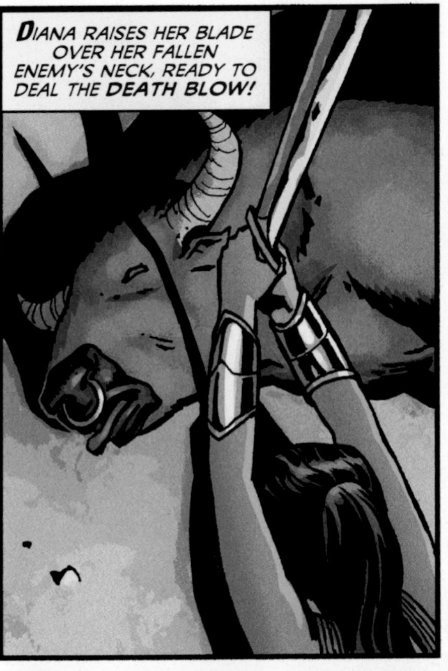
DIANA RAISES HER BLADE OVER HER FALLEN ENEMY'S NECK, READY TO DEAL THE DEATH BLOW!

BUT THEN, THE MINOTAUR'S EYE FLICKERS OPEN. IT STRUGGLES, ANGER REPLACED BY HELPLESSNESS...

IN THE GLASSY ORB, SHE RECOGNIZES...

I CANNOT.

WHAT?!
DO NOT FAIL THIS TASK, WARRIOR! THINE ENEMIES MUST BE ELIMINATED, LEST THEY RETURN FOR THINE OWN HEAD!
REVENGE IS NOT AN OPTION TO LEAVE A FOE!

THOU WISHES TO BE A WARRIOR? A TRUE WARRIOR SHOWS NO MERCY!

BUT WAR, THAT NIGHT ON THE MOUNTAINTOP...

YOU DID.

THE PURPOSE OF WAR IS TO END CONFLICT. YOU MUST STRIKE.
I WILL NOT KILL. NOT LIKE THIS.

LITTLE ONE, DOST THOU REMEMBER WHAT IT MEANS TO RAISE A SWORD AGAINST A MAN?

...YES.

AND WAR BELLOWS-- NOT WITH THE RAGE OF THE MINOTAUR, BUT HAUNTED, LIKE A WOUNDED ANIMAL!

SO BE IT!
THOU ART MY GREATEST FAILURE, DIANA OF THEMYSCIRA!
THE PATH THOU HAST CHOSEN, NOW THOU SHALL WALK ALONE!
FWOOOM

RRRRRR
!

THE MONSTER RISEN LOOMS OVER A DEFENSELESS DIANA, ITS FETID BREATH POUNDING THE PRINCESS!

WHAT IS THAT I SEE IN ITS EYES NOW? IS THAT...

RESPECT?

WE'LL NEVER KNOW, FOR THE BEAST TURNS AND SHUFFLES OFF BACK TO ITS INFERNAL ABYSS!

WHAT A LESSON I'VE LEARNED! I CANNOT WAIT TO TELL MY SISTERS-- IF I EVER GET BACK TO--
--THEMYSCIRA?! THEN I'M NOT ON CRETE, WAR FOOLED ME!
...OR DID HE?
IT FEELS RIGHT, SPARING THE MINOTAUR...
OR AM I JUST FOOLING MYSELF?
CAN MY MERCY BE A TRIBUTE FOR MY MOTHER?
The End?

DC COMICS™
SENSATION COMICS FEATURING
Wonder Woman™
#1
SIMONE
DEIBERT
VAN SCIVER
STAGGS
HI-FI
RAUCH

THERE IS A SECRET MATH IN GOTHAM, A NUMERICAL CERTAINTY THAT HAS PREVENTED THE ENTIRE SYSTEM FROM BURNING TO THE GROUND.

IT IS SIMPLY THIS: WITH THIS GROUP, ONE AND ONE NEVER EQUAL TWO.
AND THANKFULLY, ONE AND ONE AND ONE AND ONE AND ONE AND ONE AND ONE HAVE NEVER, EVER EQUALED ANY COMBINED AGGREGATE.
THEY DON'T WORK TOGETHER. THEY HATE EACH OTHER ALMOST AS MUCH AS THEY HATE US.

OR SO WE ALWAYS THOUGHT.

UNTIL ONE NIGHT, THIS PARTICULAR LOT DECIDED NOT TO BE COWARDLY AND SUPERSTITIOUS.
AND THE MATH OF GOTHAM CITY CHANGED IN BRUTAL FASHION.

AFTER THAT, THINGS WENT TO AN ICY HELL IN A HURRY.
POLICE
AND THE WEEDS THREATENED TO OVERTAKE THE GARDEN AND STRANGLE THE ROSES ENTIRELY.
IT TOOK LESS THAN FOUR HOURS TO DISMANTLE EVERYTHING THAT HELD BACK THE NIGHT IN OUR CITY.
AND THAT LEFT IT TO ME, BARBARA GORDON, ALSO KNOWN AS ORACLE, TO CALL FOR A SUBSTITUTE TEACHER FOR TODAY'S LESSON PLAN.
I'M THINKING SOMEONE WHO'S A STRICT DISCIPLINARIAN.

TOO KIND-HEARTED.

TOO COSMIC.

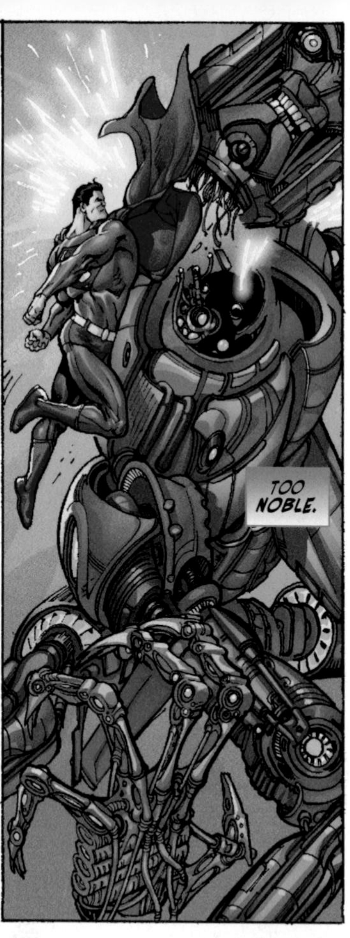
TOO NOBLE.

BATMAN WOULDN'T APPROVE OF MY CHOICE.
SO BATMAN DOESN'T GET A VOTE THIS TIME.
IT'S ME.
WE NEED YOU.
THIS IS WAR. IT'S ALL-OUT **WAR.**

SO I BROUGHT OUT THE BIG GUNS.

OH, LOOK AT THAT. LOYALTY.

I LOVE TO SEE THAT IN THESE TROUBLED TIMES.
LANGSTROM. GO HELP THESE PEOPLE UP, WOULD YOU?
WAY UP.
I DON'T... I DON'T REALLY WANT...
...AND THEN YOU'LL GIVE ME THE VACCINE? TO FIX ME?

A "VACCINE"?

BET YER WINGS, SPORT-O.

OR A POISON SQUIRT.

SIX OF ONE, OLD SON.

SKREEEEEEEEEEEE

NO. *NO!*

WELL. ISN'T THIS A KICK IN THE GROIN?
THE BET'S STILL ON, JOKER.
YES.
THE BET'S STILL ON.

WELL.

I'M HERE.

GOTHAMAZON

STORY BY GAIL SIMONE
ART BY ETHAN VAN SCIVER, PAGE 12 BY MARCELO DI CHIARA
COLORS BY BRIAN MILLER OF HI-FI
LETTERS BY SAIDA TEMOFONTE
COVER BY ETHAN VAN SCIVER WITH BRIAN MILLER OF HI-FI
VARIANT COVER BY PHIL JIMENEZ WITH ROMULO FAJARDO
ASSISTANT EDITING BY JESSICA CHEN
EDITING BY KRISTY QUINN

SHE CALLED. I KNOW IT WAS DIFFICULT FOR HER.
SHE TOLD ME TO USE "GOTHAM SOLUTIONS."
I TOLD HER, "I AM AN AMAZON."
SKREEEEEEEEEEEE
WE INVENTED "GOTHAM SOLUTIONS."
DAMN.
FATE, YOU HAVE A MEAN STREAK.
ALL DUE RESPECT TO BRUCE...
...I REALLY FAIL TO SEE WHAT ALL THE FUSS IS ABOUT.

A FEW PETTY THIEVES, LADEN HEAVILY WITH GAUDY FETISHES AND GIMMICKRY.
I'LL PUT YOUR HOUSE IN ORDER, BRUCE.
AND I WON'T EVEN NEED A CAR.

W-WAIT.
I HAVE A COUPLE QUESTIONS.

ALTHOUGH IF IT MUST BE SAID, WE DO HAVE A BIT OF A WEAKNESS.
AMAZONS ARE A CURIOUS BATCH.
GO ON.
OKAY, I'M BAD HALF THE TIME--I KNOW THAT.

SO I GO TO ARKHAM, OFTEN.
BUT I'M A DAMN HERO HALF THE TIME.
SHOULDN'T I GET A MEDAL OR SOMETHING?

ARE YOU TRYING TO TELL ME SOMETHING, MR. DENT?
WELL, JUST THAT TONIGHT, I'M YOUR WHITE KNIGHT, AND YOU DON'T EVEN KNOW IT.
OH, AND QUESTION TWO...

...WOULD YOU LIKE ICE WITH THAT?
NO ONE EVER APPRECIATES MY DOUBLE-ENTENDRES.

STAND DOWN, WONDER WOMAN.
I HAVE DESIGNS FOR THIS WASTED CITY.
IT IS TO BECOME A MONUMENT. A HEADSTONE, FROZEN IN TIME FOREVER.

YEAH. HE'S GONE A BIT TOO DEEP INTO THE MEAT LOCKER, EH, JOKER?
JOKER?

THE--
PLEASE, SIR, DO NOT KILL ME!
ANYWHERE. JUST GO.
BUT DRIVE CAREFULLY, THE ROADS ARE SLIPPERY AND THERE ARE PEDESTRIANS EVERYWHERE.

I HAVE A PERFECT ONE-LINER TO SAY OVER YOUR CORPSE!
IT'D BLOW YOUR MIND.
OH, BELIEVE ME. I'D LOVE TO.

BUT I CAN'T.
SO DRIVE.

UNLEASH HELL, MY COVETOUS COCKERELS!
WHEN IS A DEAD AMAZON LIKE A CONFUSED BAT?

WHEN SHE'S BEEN RIDDLED.

IO MADE THIS FOR ME, ESPECIALLY FOR THIS MISSION.

TCHUUK
WAUGH!
THAT DEUCED STINGS, YOU HARPY HADDOCK!
SCHUUK

ALL RIGHT. YOU CHOSE THE HIGHER GROUND, FREEZE.
LET ME BRING OUR DISCUSSION TO YOU.

YOU THINK YOU CAN DEFEAT ME WITH A BIT OF WINTER, FREEZE?
YOU THINK I WILL FALL TO MERE NUMBERS?
"THE CITY'S GUARDIAN SAID IT WOULD BE WAR.
"SO I BROUGHT MYSELF AN ARMY!"

HER.
IVY.
OH, BRUCE.

BUT YOU DO HAVE THE MOST **EXCELLENT** NEMESES...
BRING ALL THE PRETTY MEAT YOU LIKE, PRINCESS.
YOU WON'T WIN. NOT ON OUR HOME TURF, AS IT WERE.
...IT MUST BE CONCEDED.
PERHAPS I WAS A **LITTLE** OVERCONFIDENT.

FOR ONE THING, WE REALLY **ARE** RATHER GOOD AT COLLATERAL DAMAGE.
OSWALD?
kLIk
SAY NO MORE, MY BLOODY BLOSSOM!

NO.

NOT EVEN **ARES** WOULD--

FIVE MINUTES.
AMAZONS.
THIS IS NOW A RESCUE MISSION!
IT TOOK THEM FIVE MINUTES TO LEARN MY WEAKNESS.
HOW DOES HE NOT TURN TO THEIR METHODS?
THEY ARE WILLING TO MURDER INNOCENTS FOR A MOMENT'S DISTRACTION.
HOW DOES HE STAY...
...HUMAN?

I KNOW THE ANSWER.
HE IS AS INTRACTABLE AS THEY ARE.
HE IS JUST AS PRONE AS THEY TO...

...OBSESSION.

EVERY BONE IN MY BODY WANTS TO PUNISH THEM.
THEY FEAR THE NIGHT?

I'LL TEACH THEM TERROR OF THE ALL-SEEING SUN.

UH-OH. WONDER WOMAN'S GONE DARK.
DIANA? DIANA, CAN YOU HEAR ME?
I REALLY HATE TO SAY THIS.
BUT YOU HAVE TO THINK LIKE HIM, PRINCESS.
IT'S THE ONLY WAY TO TAKE THEM OUT!

SHE'S RIGHT, YOU KNOW.
THE ONLY THING THEY UNDERSTAND IS FEAR.
YEAH! AND YOU, MISS SPANGLE-BRITCHES...

...AIN'T *SCARY*, SEE?

ARE YOU HERE TO FIGHT, SISTERS?

PERHAPS I CAN SHOW YOU *OUR* IDEA OF TERROR?

NO, CALL US OBSERVERS. WE'D JUST AS SOON YOU LEFT TOWN, REALLY.

WE ALL COMPLAIN ABOUT GOTHAM, BUT WE'RE USED TO IT, VERMIN AND ALL.

NICE WHIP.

YOU OKAY, THERE, ISLAND GIRL? YOU GOTS KIND OF A FARAWAY LOOK, IF YA DON'T MIND ME SAYIN'!

IT'S A LASSO.

WHATEVER.

IT'S TRUE.

THEY'RE NOT AFRAID OF ME.

THEY'RE TESTING ME. THEY'RE TAUNTING THE COBRA TO SEE IF SHE'LL STRIKE.

WOE, GIRL-CHILDREN.

IF YOU ONLY KNEW.

THEY FEAR THE MAN IN BLACK.

BUT THEY DON'T KNOW.
THE MONSTERS AND GODS I'VE PUT TO ETERNAL REST.

IF I CHOSE MONSTERS...
...THE BAT WOULD SEEM A BLESSED REPRIEVE.

AND BEFORE THEY EXPIRED?
I WOULD FILL THEM WITH WONDER.

NO. I WILL REMAIN DIANA.

AND GOTHAM WILL CHANGE TO ACCOMMODATE ***ME.***

WHAT'S THAT, SAILOR MOPE?

WHOA, ***WHOA,*** THERE, SUGARLUMPS!
WE'RE JUST WATCHING, ALL RIGHT?
NO. TONIGHT?
YOU ***WILL*** PICK A SIDE.

TONIGHT, YOU ARE ***AMAZONS.***
YOU ARE MY PERSONAL GUARD, SISTERS.
DO NOT DISGRACE THAT OFFICE.

I HOPE YOU KNOW WHAT YOU'RE DOING, DIANA.
DO YOU KNOW WHY BATMAN'S METHODS NEVER TRULY WORKED WITH THIS LOT, ORACLE?
BECAUSE HIS PRIMARY WEAPON IS ***FEAR.***

"IT'S BECAUSE THEY ARE ALREADY SO DEEPLY TERRIFIED OF THE REAL WORLD THAT SHADOWS HOLD NO FRIGHT FOR THEM WHATSOEVER."
HARLEY...?
HEY, YOUSE GUYS!
QUIT MAKIN' WITH THE AWESOME HEIST, WHY DONCHA?
SORRY 'BOUT THIS, SWEETIE, BUT I'M AN AMAZON NOW!
JEEZ, YOU SMELL GOOD.
WHAT... WHAT ARE YOU DOING?!
EXILE.
GRIEF.
INFECTION.
IT'S NOT DARKNESS THEY FEAR...
...IT'S TRUTH.

OSTRACIZATION.

COMPULSION.

UNCERTAINTY.

THEY'RE AWFULLY QUIET, PRINCESS.
THEY'VE BEEN MADE TO FACE THEIR DEEPEST FEARS. THE ENGINE THAT DRIVES THEIR MADNESS.
NO ONE TOUCHES THE LASSO AND REMAINS UNCHANGED.

ARE YOU SURE THIS IS THE RIGHT MOVE, DIANA.
YOU DON'T FIX A BROKEN LEG BY SCARING IT, ORACLE.
IT'S TIME TO TRY THE SPLINT OVER THE SWORD.

HEH. WELL.
MAYBE YOU SHOULD RETHINK THAT WHOLE STRATEGY, DARLING?
LET MY FRIENDS FREE, OR THIS MR. NOBODY DIES GURGLING, SWEET THING.

IF I KNOW MY PUDDIN', HE'LL DO IT, PRINCESS.
YES. I BELIEVE HE WOULD.
EVEN WITH *MY* SPEED, THERE'S A RISK.

HE'S BLUFFING. HE WON'T DO IT.
SEE, WHEN WE PLANNED THIS, I FLIPPED THE COIN.
"AND THE GOOD SIDE LANDED FACE *UP*.
"SO I BET THE J THAT HE COULDN'T GO A DAY WITHOUT KILLING SOMEONE.

SEE? LIKE I SAID.
SOMETIMES I'M THE *GOOD* GUY.
WELL. DOESN'T THIS JUST CHANGE *EVERYTHING.*
HARVEY? I'VE BEEN MEANING TO SAY THIS.
YOU'RE JUST NO FUN ANYMORE.
I'M NOT TOO PROUD TO ADMIT IT.
WHILE I DO PREFER THE OPEN HAND OF COMPASSION...

I WIN, HARVEY. I WI--
...THE CLOSED FIST HAS ITS CHARMS, AS WELL.

AND I ADMIT IT... I WAS A SKEPTIC.
BUT SHE REALLY DID CHANGE GOTHAM IN HER IMAGE.
FOR A WHILE.

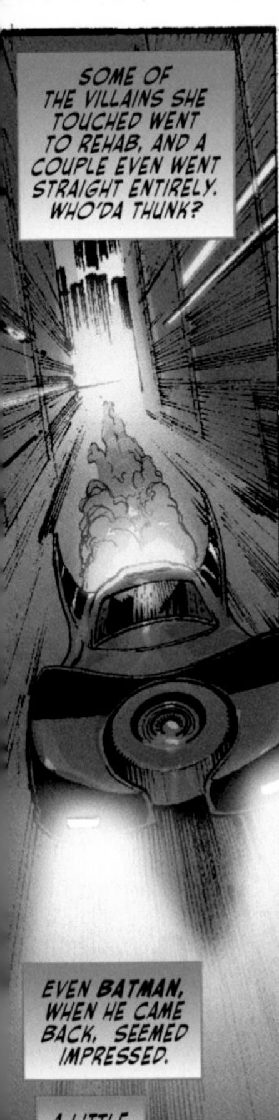
SOME OF THE VILLAINS SHE TOUCHED WENT TO REHAB, AND A COUPLE EVEN WENT STRAIGHT ENTIRELY. WHO'DA THUNK?
EVEN BATMAN, WHEN HE CAME BACK, SEEMED IMPRESSED.
A LITTLE.

I WOULDN'T HAVE THOUGHT IT LIKELY, BUT GOTHAM WILL MISS HER.
SHE WAS STRONG, BUT KIND, AND COMPASSIONATE. HUMAN.

AND BRAVE.
DID I FORGET TO SAY BRAVE?
THE END

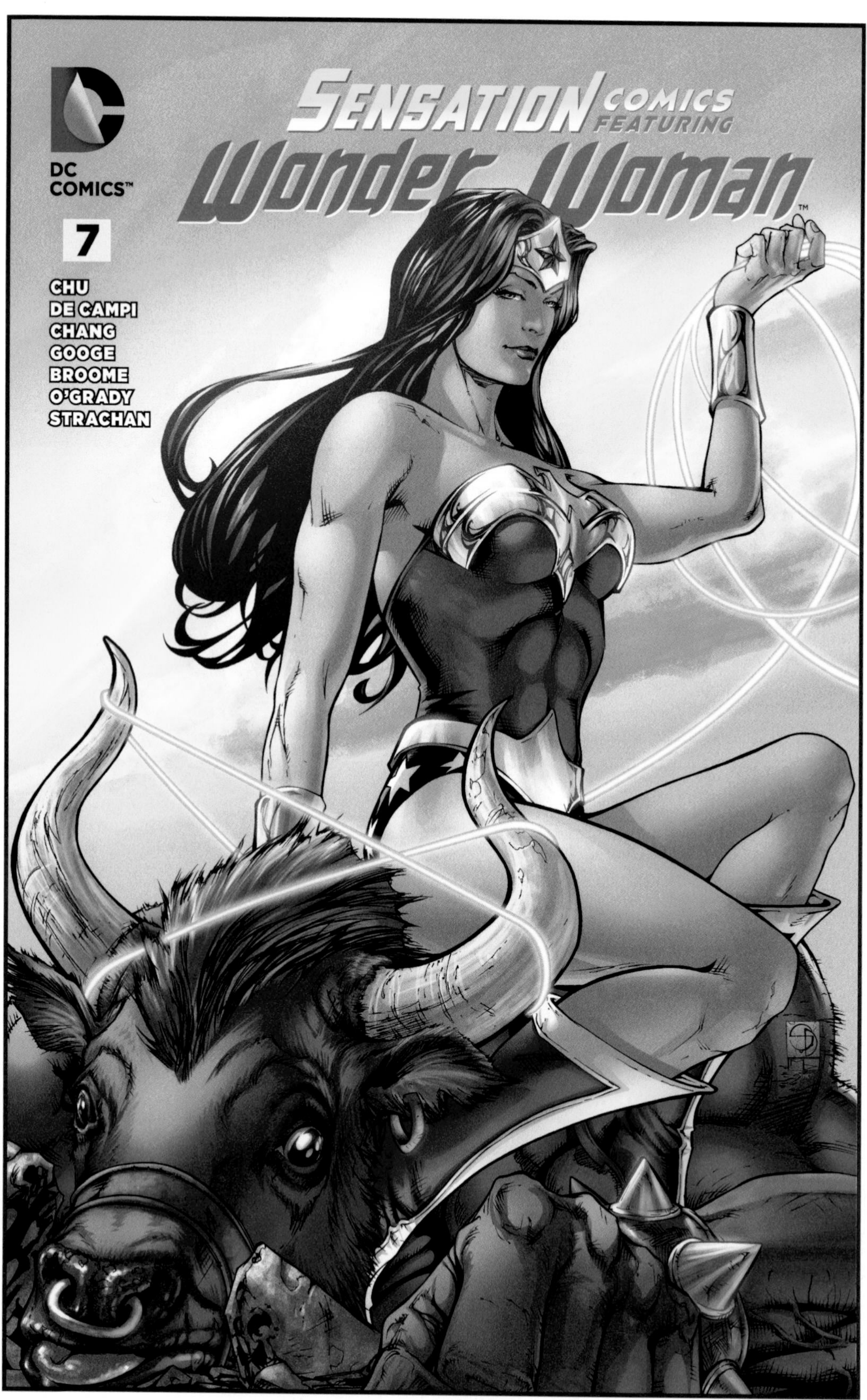
DC COMICS™
SENSATION COMICS FEATURING
Wonder Woman™
7
CHU
DE CAMPI
CHANG
GOOGE
BROOME
O'GRADY
STRACHAN

RESCUE Angel

writer: Amy Chu
artist: Bernard Chang
colorist: Wendy Broome
letterer: Saida Temofonte
assistant editor: Jessica Chen
editor: Kristy Quinn

Wonder Woman created by William Moulton Marston

I DIDN'T THINK IT WOULD BE SO PRETTY OUT HERE.
DON'T SOUND SO TOURISTY, LIEUTENANT.
IT'S MY FIRST TOUR. WHAT ABOUT YOU, CAPTAIN?
WIZ. CALL ME WIZ. MY 12TH. BUT YOU'RE RIGHT. NEVER GETS OLD.
REALLY?
NAH.
WELL, MAYBE.

SO HOW DID YOU GET YOUR CALL SIGN, WIZ?
BY BEING SMARTER THAN EVERYONE ELSE. DON'T WORRY, YOU'LL EARN YOURS SOON ENOUGH.

FOR BETTER OR WORSE. YOU DON'T PICK--WE CHOOSE.
BUT YOU'RE RIGHT--IN AN ALTERNATE UNIVERSE THIS IS A GREAT, PEACEFUL TOURIST DESTINATION.

"AND THEN THERE'S OURS...

FORWARD OPERATING BASE BENNETT, SOUTHEASTERN AFGHANISTAN.

"...WELCOME TO AFGHANISTAN."

LIEUTENANT ANGEL SANTIAGO?

I'M COMMANDER BISHOP.

THIS IS CORPORAL RILEY, PUBLIC AFFAIRS. APPRECIATE YOU DOING THIS FOR US ON SHORT NOTICE.

YO.

NOT A PROBLEM, SIR.

RILEY'S DOCUMENTING LIFE HERE ON THE BASE. PR WANTS TO SHOW THE FEMALE ENGAGEMENT TEAM ENGAGING WITH THE LOCALS...

...AND CROWLEY, OUR LAST *FET* IS... INDISPOSED.

SO, SANTIAGO, IS IT? I JUST NEED SOME GOOD SHOTS OF YOU VISITING THE VILLAGE AND THIS NEW SCHOOL FOR GIRLS THEY GOT GOING. LOOK PRETTY FOR THE CAMERA AND ALL THAT. WHAT'S THAT YOU GOT THERE?

WHAT, THIS? LUCKY CHARM FROM MY NIECE. SHE'S A HUGE WONDER WOMAN FAN.
COOL. HOPE IT WORKS...
"...THE LAST FET--CORPORAL CROWLEY? GOT HER LEGS BLOWN OFF BY AN IED JUST TWO WEEKS AGO."

SO HERE'S THE CHALLENGE, SANTIAGO. MEN MAY MAKE THE DECISIONS OUT HERE...
...BUT WOMEN HAVE THE POWER ON THE HOME FRONT. AND WE AS MEN CAN'T TALK DIRECTLY WITH THE WOMEN.
BUT YOU CAN.
ASSALAAM ALAIKUM.
WAALAIKUM ASSALAAM.
THEY SEEM CONFUSED BY ME.
THAT'S BECAUSE THEY ARE.
THEY'VE NEVER SEEN A FEMALE PILOT BEFORE?
IF IT MAKES YOU FEEL ANY BETTER, THEY THINK IT'S ODD BISHOP DOESN'T HAVE A BEARD. HERE, GIVE THIS A TRY.
I DON'T KNOW ABOUT THIS...I LIKE MY HELMET.

I'M PANRA JAN, FOUNDER OF THE NEW GIRLS' SCHOOL HERE.
ARE YOU THE NEW FEMALE ENGAGEMENT TEAM MEMBER?
LT. SANTIAGO, MA'AM.
YOUR ENGLISH IS SO... PERFECT.
I SPENT ALMOST MY ENTIRE LIFE IN CALIFORNIA. MY FAMILY LEFT DURING THE SOVIET INVASION IN 1979. I CAME BACK TO HELP. COME INSIDE THE SCHOOL AND SEE OUR PROGRESS.
THIS COUNTRY IS CHANGING. SLOWLY. WE HAVE FEMALE GENERALS IN THE ANA ARMY NOW. NOT MANY, BUT IT'S A START.
THESE GIRLS RISK THEIR LIVES EVERY DAY TO COME TO THIS SCHOOL. THEY ARE, I AM PROUD TO SAY, THE FIRST TO GET AN EDUCATION IN THEIR FAMILY.
THE TALIBAN MAY USE FORCE AND INTIMIDATION TO GET THEIR WAY, BUT THEY *WILL* LOSE.
WHY ARE YOU SO SURE?
BECAUSE, YOUNG LADY, THESE GIRLS ARE OUR FUTURE. AND YOU CANNOT STOP THE FUTURE FROM HAPPENING.
COME BACK TO SEE US. AND BRING MORE NOTEBOOKS. AND PENS, WE NEED MORE PENS...
I'D LOVE TO. THANK YOU SO MUCH--
HEY, GALS, CAN WE CUT THE CHITCHAT-- WE'RE RUNNING LATE...

"...AND IT'S GETTING DARK."
FWOOSH
YOU GOT ENOUGH PICTURES, RILEY?
NOT BAD. YOU COULD HAVE SMILED A LITTLE MORE--
BOOM
HOLY...
UNFF
IN THE TREES...TEN O'CLOCK. CAN ANYONE SEE THEM?
RATATATA
"I CAN'T SEE THEM."
RAT TA
FWOOSHHH
WHAT'S OUR STATUS--?
TATAT TA
BOOM
RATATA TA TA
NOT GOOD, SIR.

WE NEED TO FIND COVER.
DOWN THE RAVINE-- I'LL COVER YOU!
PAT
PAT
RATATAT
PAT
BISHOP!
AAGH

I GOT THIS. I'M TRAINED FOR THIS.
GOT BISHOP. NOW GET THE OTHERS.
HEY! ANYONE THERE? WE'RE UNDER ATTACK--
BZZT IDENTIFY YOURSELF--
THIS IS LT. SANTIAGO--
WHAT'S YOUR POSITION--?
C'MON, SOLDIER, WE NEED TO MOVE. NOW.
NO... ONE...LEFT BEHIND...
GET UP, ANGEL.

WHO--?
GET UP, SOLDIER. WE'RE NOT LEAVING ANYONE BEHIND.
PING
PING
HURRY.
PING
PING
HUNFF
I GOT THE LAST ONE.

RATTAT TAT
THAT'S IT.
NOW WHAT?
TATA RAT
FSSSH
FSSSH
TATA
FINALLY.
BOOM
WHY DOES EVERY SPOT HAVE TO BE SO DAMN ROCKY?! WE NEED TO GET CLOSER...
ALL RIGHT, LET'S GET EVERYONE ON BOARD.
GOD, I NEVER THOUGHT I WOULD BE SO HAPPY TO SEE *YOU*, WIZ.
WHAT ABOUT HER?
WHAT ARE YOU MUMBLING ABOUT, ANGEL?

SERIOUSLY, THAT'S WHAT HAPPENED. I'M SURE SOMEONE ELSE SAW HER. WIZ? RILEY?

LISTEN, GET SOME REST, SANTIAGO. YOU'VE BEEN THROUGH A LOT. WE'LL CONTINUE THE DEBRIEF LATER.

ALL I'M SAYING--THERE'S NO WAY SHE COULD HAVE MOVED THAT FAST AND LIFTED MEN TWICE HER SIZE, ESPECIALLY WITH HER INJURY. WHAT'S YOUR OPINION, OFFICER SHAH?
WELL, SHE'S SUFFERED A CONCUSSION, MULTIPLE INJURIES AND PROBABLY POST-TRAUMATIC SHOCK.
US ARMY

STILL, IN THE HEAT OF BATTLE, I'VE SEEN SOLDIERS DO THE CRAZIEST THINGS THAT PUSH THEIR BODIES TO THE LIMIT.

HEY, HEY, SOLDIER. WHAT'RE YOU DOIN'--BESIDES KICKING BUTT AND SAVING LIVES?
WIZ!

THE GUYS ALL WANTED TO CHIP IN FOR A LITTLE PRESENT. SO WE GOT YOU SOME READING MATERIAL WHILE YOU RECOVER.
COMICS! HOW DID YOU KNOW?

I *LOVE* COMICS.
YEAH, WELL WE DECIDED ON A CALL SIGN FOR YOU...

WONDER WOMAN.
DC
WHY IS
Wonder Woman
HELPING THE KHUND?!?
19
GAIL SIMONE
BERNARD CHANG
JON HOLDRIDGE
THE END

ART BY ADAM HUGHES

PENCILLED BY IVAN REIS
INKED BY OCLAIR ALBERT
COLORED BY ROD REIS

PENCILLED BY NICOLA SCOTT
COLORED BY JASON WRIGHT

PENCILLED AND INKED BY FRANCIS MANAPUL
COLORED BY BRIAN BUCCELLATO